"   ,"
Pete   as
clea   be
done, no matter how unpleasant it may get. Cantu turned away from Yuni and grabbed Elizabeth Pena. Joe Medellin and Efrain Perez walked up to Cantu and the bedraggled Elizabeth. Cantu grabbed her by the arms while the other boys grabbed her long legs. She barely struggled.

The three boys ambled down the not-so-steep hill and headed toward the nearby woods just north of the bayou. A footpath had been beaten down toward a large copse of towering pine trees. They looked like a bunch of delivery men schlepping a large dog-food-sized bag filled with wet cotton. Elizabeth's body put up minimal resistance. She just undulated in an awkward motion as they carried her to the woods.

Just ahead of the foursome were Derrick Sean O'Brien, Raul Villarreal, and Jennifer Ertman. They were leading the teenager on foot past the bald spot in the dirt where Villarreal's initiation had taken place almost an hour earlier, past the open forty-ounce bottle of Schlitz Malt Liquor Bull that one of the boys had dropped during the scuffle. Jennifer, unlike Elizabeth, struggled. She resisted O'Brien and Villarreal, who were much larger, stronger, and faster, but it was to no avail. They forcefully pushed her into the copse.

Other books by Corey Mitchell

PURE MURDER

COREY MITCHELL

PINNACLE BOOKS
Kensington Publishing Corp.
http://www.kensingtonbooks.com

Some names have been changed to protect the privacy of individuals connected to this story.

PINNACLE BOOKS are published by

Kensington Publishing Corp.
850 Third Avenue
New York, NY 10022

All Kensington titles, imprints, and distributed lines are available at special quantity discounts for bulk purchases for sales promotions, premiums, fund-raising, and educational or institutional use. Special book excerpts or customized printings can also be created to fit specific needs. For details, write or phone the office of the Kensington special sales manager: Kensington Publishing Corp., 850 Third Avenue, New York, NY 10022, attn: Special Sales Department, Phone: 1-800-221-2647.

Pinnacle and the P logo Reg. U.S. Pat. & TM Off.

ISBN-13: 978-0-7860-1851-2
ISBN-10: 0-7860-1851-8

First Printing: June 2008

10 9 8 7 6 5

Printed in the United States of America

For Kyle and Darrin Mitchell

You know what they say about brothers . . .

Prologue

Monday, June 28, 1993—5:00 P.M.
T. C. Jester Park
T. C. Jester Boulevard
Houston, Texas

"Where are the kids at?" the large man, with shoulder-length blond hair, asked the Texas state trooper as he walked along the side of the railroad tracks.

"Sir, you can't go over there," the trooper informed the man, who had already bounded over the side down a steep gravel incline.

"I came for my daughter, goddamn it!" the man screamed, barely glancing back over his shoulder as he quickly scooted toward the trodden circle in the grass where several Houston police officers had gathered. "No, man. Fuck you!" he screamed. The trooper slowly took off after the man, but he did not press the issue.

The large man picked up his pace as he darted toward the cluster of officers. "Does she have blond hair?" the livid father screamed at the top of his lungs. The sound carried through T. C. Jester Park like the crack of a shotgun blast.

"Is she blond? Is one of them blond?"

Randy Ertman had been looking for his fourteen-year-old daughter, Jennifer, since the previous Friday. Jennifer had gone with her best friend, sixteen-year-old Elizabeth Pena, and other friends to an apartment located on the northwest side of Houston.

Two officers stepped forward to cut Ertman off. One officer placed his hand up to prevent the angry man from advancing. The other officer told him he could not go any farther.

"I want to know if that's my daughter, goddamn it!" he screamed at the police officers.

"Sir, I'm sorry, but you cannot go any farther," one of the officers informed him again. "This is a crime scene and you cannot be here."

"I want to know if that's my goddamned daughter in there!" he screamed again, but to no avail. The officers were not budging. They would not let him through.

Ertman stared over the shoulder of one of the officers into the gaping maw of the nearby green forest. Towering pine trees hovered over the enclosed area, where even more police officers were located.

Word had leaked out that the bodies of two teenage girls were discovered in that enclosed space. Randy Ertman believed his daughter, Jennifer Ertman, may have been one of the two girls.

Randy Ertman had exerted a lot of effort to find his daughter over the prior four days. He contacted all of Jennifer's friends to see if they had any clue where she might be. He printed up thousands of flyers and posted them from Galveston to Cypress-Fairbanks. He attended an anti–death penalty rally for convicted killer Gary Graham in hopes of getting the media's attention to focus on his little girl.

When the call came in that there were two bodies found in the brush near the end of the tree line of T. C. Jester Park, Randy was speaking with newspaper and television reporters at his home in the Heights. He overheard the call on one of the reporters' walkie-talkies. The semihysterical father looked at a cameraman from the local ABC-affiliate channel 13 news division, grabbed his news van keys, and shouted out, "C'mon! Let's go." Randy jumped into the van and made the cameraman drive. They tore out of there like a scorpion shuttling over scorching asphalt.

The news van pulled up to the scene, skidded to a halt in the asphalt, and Randy leapt out of the passenger door. He noticed a large crowd of onlookers had gathered behind the invisible barrier. He was disgusted by the people. They reminded him of hungry, circling vultures eyeing rotted carrion on a deserted highway.

Randy ran from the van, jumped over the police barrier, and made a mad dash for the cluster of police officers.

"Is it my daughter?" he screamed. "Is my daughter back there?" he yelled as he advanced forward.

Sean O'Brien, an eighteen-year-old African-American male, watched the insanity unfold. He saw the van pull up to the scene and witnessed the hysterical father jump out and practically tackle one of the police officers. When O'Brien heard the man ask if one of the victims was blond, he realized it had to be one of the girls' fathers.

O'Brien sheepishly grinned. He slowly turned around and walked away.

PART I

PURE HELL

JENNIFER ERTMAN

Chapter 1

Jennifer Ertman was born on August 15, 1978, to Sandra and Randy Ertman. The Ertmans were ecstatic at the birth of their child because they were not sure if they would ever be able to conceive, since Sandra was on the wrong side of thirty-five.

Baby Jennifer was the Ertmans' own personal little miracle.

Sandra described her only child as "real sensitive, modest, funny." To her mother, Jennifer was "more child than teenager." She still seemed to act more like a young girl than a budding teenager. "She liked to play. She had a baseball card collection." Her father also said she developed a good sense of humor at an early age and that she had "the best laugh."

Her mother spoke about how Jennifer tended to act younger with the kids in her neighborhood than with her friends at school. "She would ride her go-kart or bicycle down the street. She used to pull her wagons down the street with Ishmael, a boy down the block that she grew up with, and his family."

As Jennifer got older, she kept her more childlike side out of view from her high-school friends. "When she went to school, she didn't let her friends know that she did that at home. She tried to act more like a teenager."

The Ertmans added that she was always a good kid. "We were firm with her when she was growing up," Randy recalled. "We taught her to never lie, cheat, or steal, and to treat everyone with respect." Randy added, "As long as she never lied to me, I didn't have to worry. She never lied to me, so I never had to worry."

The couple refrained from spanking her. Randy recalled yelling at her only three times in her entire life. He felt he never really had to raise his voice to her. "We only had one child and we spoiled her, but she had rules and she had to live by them."

Jennifer was always a very modest girl. She loved to swim; however, she was not thrilled about displaying her body in front of others. Her mother remembered, "In the summertime when she went swimming, I bought her big, baggy cover-ups to put on over her bathing suit when she got out of the swimming pool." Jennifer loved to swim, but she did not like to prance around in front of the other poolgoers. Her mother said she would even wear the cover-ups in the swimming pool.

Jennifer also wore long, baggy denim shorts that came down to her knees whenever she lay out by the swimming pool. She stayed away from short shorts. She also never wore a sleeveless shirt. "She dressed for comfort," her mother declared, "and she dressed baggy because she didn't like anything tight."

Jennifer was also not too big on boyfriends. "She had friends that were boys," her mother clarified, "but she did not have any boyfriends." Jennifer still seemed to retain some of her younger-child mentality when it came to boys and girls. "She didn't like boys to touch her at all."

Jennifer was proud to be a virgin. Indeed, it was her intention not to surrender her virtue until she met the right man and married him. Her virginity was her badge of honor and something she was determined to keep until the moment was perfect.

Sandra had noticed certain changes in her daughter in the previous months. To her, it seemed as if Jennifer were slowly breaking out of her little-girl phase and beginning to grow into being a teenager.

Jennifer used to wear barrettes in her hair all the time; however, she had begun taking them out so she could mimic the hairstyles worn by some of the actresses on the popular nighttime soap opera *Beverly Hills, 90210*. It's what all the girls at Waltrip High School were doing and she had decided it was time to fit in.

Jennifer also began to wear more jewelry. She had her ears double-pierced, and on top of one ear she had tiny diamond studs. She wore tiny dime-sized hoop earrings on the bottom. She also wore two long gold rope chains, one with the letter *J* on the end. The young girl also wore a total of eight rings on her fingers, including two *J* rings and one *E* ring.

Jennifer also began to put on makeup, even though her parents assured her she was beautiful without it.

Despite her newer leanings toward more mature decorations, Jennifer also wore a Walt Disney Goofy watch, which was a gift from her parents from the previous Christmas.

She was not entirely ready to give up her childhood.

There was another overt sign that the Ertmans' baby daughter was growing up. When she turned thirteen, she asked her parents for her own set of house keys. It was not for sneaky ulterior motives. The Ertmans had two doors in the back of their home. One was the regular door and the other was a door made of metal burglar bars, which were necessary because they lived on a nice street in one of the lower-quality areas of the Heights.

Jennifer wisely said, "Mom, can I have my own keys so I don't have to keep bothering you?" Sandra believed her daughter had proven she was responsible enough, so she had an extra set of keys made for her.

The Ertmans also purchased a unique gift for their daughter that showed she was quickly growing up: a pager.

Jennifer received a Southwestern Bell pager for Christmas in 1992. Sandra was reluctant to give it to her at first. During the '90s, pagers had a stereotypical connotation as a tool for drug dealers. Jennifer insisted she wanted one because it was a way to keep in touch with her friends. This was before the mass proliferation of cell phones. Sandra and Randy discussed the issue with Jennifer, and the couple decided that because Jennifer was now attending Waltrip High School, she would not be in the Heights area, where they lived, as much. The family agreed it would be a smart purchase, so they bought her one. Sandra actually felt better about it because now she knew she could get in touch with her daughter much quicker in the event of an emergency.

Thursday, June 24, 1993—4:00 P.M.
Ertman residence
East Twenty-fifth Street
Houston, Texas

Sandra walked into her daughter's bedroom. Jennifer was getting ready to visit her best friend, Elizabeth Pena. Sandra glanced at her daughter, who was standing next to a mirror, brushing her hair. She was amazed at how much her daughter had grown, and she was proud of what a wonderful person she was turning out to be. Jennifer made straight A's in school, had nice friends, never got into trouble, and loved her parents.

"Dad's taking you over to Elizabeth's," Sandra informed her daughter. It was usually her mother who drove Jennifer everywhere. "I'm going to go over to Apple Tree to pick up some groceries."

"Okay, Mom," Jennifer acknowledged while continuing to brush her hair.

"I love you, honey." Sandra walked toward her daughter. "I'll talk to you later." The mother leaned over and gave her daughter a peck on the cheek.

"I love you, too, Mom." Jennifer smiled as her mom exited her bedroom.

Sandra felt safe about letting her daughter go out for the night with friends. Jennifer had her pager and also cash in her purse. Her mother always left $35 on Jennifer's dresser every Thursday for allowance. Jennifer also received the same amount on Sundays and she always kept a $10 bill in her pants pocket in case of emergency or if she needed to call a taxicab. Sandra made sure her daughter knew that if she ever needed a ride home, all she had to do was get to a pay phone and call her parents. They would come get her—no matter the situation.

Sandra left her home feeling upbeat. She knew her daughter was a good girl and knew how to stay out of trouble. Randy marveled at how close the two ladies in his life were. He watched as Sandy and Jenny communicated more "I love you's" without verbalizing them. They shared a unique and special bond that only a mother and daughter could experience.

Jennifer and her dad left fifteen minutes later.

Randy dropped Jennifer off at Elizabeth Pena's house on Lamonte Lane, approximately four-and-a-half miles away from their home. Jennifer did not lean over to give her father a kiss good-bye. She had recently gotten out of the habit due to embarrassment, being a teenager and all.

"Be home by midnight," her father reminded her.

"I will, Dad. I love you." Jennifer said good-bye.

"I love you, too, honey," Randy responded as he drove off. The self-described overprotective father did not like to leave his daughter on her own; however, he knew she was growing up.

ELIZABETH PENA

Chapter 2

Elizabeth Christine Pena was born on June 21, 1977, at Memorial Hermann Northwest Hospital, in Houston, Texas, to her parents, Melissa and Adolpho "Adolph" Pena. Melissa was eighteen years old at the time and Adolph was twenty-one.

Melissa's water broke the night before and Adolph rushed her to the hospital. At 2:00 A.M., after several hours of waiting, the nurses informed Adolph he could go home and get some sleep. Sure enough, less than two hours later, he received a call that his first child had been born with no complications.

"That was one of the most precious times of my life," Adolph recalled. "That firstborn child. There's nothing like the first one." He described his immediate attachment to his daughter as "pretty special."

Adolph and Melissa used a baby-name book to select "Elizabeth." They were an ecstatic young couple looking forward to sharing their lives and love with their baby daughter.

The Penas had met just over two years before. Adolph, whose parents and grandparents grew up in San Antonio, Texas, moved to Houston with his parents in 1975 after his dad received a better job offer. He was the only child left in the house and the three of them packed up and moved southeast to Houston.

Soon thereafter, Adolph went to a Crosby, Stills, Nash & Young concert at Jeppesen Stadium, the former home of the Houston Oilers football team and also the University of Houston Cougar college football team. There he met an attractive white girl named Melissa Moore. The two hit it off as friends and promised to get together after the concert. One thing eventually led to another and they found themselves in love, married, and with child.

The Penas lived a quiet, relaxed life in their quaint home on Lamonte Lane, in northwest Houston. Their home was located on a pine-tree-lined suburban street less than a quarter of a mile away from Stevens Elementary and less than half a mile away from T. C. Jester Park, with its clean bicycle paths and shade trees for people who sought exercise.

Adolph described Elizabeth as a "normal little kid who loved to play out in the backyard and swim in her little plastic swimming pool."

Elizabeth was two years old when she was joined by her little brother, Michael. As brother and sister grew older, they fought constantly about the silliest things. Michael picked on Elizabeth, and she told on him. They always seemed to be at each other's throats, even though they loved one another tremendously. They shared a bedroom for ten years and slept in bunk beds together.

Adolph laughed when he talked about how Elizabeth and Michael used to fight. "It was always some piddly bullshit stuff. 'Oh, Mom, he's looking at me' or 'Oh, he's touching me.' Just piddly, silly kind of stuff. Just bullshit, like brothers and sisters do."

When the two oldest children became teenagers, they "kind of went their separate ways," according to Adolph.

"He got into basketball and baseball. She couldn't stand PE. She didn't like sweating. She was into her things. So, finally, they quit fighting with each other."

According to Adolph, Elizabeth was still very much a girly-girl. She loved to dress up and look good. It was apparent early on that she was a beautiful little girl. All of the Penas' friends and family members would comment on what a lovely young lady Elizabeth was from an early age.

Elizabeth had very curly hair and loved to have it fixed up, but she hated having her hair washed. Her father and mother used to wash it in the sink and Elizabeth would scream at the top of her lungs while she was doused in water. No one knew why, but it became a source of humor for the entire family.

When Elizabeth was almost ten years old, the Penas welcomed their third child into the fold—a baby girl named Rachael. Elizabeth immediately took to Rachael and constantly doted on her little sister. She adored Rachael and did everything she could to help her mother take care of her.

"She just thought that was the neatest thing," Adolph recalled of his oldest daughter's fascination with the newest addition to the family. "She thought the world of Rachael." By the time Rachael turned four, Elizabeth had already taken her under her wing and loved playing with her.

Elizabeth was a decent student in school. Her father believed she was "intelligent, but lazy. She did what she needed to do to get by. As far as books were concerned, she would do what she had to do to pass. One of those types of people." Elizabeth was not interested in excessive studying or making the honor roll. According to Adolph, she was only a C to C-minus student. She was more interested in enjoying herself, looking pretty, and making lots of friends.

The older she got, the more everyone noticed her.

She grew into a stunning, thin young girl, with long, dark hair. She was one of the most popular girls in each of her schools from Oak Forest Elementary to Stevens Elementary.

Her parents would not let Elizabeth attend F. M. Black Middle School, even though it was located just three blocks down on Lamonte Lane. Her parents believed there were too many bad things going on at Black, so they sent her to a private Catholic school.

Her father even warned her about "men of all ages." He told her that most men were only interested in one thing and that she should always be wary of their intentions. He told her that since she was so beautiful "men would try to take advantage" of her and that she should not "trust anyone" and "always be aware of your surroundings."

Adolph did not mind if his little girl had a boyfriend; he just wanted to make sure she was friends with the boy for a long time before they started dating, "Just like me and her momma did." He worried about his little daughter having sex and getting pregnant.

While Adolph fretted about his daughter's blossoming into a woman, Melissa Pena could still see the little-girl quality within her oldest daughter. She described Elizabeth as "fun-loving, goofy, silly, liked to talk on the phone, sweet, gentle, and kind." Elizabeth was "young and carefree," with no plans.

"She thought she had a full life in front of her," Melissa recalled.

According to Adolph, Elizabeth had always been a good kid until she turned fourteen. "She started hanging out with the wrong crowd. A bunch of crazy little kids. She didn't give a damn about nothing. She wasn't using any drugs or drinking any alcohol. She just kind of liked to get into trouble. Never went to jail. Never in trouble with the law." Adolph did not think the kids she hung out with were bad; they just seemed bored with life. "There were no gang members, no drug dealers, no rapists, no killers. They were just bored and lifeless."

This had been why the Penas enrolled Elizabeth in St. Pius X Catholic private school, located in downtown Houston. This turned out to be a bad move, as Elizabeth got into even more trouble. She was removed from the private school after only six weeks. She also had her first sexual relationship with a boy during this time frame.

"I don't know what it was," Adolph recalled, "but something about her from the age of fourteen to fifteen just went a little wild. She just seemed to want to get into trouble."

Elizabeth took out most of her teenage rebelliousness on her parents. "We would argue with her about coming home late or staying on the phone too long or for hanging out with the wrong type of people." Elizabeth would retaliate by running away from home twice.

"She'd sneak out the window and go to somebody's house," Adolph mused, "and I wouldn't find out about it until the next day. I'd be like, 'Where in the hell they at?'"

Elizabeth usually ran away because she was upset with her parents over something trivial. "She had gotten pissed at us and went and stayed with this one gal over at her house. She was harboring her for like two or three days." Adolph ran into the girl's father out in public and said to him, "Dude, do you know you can go to jail for harboring a minor? All you had to do was tell me, 'Hey, your girl's over here.'"

After Elizabeth was kicked out of St. Pius X, she was devastated and determined to start anew. She thought about the types of people she hung out with and came up with an insightful realization—she truly only had three to four friends she knew she could count on to help her out, no matter what.

One of those friends was one of her newer girlfriends,

Jennifer Ertman. Even though Jennifer was more than a year younger than Elizabeth, she would prove to be a positive influence on the older girl. Jennifer did well in school, obeyed her parents, and made plenty of friends as well. Elizabeth followed her new friend's lead and began to turn her life back around.

"I don't know what happened to her," Adolph recalled, "she was a totally different person. When she turned fifteen, she just straightened up her act.

"I don't know what somebody said to her or what she had seen but she turned back into a little princess. She started doing well in school. She totally turned herself around all by herself. It was kind of odd," Pena marveled.

The Penas were very happy Elizabeth befriended Jennifer. "She was an extremely good kid," Adolph recalled. "I can't imagine her being bad, with a dad like Randy.

"Jennifer was a little doll," Adolph continued. "Every time she'd come into the house, she would make it a point to come over and say, 'Hello, Mr. Pena,' even if I was in another part of the house. She was a very, very polite young lady."

Jennifer and Elizabeth both attended Waltrip High School and had recently completed the ninth grade. The year at Waltrip with Jennifer by her side was the best year Elizabeth had spent in ages. Her grades were improving, she pared down her friends to those who truly cared for her, and she met a young boy with whom she fell into teenage love. It appeared as if things were back on the right track for Elizabeth Pena.

For the last few years, Adolph and Melissa would take the family to Florida for a week to ten-day vacation. It was all about fishing and sunbathing. The boys went fishing, the girls went sunbathing.

"I was coming back from Florida and everybody was

just happy. The kids were in the van. I looked up and saw my beautiful girl in the rearview mirror and thought to myself, 'What would happen if I didn't have these kids?'" It was a fleeting thought that Adolph had never had before. As quickly as it came into his mind, he shook it out. He looked up into the mirror and caught his daughter's attention.

"I love you, sweetie," Adolph told Elizabeth.

She smiled. "I love you, too, Daddy."

RAUL VILLARREAL

Chapter 3

Seventeen-year-old middle-school dropout Raul Villarreal sat around the house of his parents, Louisa and Omar Villarreal. Being unemployed had become a common occurrence for the young man. As a result, he was forced to live with his parents, where he did not have to pay rent or do many chores. The Villarreals lived in a quaint but poor neighborhood, and the family needed every penny it could get its hands on.

That did not stop Raul from asking his mother for a quarter so he could go play video games down at the local convenience store. His mother agreed and gave him the change. Raul bolted out the door and headed over to the store, where he planned to kill some time playing his favorite video game, *Street Fighter II*, the popular sequel to the combat-fighting game that reinvigorated arcade-style video gaming.

* * *

Raul Omar Villarreal was born on September 25, 1975, in Houston, Texas. He was the third child, behind twin sisters, Laura and Elizabeth, who were born one year earlier to his parents.

Raul was a healthy baby born into a relatively poor family. His father, Omar, worked as a repairman with a specialty of fixing refrigerators and air conditioners. He never brought home much money, but always had food on the table for his kids, a roof over their heads, and was always there for them when they needed him. Louisa was a stay-at-home mom who doted over all of her children equally.

What the Villarreals lacked in finances, they made up for in how they treated their children, which would later include three more. Omar and Louisa made sure the kids were clean, well-fed, and they also stressed the need for a good education and a strong belief in religion.

The Villarreal family led a normal, unspectacular life. Omar worked, Louisa looked after the kids, the family attended church, the kids went to school, and they played sports. All fairly normal and routine for kids growing up in Houston, Texas.

The Villarreals had a nice but small white wooden house located on Chapman Street. The house was practically encaged with burglar bars on all the windows and all the doors. It was not uncommon for a van to be parked on the tiny strip of grass between the front of the house and the narrow street.

The Villarreals made friends with their neighbors, joined in on barbecues with them on the weekends, and frequented the Trinity Baptist Church, less than two miles away from their home. Raul first attended church when he was six years old and pretty much went every Sunday.

Raul was not exactly the world's best student in elementary school. He managed to get by, but he struggled with many of his classes.

After elementary school, Raul was somehow allowed to graduate to Marshall Middle School, located less than two miles away from his family's home. He did very poorly and was retained twice during his academic career. In other words, he flunked out of two grades, which he was forced to repeat.

When he was thirteen years old, Raul met Pastor Rudy Sanchez, from the Trinity Baptist Church. Pastor Sanchez had known the Villarreal family for a while. He knew Raul was a very polite, obedient, quiet young boy who usually came to church every Sunday, sat quietly in the pew, and was respectful toward the setting for the invocation of Jesus Christ. Pastor Sanchez also knew Raul made his "commitment to Christ" when Raul was twelve years old.

Pastor Sanchez noted Raul was also consistent with his appearances in Sunday school after each sermon. He was usually quiet, attentive, and a good listener. He never got into trouble with his teacher or the other Sunday-school attendees. He was well-liked by his peers, even though he was very quiet.

Trinity Baptist Church had more than six hundred parishioners at the time. Despite the large numbers, Pastor Sanchez made it his personal mission to get to know and help as many of them as he possibly could. He took a particular interest in the Villarreal family when Omar Villarreal became sick. Since Omar was the sole breadwinner in the family, Pastor Sanchez was worried about their financial well-being and how it would affect the family emotionally.

To help out, the pastor visited the family on a periodic basis to see how they were making ends meet. Every time he visited the Villarreals in the tiny wooden home, Raul answered the front door.

"Hello, Raul," Pastor Sanchez greeted the boy. "Are your parents home?"

Raul usually would not say anything, but simply nod his head affirmatively. He would scoot back to open the door and wait until the pastor stepped inside. Too shy to say anything, Raul slipped away from the front room. Within seconds, Louisa Villarreal would enter the foyer and greet Pastor Sanchez.

Raul usually scampered off, back into his room.

When Pastor Sanchez did see Raul in the Villarreal home, he described him as "quiet and respectful of his parents."

Pastor Sanchez always enjoyed his visits with the Villarreal family. He could tell that all six of their children were loved. When the pastor would visit, he spent the majority of his time chatting with Louisa, since Omar was "a very quiet man."

Unfortunately, Pastor Sanchez's ministrations did not solve the Villarreals' problems. Omar's downtime from work cut into what little financial budget the family had. As a result, Raul used to go to school in less than pristine clothes. He was embarrassed to be seen by other kids at school, who teased him for his pauper's wardrobe, he claimed.

In February 1991, at age fifteen, Raul approached his mother. He told her he no longer wanted to go to school. He was tired of the taunts and he wanted to do something about it. He begged her to let him quit so he could join his father and earn extra money for the family.

Louisa was mortified. She did not want her son to quit school. She had always stressed the importance of a good education, and even though Raul had been kept back twice, she still believed he had what it took to succeed in school and in life.

Raul won the argument. He informed his mother he was done. He was dropping out of school.

He was only in seventh grade.

Louisa was crestfallen. She visited Pastor Sanchez to see if he could provide counsel to young Raul, but it was too late. Her boy was determined to make a living and contribute to the family. Nothing was going to stop him.

Raul also stopped going to church around the same time. He gave no explanation why.

Raul began to work with his father repairing air conditioners and refrigerators. It was very labor-intensive work, which he did not enjoy. He did, however, like the paycheck that came with the work. He would readily give up 40 percent of it to his parents every payday.

Louisa continued to stress the importance of a good education and convinced her son to take the GED, a battery of five tests that a person can take to earn the equivalent of a high-school diploma. Raul had the opportunity to participate in a tutoring center to prepare for the exams; however, he failed to complete his studies and never even took the tests.

Raul felt no need, as he was making the beginnings of a living and he enjoyed the money.

He was, however, getting very bored with his social life. He began to hang out with his cousin Eddie Sanchez, whose mother was sister to Raul's father. Raul and Eddie were almost the same age.

The cousins used to spend a lot of time together when they were little, because they lived within just a few blocks of one another. That changed when Eddie's parents moved to another part of Houston, which was more than twenty minutes away. Eddie was only six at the time. As a result, he was unable to drop by as he pleased and see his cousin. The two became less close over time; however, they occasionally attended Trinity Baptist Church together. Eddie stopped going to church when he was only eight years old.

As the boys got older and were a bit more mobile, they got back into the habit of spending time together. Practically every weekend, the cousins made sure they got together whether it was sitting around a picnic table eating barbecue, catching the latest football game on television, or spending the weekend down at the beach in Galveston. The cousins had reignited their relationship and became much closer. They even went on a couple of double dates together.

Eddie dropped out of school one year after Raul had. He never took his GED, either—something the cousins had in common.

Eddie trusted his cousin implicitly. He never worried about Raul being around his common-law wife, Rene Spinks, and her young child from a previous marriage. Eddie and Rene would have another baby when Eddie was only sixteen. Eddie had no problem letting Raul hang around his wife or his two kids when he was not around, because he believed his cousin was a solid, safe, nice guy.

Raul was nice enough that Rene suggested to her sister, Kate Dickson, that she go out with him. The couple hooked up, but it was not meant to be. According to Eddie, Kate wanted to date more than one guy and had no desire to be tied down. She even told Eddie that Raul was almost too nice and that she wanted "somebody more aggressive."

Kate described Raul as a "perfect gentleman" who never cursed in front of her. She also said he was too shy and had not even attempted to kiss her. In the end, after only three weeks, she found Raul to be too boring and dumped him. According to Eddie, Raul did not seem too bummed about it. Luckily, the failed relationship between Raul and Eddie's common-law sister-in-law did not adversely affect the two cousins' relationship.

Raul had struggled in school and he struggled in relationships with the fairer sex. He was also bored with manual labor and wanted something different. He spoke with his mother about her newest vocation. She was attending nursing school at the Polytechnic Institute, along with two of Raul's sisters. She convinced her son it would be a wise move for him to join them. He took her up on the offer. He informed his father he would be quitting the air-conditioning business and enrolled in nursing school.

Raul enjoyed the work and he even enjoyed spending extra time with his mother and sisters. He did not make many friends while in nursing school, electing instead to eat lunch and spend most of his break times with his family.

The majority of his fellow nursing students found him to be pleasant, hardworking, and relatively quiet. They tended to like him, but were not close to him.

There was one exception. Andrea Flores, one of his fellow students at the institute, befriended Raul in September 1992. She, too, hoped to become a nurse.

Andrea described Raul Villarreal as calm and easygoing; she noticed he made good grades. She claimed he got along well with everyone at Polytechnic Institute.

The nursing program lasted only four months. Raul had no problem with the curriculum, showed up for classes, and was an eager participant in all variations of training. He passed the program with flying colors.

Raul, along with his two sisters, his mother, and Andrea all received their nursing certificates on January 15, 1993. It was one of the proudest days in his young life.

Unfortunately, landing a job was a completely different story for Raul. He went through all of the usual channels to seek out a nursing job, but he always came up empty-handed. No one would hire him. His sisters were hired. His mom got hired. Andrea was hired, but no one would hire Raul Villarreal.

Raul's state of unemployment led to a deeper state of depression. He was finished with school, jobless, and had no girlfriend. He felt unwanted and unneeded. He went from helping his family buy food and clothes to having to wear worn-out, out-of-style clothes.

Raul sought out new friends to help break up his monotony. The main person he hung out with was a young boy, roughly Raul's same age, named Efrain Perez Jr. According to Eddie, Efrain and Raul lived on the same street when they were younger and had known each other for nearly five years. He noted that despite the fact the Perez family had moved away from the neighborhood, back in 1989, Efrain and Raul still managed to hang out together. Eddie described Efrain as a guy who "liked to be on the streets."

Raul's mother did not like Efrain. She claimed he only came over to their house twice since 1989. Each time, she did not want her son to have anything to do with him. Whenever Efrain showed up in her front yard, Louisa would yell at her son to come inside the house and reiterated that she did not want him playing with Efrain.

Louisa and Raul would run into Efrain when they went out grocery shopping as well. Every time she saw Efrain, she later warned her son he "was not doing very well," and insisted that Raul better be careful because Efrain was "always getting into trouble."

Louisa said of Efrain Perez, "He was on a bad path." She heard he was mainly interested in making a name for himself out on the streets. "I had heard about his fame," Louisa warily recalled.

There were still many people looking out for Raul Villarreal's best interests. One was family friend Benitas

Arias. She knew Raul since he was thirteen years old and described him as "a peaceful person." The older woman trusted Raul well enough that she would leave him alone with her own daughter who was a year older than Raul.

Arias became close enough to Raul and friendly enough with the Villarreals that she would invite Raul over to spend the weekends at her house. She never had any complaints about the young man and thought he was a "nice boy."

Another adult authority figure who took a keen interest in Raul Villarreal was Pastor Guillermo Tamez, from the Living Work Church.

From his days of being a fellow parishioner at Trinity Baptist, Pastor Tamez had known Raul since Raul "was just a baby." Tamez enjoyed the Villarreals' company and was especially fond of Raul. He kept up with the family over the years and liked to hear updates about the boy as Raul got older.

Tamez often met Raul at church and would talk to him about his life, especially when Raul was between fifteen and seventeen. The pastor sensed Raul was troubled and he wanted to be there to help him on his path. He had great faith in Raul and believed he simply needed additional support and guidance. "He was interested in him" and wanted to "try and help him out because the boy lacked self-confidence."

Tamez would sit and counsel with Raul on a one-to-one basis at the church. He eventually spent some time at the Villarreal household, where he would talk with Raul and the rest of the family.

Tamez feared Raul's boredom would lead him down the wrong path of bad choices. Top of the list was joining a gang. The pastor had seen too many kids' lives forever damaged by their association with gangs. He wanted to steer Raul away from that dead end.

Tamez feared that route for Raul because he knew the

young boy was book-smart, but not street-smart. The pastor described the young boy as "a follower, not a leader." He added that Raul was not "a hard-core person."

Tamez was also somewhat critical of Raul's father and his relationship with his son. He claimed that the father "did not pay enough attention" to Raul. He also lamented the fact the boy had to purchase his own clothes with his own money.

Pastor Tamez could not tell if what he said to Raul had actually sunk in.

Apparently, it did not.

Raul's boredom led him down an even more destructive pathway: drugs and alcohol. Raul's mother found out he was sniffing inhalants to get high—specifically, Texas shoe-shine, which is a local-brand shoe-shining spray that contains toluene. She also found out he had been sniffing for quite some time. ("Texas shoe-shine" is now slang for huffing inhalants.)

Raul was referred to a drug-and-alcohol counselor by a gentleman named Tommy Acosta, who worked for the Chicano Family Center, which helps low-income families.

Raul's counselor, Norberto Torres, definitely agreed Raul was a sniffer. Instead of Texas shoe-shine, however, Torres believed the young man's inhalant of choice was Freon, which was more readily accessible because of his father's air conditioner repair service. Raul denied sniffing Freon or anything else. Torres informed Louisa Villarreal that it was quite common for sniffers to deny any wrongdoing.

Raul's problem worsened, according to his mother, so she decided to take drastic action to save her son. With Torres's guidance, they hoped to stage an intervention to help Raul with his drug problem.

On Wednesday, June 23, 1993, Torres arrived at the Villarreal home at 3:00 P.M. to plan out a strategy with Mrs. Villarreal. They all agreed to meet at the Houston

Recovery Campus at 3:30 P.M., on Friday, June 25, in two days. Louisa Villarreal prayed she could convince her son to go with her to meet Torres and help him with his drug problem.

The next day, Raul strolled up to the convenience store and saw his good buddy Efrain Perez in the parking lot working on his family's truck.

"What up Junior?" Raul inquired of his friend, using the name Perez most often went by.

"Fixin' this piece of shit ride, bitch," Efrain responded. "What the hell you up to?"

"Just killin' some time. Gonna play a little *Street Fighter*. Whoop me some ass." Raul laughed.

Efrain Perez nodded toward Raul, then stuck his head back under the hood of the truck. Raul headed into the store to get his game on.

EFRAIN PEREZ JR.

Chapter 4

Efrain Perez Jr. was born on November 19, 1975, in his grandmother Eusebia Guerrero's home on East Monroe Street, in Brownsville, Texas, to Maria "Louise" Perez and Layo Guerrero, whose name strangely was not included on his son's birth certificate.

The coupled lived in the tiny, cramped quarters of a ramshackle pink wooden-framed house. The family employed the services of a midwife to birth baby Efrain. His arrival in the world was greeted by his one-year-old sister, Gabrilla, who was also born in the Guerrero home.

The excitement of a newborn was short-lived, however, as Louise and Layo, who were constantly fighting about something, decided to go their separate ways.

Louise packed her bags, took Efrain and Gabrilla with her, and moved out of the Guerrero household. The relocation was not too dramatic, as they literally moved just one block away.

Louise made a go of it alone. She took care of Efrain and Gabrilla, kept her place up, and also worked a job as a housecleaner. On the days when she had to go to work, she relied upon Efrain's grandmother Eusebia to watch after her baby boy and girl.

Their stay was short-lived, for Louise met a young man named Ismael Castillo and married him. The new family moved, this time eight blocks away from the Guerreros, into a tiny wooden house with two rooms for the children, a master bedroom, a living room, and a kitchen.

The distance made it much more difficult for Eusebia to stop by and babysit. She had to take the city bus to get to the kids' new home. She also worked a demanding job packing shrimp and it became physically harder for her to take care of her grandkids.

Louise, however, was eventually forced to send her son off to live with his grandmother and aunt. Efrain spent several years there and grew quite attached to both ladies.

Efrain was very fond of his aunt Doria Elia Casias. She lived in Rio Bravo in the late 1970s and early 1980s, and Eusebia used to bring Efrain and Gabrilla to visit her once a month. They would also make return visits for special holidays, such as Easter and Christmas. Doria loved the children as if they were her own.

Efrain and Gabrilla were ecstatic to find out Aunt Doria would be moving to Brownsville on New Year's Eve, 1981. Efrain was only six, but he knew Doria was coming to live with them and he could see her as often as he liked.

But by 1984, Louise sought out better employment opportunities in Houston and took Efrain and Gabrilla with her. Four years later, when Efrain was a young teenager, he wanted to move back to Brownsville and live with his grandmother. Efrain asked his mother if he could and she agreed.

This routine between Houston and Brownsville was a continuous scenario. Trying to keep up with how many times Efrain moved back and forth between Brownsville and Houston is nearly impossible.

While he lived in Brownsville, Efrain attended Resaca

Elementary School, home of the Mighty Chiefs. He went through grades one through six, on and off. He was always a very good student, was actively involved in school, and had plenty of friends. As he got older, he became interested in music and joined the school band. Efrain also stayed out of trouble and hung out with some of the better kids who made good grades.

In 1989, when Efrain was fourteen, he attended Cummings Junior High School, also in Brownsville. By eighth grade, he was enrolled in an honors course for every subject except reading. Eduardo Martinez, his earth science teacher, remembered Efrain as a good student who never got into trouble and never missed a single class. Martinez recalled Efrain's two best buddies at the time were Pete Lopez and Tony Chavez. They were both bright students and good kids.

By February 1990, Louise wanted her son to come live with her again in Houston. Aunt Doria, however, did not want her nephew to go. It was the beginning of the second semester of eighth grade at Cummings for Efrain and she wanted him to have more stability. She was afraid that another abrupt upheaval would damage him. Furthermore, she felt as though Efrain was her own son and did not want to surrender him. She and Eusebia had made sure that Efrain was taught to respect and to obey. They also taught him manners, gave him a curfew, and made sure to discipline him when he got out of line.

Doria knew, however, she had no choice. Efrain was forced to withdraw from Cummings Junior High and transfer back to Houston yet again.

Eusebia was not thrilled about the prospect of Efrain leaving, either. She worked hard with him and believed he would turn out to be a good little boy. She was afraid another move would throw him off the right track.

She prayed for her grandson that he would make a

seamless transition and not get mixed up with the wrong crowd.

Efrain was sent to Marshall Middle School upon his return to Houston, but was transferred after only two weeks to Hoffman Middle School. According to James Royster, Efrain's English as a Second Language (ESL) teacher, Efrain was a "bright student" who hung out with the kids from his class. All of the ESL students were Hispanic and came from another school called Shotwell Middle School. Royster believed Efrain always hung out with the Hispanic kids because he was more comfortable around them.

According to Royster, Efrain and his new buddies used to walk confidently through the school corridors side by side. Despite Efrain's seemingly intimidating presence, Royster declared he never saw the young man engage in aggressive behavior with any of the other students. He also believed Efrain was more than able to make decisions for himself. He was definitely not a follower.

Despite Efrain being a bright student, he started to get into trouble at school. According to Royster, he recalled having to break up a fight in the school hallway one day between Efrain and another boy. Royster was not sure what happened, but he came across the two boys swinging wildly at each other. Both boys were cursing and throwing punches.

Royster grabbed Efrain and pulled him off the other boy. Despite Efrain's rail-thin stature, he put up serious resistance to his teacher.

"I had to get him into a different area to settle him down," Royster recalled. "I had a tough time getting him settled down."

Efrain met another young boy in his same grade, named Joe Medellin, who was also part of ESL. They became close friends.

In September 1991, Efrain graduated from Hoffman

Middle School to Eisenhower High School. Assistant Principal Greg Colschen's most relevant memory of Efrain is that he skipped too many classes. Colschen was surprised, because he knew Efrain had done well in middle school, but now it seemed like the teenager was "uninterested in school." Colschen called Efrain into his office numerous times to discuss his absenteeism, but Efrain never gave him any good reasons why he was cutting class. Colschen did note that Efrain had been spending more time with a group of kids from his Heather Glen Subdivision, including Joe Medellin and another boy, named Peter Cantu.

Colschen attempted to contact Efrain's parents to discuss their son's truancy; however, he was never able to reach them. He even wrote and mailed the family certified letters, which were ignored.

Wednesday, December 18, 1991—7:00 P.M.
Foundry United Methodist Church
Jones Road North
Houston, Texas

Mary Jo Hardy drove her 1989 Dodge van from her job as a relief pharmacist to the Foundry United Methodist Church so she could attend choir practice. She parked her vehicle, locked the doors, and headed inside the church.

After more than two-and-a-half hours of tension-relieving singing, she called it a night and said good-bye to her fellow choir members. Hardy headed outside the church toward the spot in the parking lot where she parked her van. She knew she was tired from the long day, but she felt as if she were losing her mind.

Where is my van? she thought.

She walked to the exact area where she had parked it and only discovered a pile of shattered glass. Someone had broken into her van and had stolen it, along with a truck that she had parked beside.

Visibly upset, Hardy returned to the church, where she located a telephone and contacted the Jersey Village police. One of her fellow parishioners offered her a ride to her home in Cypress-Fairbanks, which she accepted.

Thursday, December 19, 1991—12:30 A.M.
Houston, Texas

Harris County sheriff's deputy D. C. Bair and his partner, Deputy Tom Davis, were driving their marked car on the north side of Houston, near the 9000 block of Ella Boulevard. The two deputies were assigned to the "hot spot division," a narcotics enforcement team that traversed the city. This particular evening found the officers cruising near Loop 610 looking for anything unusual.

They definitely found it.

Deputy Bair nudged Deputy Davis as they came upon a unique situation. "Check it out." Bair nodded toward the vehicles in front of him. They watched as a blue Dodge van pushed a 1984 two-door blue Chevrolet Monte Carlo along the road at a snail's pace. The blue car had apparently broken down and was being assisted by the blue van.

Deputy Davis put in a call to dispatch with the plate numbers of the van. As the two men waited for a response, they slowly drove up beside the two vehicles. Deputy Davis glanced into the van and saw a young, thin Hispanic boy behind the wheel. The driver ignored the deputy and focused on the car in front of him. The deputies then pulled alongside the blue car and saw another young Hispanic boy driving it.

"We've got a make on the vehicle in question," the dispatcher informed the deputies. "The blue Dodge van was reported [as] stolen, to the Jersey Village Police Department late last night, from the Foundry United Methodist Church parking lot."

Deputy Bair flipped on his police car lights and Deputy Davis pointed to the drivers to pull over to the side of the road. Since the van was stolen, the officers were prepared to bring its driver into custody. Deputy Bair exited his cruiser and walked up to the van's driver's-side door. He peered into the open window and asked the boy for his identification. The boy, who looked rather bored by the whole affair, complied and handed his driver's license over to the deputy.

The driver of the stolen van was Efrain Perez.

Deputy Bair asked Perez to step out of the vehicle. He then arrested the juvenile and put him in handcuffs. Perez did not put up any resistance.

As Deputy Bair placed Perez in custody, Deputy Davis ran a check on the license plate of the Monte Carlo. Information came back that it, too, had been stolen. Deputy Davis waited until Deputy Bair patted down Perez and then guided him into the backseat of the sheriff's vehicle.

Deputy Davis informed Deputy Bair that the other car had been stolen as well. Deputy Bair walked up to the Monte Carlo and asked the young man inside to produce some identification, which he did.

The driver was Joe Medellin.

Deputy Bair also cuffed Medellin, patted him down, and stuck him in the cruiser. The deputies drove Medellin to his parents' home and released him. The deputies, however, then drove Perez to the West Ellis

Detention Center, where he was charged with unauthorized use of a motor vehicle.

Perez had broken the steering column on the van, as well as the knee panel and ignition. Basically, he hotwired the vehicle. The same things were damaged in the Monte Carlo, in addition to both car stereos being damaged during unsuccessful attempts at stealing them.

The entire time he was in Deputies Bair and Davis's custody, Perez appeared nonchalant. Bored, almost. It all seemed rather humorous to him.

Mary Jo Hardy received a phone call at 2:00 A.M. from the police that her van had been recovered. When she picked it up, she discovered it had been thoroughly trashed and most of her belongings, including a baby's car seat, were gone.

Saturday, January 4, 1992—1:30 P.M.
Del-Mar Bowling Center
Mangum Road
Houston, Texas

Since 9:00 A.M., Cathleen Buford and her husband, Greg, had been enjoying a relaxing day at the Del-Mar Bowling Center. They were there to watch their nephew bowl in his youth league.

Right after lunch at noon, Greg slipped outside the bowling alley to retrieve his bowling ball so he could partake in some fun with his nephew. After bowling for nearly ninety minutes, Greg and Cathleen said their good-byes to their nephew and headed out of the facility. Once they arrived at the spot where they parked their car, they stopped dead in their tracks. Another car had parked in the exact same spot where they had parked their red 1988 Pontiac Firebird. The couple panicked, ran around the parking lot trying to find their vehicle, in case they just did not remember exactly where they had parked. It was all for naught. Their car had been stolen.

The couple returned to the bowling alley, met up with their nephew, told him what happened, and then called Cathleen's sister and asked her to come pick them all up. They also called the police department to report their car had been stolen.

Later that evening, Cathleen's sisters offered to take Cathleen out to the movies to help take her mind off her stolen car.

After the movie, at approximately 10:30 P.M., as the women drove from the movie theater to Cathleen's sister's house, they passed the bowling alley where Cathleen's car had been taken. They crossed onto Thirty-fourth Street when Cathleen, who had been looking out the window for her car on the entire trip back, spotted her Firebird in front of the Taquerias Arandas Mexican restaurant, which was located in a strip center at the 4700 block of West Thirty-fourth Street. She hollered at her sister to pull into the restaurant parking lot. They drove right up next to the car. Cathleen checked the license plate to make sure it was hers, and it was. They pulled out of the Taquerias Arandas parking lot and drove across the street to the Kentucky Fried Chicken parking lot. They called the police from a pay phone; she then called her husband.

Greg Buford stayed at home that evening to watch football on television. When Cathleen called to tell him she found her car, he told her to sit tight and he would be right over. Greg pulled up to the restaurant, checked out the car to make sure it was his wife's, and then walked over to the Kentucky Fried Chicken parking lot, where his wife had parked. He told her to stay put and that he was going inside to see if he could find the culprit.

Greg walked back over to Taquerias Arandas and into the restaurant. He looked around for anyone that seemed suspicious. There were only three occupied tables—one was a dressed-up couple, who appeared to be on a date; one table had a black couple with kids; at the third table sat three young Hispanic males eating their food. Greg walked up to the counter and quietly asked for the manager of the restaurant.

When the manager walked up, Greg greeted him and asked, "Do you know who drove that red Firebird here?" He tilted his head toward the location of the car, trying to be as discreet as possible. The manager, who did not speak English, shook his head no. Greg then asked one of the restaurant staff members if he knew who had driven the red Firebird. The young man motioned to the table with the three Hispanic boys near the back of the restaurant, confirming Greg's suspicions.

Greg turned away from the staff member to look at the boys. He was nervous because he was outnumbered, three to one. He became even more nervous when he saw what he described as "the glint of a metal barrel that looked like a revolver," on the belt area of one of the three young men. He did not want to alarm anyone, so he did not say anything about the possibility that one of the boys might be carrying a weapon. Instead, Buford asked the manager if he could borrow his telephone in the back, which he used to contact the police. He thanked the manager and then walked out of the restaurant.

As he walked back toward his wife, over one hundred yards away, Greg was scared as hell. He was nervous, but he was damned if they were going to leave that parking lot with his wife's car. Greg walked up to his wife and told her that the thieves were inside the restaurant and that he had also called the cops.

It would not take long for the situation to escalate.

Less than one minute later, Cathleen watched as the

three Hispanic male teenagers walked out of the restaurant toward her car. Greg stood next to her and witnessed the entire scene as well. Cathleen was nervous as she saw one of the young men lean up against it as if he were in no particular hurry.

One minute after that, a Houston police car, with siren blaring and lights flashing, pulled into the Taquerias Arandas parking lot. The boys froze in their tracks and looked like deer caught in the headlights of an oncoming diesel.

Officer Kenneth Bradshaw, who was driving the police car, barked out, "Stop right there. Don't move!"

Suddenly the youths snapped out of it and took off running toward Mangum Road. Mirroring an episode of *Starsky & Hutch,* Officer Bradshaw bolted out of the squad car and took off after one of the boys. The other juveniles, Efrain Perez and Joe Medellin, stopped running, once they realized a police officer had taken chase after them. The third boy was able to make his way eastbound across Mangum Road, so Officer Bradshaw focused on him. As he ran after the suspect, he radioed in for a Fox unit, or helicopter assistance. Bradshaw resumed his sprint after the young man until he reached the Silver Creek Apartments complex. The officer lost track of the fleeing suspect in the maze of apartments. It took less than two minutes.

Meanwhile, Officer Gerald Crawford exited the squad car and hollered at the two surrendered miscreants: "Get down on the ground, now!" One boy turned around as if he were going to walk back into the restaurant, while the other boy, who had his hands buried deep in his pants pockets, continued to walk off. Officer Crawford was compelled to brandish his revolver and point it at the second boy. "I said, get down! Now!"

The other boy flopped to the ground and yelled out, "Joe, stop."

The suspect eventually halted after a few more steps. Crawford approached him and stated, "Take your hands out of your pockets, slowly." The boy, who looked rather nonplussed about the whole affair, smirked, lifted his arms up, and removed his hands from his pockets. In the process of doing so, a gun fell out.

"Put your hands up in the air, now!" Officer Crawford yelled at Medellin.

Joe Medellin reluctantly did as he was told. He did not even flinch at the sight of the gun that had fallen from his pocket.

Officer Crawford scurried toward Medellin, grabbed him, and pushed him up against a wall. He then proceeded to pat the boy down, saying, "Get down on the ground, now."

Medellin complied with the officer and slowly worked his way facedown to the parking lot's surface. Crawford withdrew a pair of handcuffs and restrained the juvenile. Crawford looked back toward the other boy on the ground and decided he was not going to make a break for it.

A few minutes later, a heavily breathing Officer Bradshaw returned to the parking lot, where Officer Crawford had the two boys in custody. Bradshaw informed Crawford that the third suspect had escaped. Officers Crawford and Bradshaw lifted the two suspects off the ground and escorted them to the back of the squad car.

Officer Bradshaw walked over to Cathleen and Greg Buford. He confirmed that it was indeed their vehicle that had been stolen and recovered. Officer Crawford then showed Greg how to ignite the Firebird so he could drive it home. The officer knew that GMC cars were fairly easy to steal; however, the thieves had to really know what they were doing to be able to steal them successfully.

On the drive to the police station, the officers were able to coax some information out of one of the boys. They found out that their names were Efrain Perez Jr.

and Joe Medellin. Perez was not speaking, while Medellin nervously began to chatter with the officers. The officers could not convince Medellin or Perez to give up the name of the third person, who had escaped.

Perez and Medellin were transported to the Juvenile Division located at the downtown central station of the Houston Police Department (HPD). There they were processed and questioned by a detective. Inexplicably, neither boy was charged with any offense.

Wednesday, February 5, 1992
Houston, Texas

One month after Perez and Medellin's arrests for the unauthorized use of a motor vehicle, Perez appeared in the juvenile delinquent court for the theft of Mary Jo Hardy's van from a church parking lot. Associate Judge Ramona John placed Perez on juvenile probation and declared he "is in need of rehabilitation" and that for his own safety, and for those around him, he "should be placed in the custody of the child's mother."

In order for Perez to successfully complete his probation, Judge John created several orders that were to be followed by the young man for one year:

- must attend the Juvenile Alcohol and Drug Awareness Program,
- must attend a peer pressure workshop,
- must attend a legal awareness workshop,
- was to have no contact with Joe Medellin.

Perez was given additional rules by Judge John that he had to adhere to during his probationary period. These included:

- reporting to a Juvenile Division officer in the event that he changed addresses,
- must attend school and "all classes every day,"
- must stay within the boundaries of Harris County and only be allowed to leave upon receiving permission from a juvenile probation officer,
- must not violate any laws of the state of Texas or any other place,
- must not leave his "court placement," in other words, his mother's home, without lawful permission,
- must be home every evening by nine, Sunday through Thursday, and eleven on Friday and Saturday; not allowed to leave his home until 6:00 A.M. every day,
- must not operate a motorized vehicle without permission from his juvenile probation officer,
- not allowed to have a driver's license during his probationary period,
- must submit random urine samples to the Harris County Juvenile Probation personnel; a positive result for drugs including marijuana or "dangerous drugs" would result in "adjudication of delinquent conduct" or revocation of probation.

Perez signed the probationary report, which also included the statement, "If I commit an offense after my 17th birthday, I could be tried as an adult in criminal courts." It was also signed by his mother.

After several drop-ins by Maria Guerra, Efrain Perez's probation officer, Perez stopped by her office on April 21, 1992. Perez had no telephone in his home and his parents were usually gone to work whenever Guerra would stop by for a visit. As a result, she sent him a letter asking him to come by her office.

Guerra wanted to discuss Perez's mandatory counseling programs ordered by the judge. She referred the boy to the Association for the Advancement of Mexican Americans (AAMA), a group that conducts therapy for Hispanic families and attempts to help at-risk youth.

Perez and his parents went to one therapy session.

In the meeting, the AAMA representative discerned that the parents were unable to control their son and they worried about his abuse of alcohol and drugs and believed he might be dealing drugs.

By June 1992, Guerra received a notice from AAMA that they had closed Perez's case because no one from the Perez family ever showed up again after that initial meeting. As a result, Guerra, who could have revoked Perez's probation, instead opted to send the boy to a Council on Alcohol and Drugs Houston (CADH) counselor, whose focus was on drug and alcohol abuse. The meetings were to take place in the same building where Guerra worked on Antoine Drive, which is easily accessible by the Houston METRO bus system.

Perez was scheduled to meet with the CADH counselor six times during the month of June. He made it to two sessions. The counselor dropped the case.

Guerra noted, however, that Perez did attend his mandatory peer pressure workshop. He was only required to attend one time. Guerra stated the workshop was very beneficial to younger kids who might be persuaded to join up with other people who are prone to making bad choices.

As far as Perez's attendance at the legal awareness workshops, he was supposed to attend six consecutive weeks of sessions. He missed three of them.

Guerra also spoke about Perez's final condition that he was not supposed to have any contact with Joe

Medellin. Guerra was fully aware of the other boy, because she was his probation officer as well. Needless to say, Guerra knew Perez was in violation, because he and Medellin used to walk into Guerra's office together. Guerra was appalled by their obvious disregard for authority and restrictions. She reminded the two young men they were not allowed to be together and they needed to go their separate ways.

Guerra's reason for not reporting the two boys to their judge sounded unusual. She stated, "There's no way for me to say they did come together. They continued [to be] friends." She notated the violation, however, and stated, "It wasn't enough for me to take it back to the court."

Guerra, who had a caseload between sixty and seventy juvenile delinquents, lamented the fact that she was never able to monitor whether or not Perez violated his curfew. Her method of monitoring consisted of calling the delinquent's home phone number and asking if he was home. Since the Perez family did not have a telephone, she was never able to check on his status.

Guerra was able to visit the Perez household on a few occasions. She spoke with his parents in regard to him breaking curfew. From their conversations, Guerra gleaned that the Perezes had no control over their son. He came and went as he pleased, and he almost never adhered to his curfew guidelines.

Chapter 5

Cypress-Fairbanks High School eleventh grader Gary Ford was excited because his boss was letting him off work three hours early. The avid football-card collector needed to pick up a weekday job to go along with his weekend job at the Traders Village, a large flea market, where he sold playing cards to kids. He intended to walk over to a nearby Burger King so he could apply for a job as a cook, which would give him work during the week, but first he needed to walk home to his Chimney Hill neighborhood. It was the same path he trudged on the weekends to and from work; it usually took him fifteen to twenty minutes to complete. The fashionable young man was resplendent in a black Los Angeles Raiders jacket he had purchased six months earlier and a pair of red-and-maroon Air Jordan sneakers. He was carrying a box of football cards.

Ford also carried a steak knife in his pocket. He

claimed it was because he was "not real popular with the gangs in the neighborhood, because I tell little kids not to join them." Ford did not have a good relationship with the Latin Kings, a Hispanic gang that patrolled his neighborhood. That day he would have no run-ins with the Latin Kings.

As he strolled down Log Cradle Drive, Ford watched his friend Douglas Gordy playing football with some of the little kids from the neighborhood.

Ford continued down Log Cradle Drive, until it intersected at Blazey Drive. As he shuffled up to the intersection, he noticed someone walking in his general direction from Log Cradle on the same side of the street. It was a teenage boy wearing a dark baseball cap, dark pants, and a khaki shirt. Ford thought the boy looked Vietnamese. He had no idea who the kid was coming toward him.

As the two crossed paths, the other boy slowly changed direction then and began to walk back toward Ford. The boy approached within three feet and said, "Do you know Refugio?"

Ford slowed and responded, "Yeah, man. He's cool."

"Are you part of the Latin Kings?" the boy asked.

"I ain't no part of no gang," Ford retorted in a pissed-off voice.

The other boy seemed relieved. "Well"—he smiled at Ford—"I want your jacket."

Ford was not happy. He had saved up enough money working at Traders Village to purchase his prized possession. He was a huge fan of former Raiders running back Bo Jackson and wanted to adorn himself in his favorite player's team colors. He looked the other boy up and down and smirked at him. He was not going to give up his jacket.

At least, not until he saw the gun in the boy's waistband.

Ford got real nervous, real quick. "Okay, man," he stammered as he looked around to see if there was anyone else ready to jump him. He was not willing to risk his life over a jacket. Ford lifted one hand up in resignation as he knelt down on one knee to lay down his box of football cards.

"If you do anything stupid," the boy warned, "I know where you live and I will shoot your mom."

Ford bowed his head toward the pavement. "You don't need to talk any shit, man," he said to his mugger.

The boy quickly responded in a calm manner, "Fuck you. I will kill and rape your mom."

Ford recalled that the boy seemed to relish the thought.

The boy pointed at Ford with his left hand, but did not say a word. Ford began to remove the Raiders jacket. He rolled it up and looked up at the boy. He motioned as if he were going to hand the jacket over. Instead, he threw the jacket straight up in the air to distract the boy while he took off running for cover behind one of the parked cars. He changed his mind, however, and decided to take on his assaulter. Ford charged toward the boy. He knew he had the steak knife in his pocket, so he felt he had a chance. He tackled the boy, the two collapsed to the pavement, and the gun fell loose from the other boy's pants. The revolver skidded down the pavement about three feet away from the two boys. Ford began to lunge for it when a maroon car pulled up in front of him and a "bunch of Mexican dudes jumped out."

Ford realized he was outnumbered. "Fuck this," he said, and took off running. He spotted a trash can and aimed to jump behind it for cover. As he leapt over the can, he heard several popping sounds. It was gunfire.

Ford became distracted, crashed into the garbage can, and crumpled to the ground in the heap of trash. He thought the extra *pops!* were simply him smashing into the garbage can.

Ford rolled around in the trash until he was able to orient himself. He looked up, only to see a group of kids running toward him. Instinctively, he clutched the knife and turned toward the mob so as to protect himself.

"Yo, man. You been shot," one of the kids told him.

Ford was confused. He thought these people were the same group of guys who had hopped out of the car. He looked over the kids' heads and saw the boy who mugged him jumping into the car, which sped off. He then looked back at the street and flopped down on it.

Ford had been shot in the chest and in the middle of his shoulder blade. He was bleeding badly.

"Call 911!" one of the kids shouted.

Several people in the neighborhood poured out of their homes to help the boy.

"Get away from me!" Ford screamed at the onslaught of more than one hundred people rushing toward him. It was only a matter of seconds before Ford began to feel woozy and nearly blacked out. He could barely lift his arm. "I am shot! I am shot!" he screamed out. "Somebody get my mother!"

The next thing he remembered was being whisked away in a Life Flight helicopter and taken to Memorial Hermann Hospital. While in a severely groggy state, he was interviewed by a reporter from the *Houston Chronicle* and also a local television news station.

"What happened?" the reporter asked.

"I told that dude that I don't like gangs and that he wasn't gonna mess with my mom," Ford sputtered.

He was relieved to find out the other kid had not stolen his jacket.

He was less thrilled to find out he would have to undergo surgery to his stomach to stop some internal bleeding. The doctors also searched around to locate and remove the bullets. They found them, but determined they would not be able to take either one out.

Ford did not have a clue that the person who approached him in the street and attempted to steal his jacket was Efrain Perez. He did not even know Perez. He did believe the man who approached him was also the same person who shot him.

Perez would never be caught for the attempted murder of Gary Ford.

By the spring of 1992, the Eisenhower High School administration had had enough of Perez's absenteeism. He was expelled from school for nonattendance. He sat out that spring and summer and hung out even more with Medellin and Cantu.

Eisenhower High School allowed Perez to reenroll the following September. It was not long before Perez found himself in trouble again. Just a few weeks after the semester began, Perez got into a big fight on campus between guys from his Heather Glen Subdivision and a group of boys from a nearby subdivision. The animosity spilled over from the streets onto the school grounds.

The brawl started at 7:15 A.M., with more than a dozen boys wailing at one another. The fight escalated, teachers came rushing outside their classrooms to stop it, and the groups broke off and started fights in different locations. After the melee seemed to die down, Perez broke off from the pack and started another brawl.

Greg Colschen was alerted to this fight via his walkie-talkie. When he arrived at the scene, he spotted Perez standing by two other boys who were fighting. Perez was not partaking in the action, just standing there observing. Colschen managed to break up the fight.

Suddenly Perez took a swing at one of the boys. Colschen quickly restrained him, which was not too difficult considering Perez was clutching his left hand.

It appeared to have been broken. Colschen rushed the boy over to the nurse's office to have his hand examined. Colschen knew that Perez's hand was in bad shape, so he went to his office to contact Perez's parents. However, there was no telephone number to call because they did not own a phone.

After the nurse checked Perez out, Colschen informed the boy he would drop him off at his home. When they arrived at the Perez house, a young man answered the door. Colschen had no idea who he was, and Perez was not talking. Perez sauntered inside and did not bother to thank Colschen for bringing him home or even bother to glance back at him.

According to Colschen, Perez was expelled from Eisenhower High School for fighting. The school followed up with a certified letter informing Perez's parents of a hearing date for his possible expulsion. The letter was received, but neither Perez's mother nor stepfather responded to it.

When Perez's expulsion hearing date arrived, no one—not even Efrain—showed up for it. He was expelled from school and placed on home-based instruction for the rest of the school year. Perez made no attempt whatsoever to comply with the home-based instruction, and his parents never pushed it on him. Eventually Efrain Perez Jr.'s educational career had ceased. He was now officially a "dropout."

According to Colschen, Perez's "reactions were always more of nonreactions. He just was not really interested in being in school and it really didn't matter what the consequences were" for his actions. Colschen added that Perez never expressed any hostility toward him or anyone on the staff. He believed Perez was just unaffected by most other people.

Colschen wondered how much negative influence Perez's friend Joe Medellin had on the former honors student. The assistant principal described Medellin as a person "not interested in being in school." Colschen added that Medellin "caused problems for other students at school."

It appeared that Efrain Perez was one of them.

Perez lied to his probation officer, Maria Guerra, about his expulsion. He told her he wanted to drop out of school so he could go to work with his stepfather, Ismael Castillo.

Guerra was skeptical, but Perez was a smooth talker. Eventually he convinced the seasoned officer it would be the best move for everyone. She agreed on the condition he attend night classes to help him prepare for the GED. Perez agreed, but never showed up for the classes.

Guerra described her situation as "having her hands tied." She bemoaned the fact that she could not truly punish Perez for his inability to do what the judge ordered him to do. "He might have been violating some of those rules of probation," she recalled of Perez, "but he had not really officially violated the law enough for our legal department to accept it."

Perez routinely failed to show up for his monthly meetings with Guerra. He skipped out in July, August, September, and November of 1992, and never showed up. According to Harris County assistant district attorney (ADA) Marie Munier, Perez's probation record was terminated on February 3, 1993. Munier criticized Guerra's handling of Perez's probation and believed she "let him slide," when there was no apparent effort to extend his probation.

* * *

Friday, December 4, 1992—4:00 P.M.
Oak Forest Apartments
Afton Street
Houston, Texas

Thirty-six-year-old Jose Arellano drove all the way from Fresno, California, to Houston, Texas, in his big 1985 red Blazer just so he could attend the wedding of his cousin Jose Acosta and spend some time with his other cousin, the similarly named Jose Ariel Acosta.

The husband and father of three was looking forward to seeing his cousins and relaxing at the wedding. He had driven straight through and the wedding was about to happen the next day. Arellano was also excited because this was his first time in Houston.

After the wedding ceremony the following day, a group of three teenage boys walked intently toward Arellano and Ariel Acosta. Arellano did not think anything of them until one boy dressed in a long coat and a backward baseball cap walked right up into his face.

"Give me your money," the first boy demanded.

Arellano was dumbstruck. Since he only spoke Spanish, he did not understand the boy. When he did not respond appropriately, one of the two boys behind the lead boy pulled out a gun. Arellano saw the weapon and instinctively thrust his hands up toward his chest to protect himself.

The gunman held the weapon with both hands and fired it at Arellano's chest. The bullet ricocheted off the bone of his upper arm, which caused the bullet to slow down when it entered his body. Arellano rolled to the ground in an attempt to get away from the shooter. He hoped he could make it underneath a flatbed truck, which was parked in the street. As he rolled onto his stomach, he saw the third boy coming in his direction.

He's going to kill me, Arellano thought as the three boys quickly advanced toward him. He painfully attempted to roll toward the truck. Without warning, another *pop!* was heard. He instantly felt a searing white-hot pain in his upper back. He had been shot, a second time, between the shoulder blades by the second boy in line.

Arellano passed out on the street.

At the same time, the first boy pointed his gun at Ariel Acosta, pulled the trigger, and slammed a bullet into Arellano's cousin's chest. It was the last sound and last sight Arellano remembered before he fell unconscious.

Efrain Perez, a boy Arellano did not even know, shot him in the arm and chest. Arellano later cried as he realized Perez had killed his cousin Jose Ariel Acosta.

Perez and his two companions, Joe Medellin and Peter Cantu, took off running and never collected any money from Arellano. Jose Acosta ran to his brother's side.

He was too late.

No one was ever charged with the murder of Jose Ariel Acosta or the attempted murder of Jose Arellano.

Sunday, June 6, 1993—10:30 P.M.
Memorial Hermann Northwest Hospital
North Loop West
Houston, Texas

Peter Cantu swerved his red Ford pickup truck into the emergency area of the Memorial Hermann Northwest Hospital. In the backseat of the car were Joe Medellin and Frank and Ramon Sandoval. In the passenger seat sat Efrain Perez. He was bleeding from his chest. He had just been shot.

Cantu pulled up to the curb and jumped out of the

car. He was joined by Medellin and together they removed Perez from the front seat.

"Those motherfuckers," Cantu swore through gritted teeth as he assisted his friend into the hospital.

They managed to escort Perez into the emergency room (ER). Cantu was getting impatient.

"What is taking so long?" he screamed at a nurse. Eventually some medical personnel came out to tend to Perez. Cantu and Medellin stood by their friend and began to talk about who shot him.

"We're gonna make them pay," Cantu said. Both he and Medellin were getting more incensed. They were also obstructing the hospital staff.

Security guard Joseph Similien spotted the conundrum and approached. He was informed by one of the nurses that the two young men were in the way and they could not tend to Perez's gunshot wound.

"Don't tell them anything," Cantu whispered to Medellin as Similien approached. The security guard overheard their conversation. "Don't tell them what happened," Cantu added, and then took off running. He yelled out, "I'm gonna get those motherfuckers!"

Similien did not attempt to stop Cantu, but called a patrol officer to locate him. He then walked up to Medellin and asked him to step away so the staff could help his friend. They walked to the lobby. Similien wanted Medellin to stick around so he could tell the police what happened to Perez, despite the fact the guard believed Medellin would lie to them.

Within a few minutes, Cantu reentered the hospital with the Sandoval brothers in tow. Soon thereafter, Houston police officer Mike Knehans walked into the hospital. He spoke with Similien to get the lay of the land; then he decided to go directly to Cantu.

"What's your name, sir?" Knehans asked Cantu.

"What do you need to know that for?" sneered Cantu.

"I need to know this for the investigation. What's your name?"

"Peter Cantu."

"What's your date of birth?"

"May 27, 1978," Cantu lied, making himself three years younger.

"You're fifteen?" Officer Knehans asked skeptically.

Cantu smiled back at the officer.

"Tell me what happened," the officer queried.

Cantu began to spin three or four different versions of the incident. He would not give the officer a straight answer about how Perez had been shot. He told him it occurred near North Loop and Airline Drive. Then he changed it so it occurred closer to the hospital. The story never stayed the same two times in a row. He also lied about the car that pulled up next to them and whose passenger shot Perez. He first said he did not know the color. Then it was a gold car. Then blue.

Knehans could not believe the balls on this kid. The whole time Cantu was lying to his face, he was also acting "arrogant" and "cocky."

"Son, I know you're lying to me," Knehans informed Cantu, who simply smiled sarcastically back at the officer. Knehans gave up and moved on.

Cantu walked away and grinned at Medellin, as if to gloat, *You see, that's how it's done.*

Officer Knehans never found out who shot Perez or why.

Perez's wound was superficial and he was released within hours.

Chapter 6

Raul Villarreal finished up his game of *Street Fighter II* and headed out of the store. He was ready to walk back home. As he slipped out the door, he spotted Efrain Perez, who was still working on his ride. He walked back over to his friend.

"Dude, what's wrong with this piece of shit?" he playfully asked his buddy.

"It's a piece of shit." Perez laughed.

Raul laughed as well. "So what you got goin' on tonight?" the taller, heavier young man asked.

"Nothin', man. Maybe drink a few beers. You wanna join us?" Perez asked.

Raul was excited. He knew Perez hung out with some pretty cool guys and he wanted to get into their inner circle somehow. "Yeah, man. I guess that'd be cool. Where and when?"

"C'mon over to my place around five-thirty and we'll head on over to the house of a buddy of mine. Cool?"

"Yeah, dude, that'll work."

"And bring some beer," Perez ordered, and then stuck his head under the hood yet again.

"All right," Raul shouted back.

The video gamer had a loftier bounce in his step as he headed back to Chapman Street and his parents' house. He hoped this night might lead to building some new relationships with some new friends so he could get out of the house more and get his parents out of his business. He was sick of feeling like a little kid.

Raul stopped briefly to speak with his mother. He told her he ran into Efrain Perez at the convenience store and that he was fixing his family's truck. She again warned him to stay away from Perez, and added that he was "bad news." Raul ignored the comment and went into his room and waited.

The next two hours crawled by for Raul. He was itching to get out of the house and meet up with Perez. Around 5:30 P.M., he took off. He did not tell his mom anything, and when she discovered he was not in the house, she became worried. She later said she "didn't see him no more" and was very concerned because "he never disappears from the house."

When Raul arrived at Perez's, the first thing the tall and skinny Efrain asked was "Where's the beer?"

"Dude, I'm not old enough to buy beer." Raul shrugged.

"That is lame." Perez snorted in disgust. "C'mon, I know where we can get some." The two boys hopped into Perez's car.

Perez drove over to the house of another buddy of his, Peter Cantu. If anybody would have beer on hand, it would be Cantu, Perez assured Raul.

"Cool," the new guy said. The two young men sped out on the gravel as they headed for their first beers of the evening.

* * *

Thursday, June 24, 1993—5:30 P.M.
Houston, Texas

Elizabeth Pena and Jennifer Ertman, meanwhile, were headed for their first tacos of the night. The girls decided to walk to a nearby Mexican restaurant and buy some of their favorite food. They purchased it and were on their way back to the Pena home when a car pulled up directly beside them. The girls were a bit leery, but then Elizabeth began to smile.

The man in the car rolled down his window and said, "Hey, what are two cute girls like you doing walking down the street alone?"

"Dad!" Elizabeth squealed. "Leave us alone. We'll see you later." Elizabeth smiled and waved as her dad drove off. The girls kept walking and laughing.

Thursday, June 24, 1993—6:00 P.M.
Cantu residence
Ashland Street
Houston, Texas

Efrain Perez pulled his car into the well-kept driveway of Peter Cantu's family's house. He noticed his friend fooling with his red Ford pickup truck. Cantu looked up at Perez, nodded, and went back to working on his truck. Perez pulled up, killed the engine, and he and Raul stepped out of the ride. Cantu looked up again and glanced over at the noticeably larger Raul with suspicious eyes.

"Who's he?" Cantu barked at Perez.

"He's cool, man. He's cool," Perez assured his friend. "This is Raul. He wants to hang. He's cool, man."

"What's up, man?" Raul nodded toward Cantu, who ignored him.

PETER CANTU

Chapter 7

Peter Cantu was born in Austin, Texas, on May 27, 1975, to Suzie and Rudolph "Rudy" Cantu. Peter was the third boy, after his older brothers Rudy Jr. and Joe. A younger sister, Sabrina, was born several years later.

Suzie was born and raised in Austin and later met Rudy when she was fifteen. She only managed to make it through tenth grade. Her husband was born with a "crippled foot" and suffered from epilepsy, but he was a strong man and a good provider for his family with income earned from his job as an office furniture deliverer.

The Cantus held family close to their hearts. They were especially fond of Rudy's father, who lived on a ranch. The family used to visit Grandpa almost every weekend. Little Peter loved to spend time with his grandfather fishing on the lake or riding on the large lawn mower to cut the grass. It was almost like having two dads.

Suzie believed Peter was always a "pretty good kid," but she had to get on him about cleaning his room or picking up after himself.

When Peter was four, his mother took him to a speech therapist to work on his poor speaking skills. The Cantus lived in Austin until Peter was four-and-a-half years old.

They packed up their belongings and headed southeast to Houston.

By the time Peter was ready to attend school, Suzie noticed that he would get frustrated when he would speak. He would get "all the words combined in one" when he spoke and had difficulty communicating. Unfortunately, Peter's speech problems became the brunt of amusement for some of his fellow kindergarteners at Hohl Elementary. His mother claimed the kids used to tease him constantly.

Peter was never a very good student. It was evident by first grade at Janowski Elementary, where he did poorly in every subject, except math in which he exceeded, scoring in the upper 92 percentile. His reading and language skills were especially poor as he scored in the bottom 7 percentile

In second grade, he improved his scores across the board; however, he was still far behind most kids his same age.

Peter did even worse in third grade. He made D's in almost every subject. His mother blamed it on the deaths of an aunt and his beloved grandfather. Peter crawled into a shell after the death of his grandfather. His mother noticed he no longer wanted to talk to anyone, he tended to back away from people who attempted to get close to him, and he would never cry.

"He just did not show me grief when his grandfather passed away," Suzie recalled. "He blamed himself when his grandfather died, but I don't know why. He took it very hard."

Suzie Cantu added it was extra difficult for Peter because his grandfather was laid to rest on Peter's birthday. "It bothered him tremendously," she declared. "On his birthday, the only thing Peter would do was ask to take him to go see his grandfather at the cemetery. So we used to take him all the way out to Gonzales, Texas, because that's where he is buried. That's all he wanted for his birthday. He didn't want birthday cake. He didn't want a party. He didn't want anything. Just to go visit the cemetery."

Peter also blamed his poor performance that year on his teacher. He claimed his teacher used to "pick on him a lot" by "poking him on the shoulders." Suzie Cantu added that her son would come home from school with "all sorts of bruises on the side of his shoulders."

Suzie attempted to deal with the problem, but she was allegedly always rebuffed by the school. She claimed she spoke to the school's principal, who told her they could do nothing because the teacher was part of the staff and she was only a parent.

Whatever the reason, Peter was retained for the third grade, which meant he would be required to repeat the grade.

After finally completing third grade, Peter transferred to Garden Oaks Elementary, where he reverted back to his poor performance. Once again, he made nothing but D's and F's. He was retained for fourth grade this time. Before even reaching junior high school, he had already flunked out twice.

Peter Cantu was an eleven-year-old in a classroom full of nine-year-olds. It was not easy for him to relate to his classmates, but he made a go of it in his second shot at fourth grade. He started off promisingly, showing up to class regularly and even making decent grades of B's and C's. He did well enough to make it out of fourth grade.

On June 24, 1986, eight-year-old Darren McElroy pedaled his bike home from another day at the year-round Janowski Elementary School. As he came to the intersection of East Crosstimbers Street and Bauman Road, he pulled his bicycle up to the 7-Eleven convenience store so he could go inside to play video games, especially any of them having to do with the movie *Star Wars,* as was his normal daily routine. He was very proud of his bike because he won it for collecting the most money to help support muscular dystrophy. Darren's little brother suffered from the disease, so the bike had even more significance for him.

Darren proudly rode his bike around like a grown-up motorcyclist would ride a brand-new shiny chrome-plated Harley-Davidson. It was a very unique bike because it was spiffed-up with several 7-Eleven Southland Corporation logo stickers. He gingerly placed the bike next to the front door on the outside of the store and went inside, ready to conquer Darth Vader and his band of Imperial stormtroopers.

The bespectacled lad finished up saving the planet and headed out of the store. As he stepped outside the large glass front door, he saw his prized bicycle. He made sure everything was in order, hopped on, and continued on his way home. The young boy was less than one hundred feet away from the 7-Eleven when he noticed someone in his peripheral vision. He spotted an older boy slightly behind him, but he did not pay any attention to him. As he continued to casually pedal his bike, he noticed another older boy on the other side, also behind him. He continued to pedal and did not think much of them.

Suddenly he heard running footsteps, so he glanced back over his shoulder. The two older boys were heading for him in a full-tilt sprint. Darren realized they were coming after him, but by the time he got up the energy to pedal faster, they had already caught up to him. One of the boys pushed the eight-year-old off his bicycle, and Darren rolled into a ditch, scratching his expensive glasses. The other boy grabbed the bike by its handlebars and swung it in the air before it hit the ground.

The boys laughed as they took off with the young boy's

bicycle. The boy who pushed Darren off his bike called out to his companion, who had ridden off on the bike, "Hey, Peter!" and ran after him.

Darren McElroy dusted the gravel and dirt off his clothes and began to walk home without his bicycle.

Once Darren finally arrived at home, he was greeted by his mother, Nancy McElroy, who instantly noticed that he was scuffed-up. He was also crying. After realizing her son was okay, Nancy took him inside, grabbed a telephone, and called the police. She reported that her son's bicycle had been stolen by a couple of preteen boys, and her son had been assaulted in the process. Nancy even went looking for the perpetrators back at the convenience store. She asked a group of teenage boys if they had seen the altercation and robbery, but they all claimed not to have seen anything. She even offered them $10 to help her locate her son's bicycle, but to no avail.

Two hours later, Peter Cantu came riding up the McElroys' driveway on Darren's bicycle. Nancy came outside to greet the young boy.

"I heard that you were looking for this," the irascible youth stated. "I found it near the convenience store and was told it belonged to your son."

"Yes, that's his bike," Mrs. McElroy acknowledged.

"I also heard you were giving out a reward for it," Peter said.

"Yes, here you go," the mother said as she handed the small boy a $10 bill. Before she could ask him how he had found the bike, he snatched the bill out of her hand and spun around to take off.

He did not look back.

Nancy McElroy stored her son's prized bicycle in the family garage. Two days later, it was stolen and never seen again by Darren McElroy.

Three weeks later, however, on July 16, someone

came knocking on Peter Cantu's door on Melrose Street. Houston Police Department Juvenile Division officer Charles Niemeier paid the eleven-year-old a visit. Officer Niemeier, despite wearing a service revolver, considered his position to be one of a counselor. He usually could reach the kids by discussing their problems with them or with their parents. It was rather unusual for the officer to be making a house call on such a young perpetrator. The youngest he dealt with were usually twelve- or thirteen-year-olds.

Officer Niemeier knocked on the Cantus' door and was greeted by Mr. Cantu. The officer explained why he was there and requested to speak with Peter. Mr. Cantu quickly opened the door to let the officer inside. He then excused himself and called out for Peter to come into the living room.

As soon as Peter entered and spotted the police officer, he knew he was in trouble. Officer Niemeier informed the family Peter had been accused of first assaulting and then stealing a bicycle away from eight-year-old Darren McElroy. The officer added that Peter was also accused of stealing the same bicycle a second time, two days later. He placed Peter under arrest and took him into custody.

When a Juvenile Division officer arrests someone and places him in custody, it simply means the juvenile has his rights read to him and is questioned by the officer in front of the juvenile's parents or guardian. Officer Niemeier questioned Peter for nearly twenty minutes about the incidents.

Upon completion of the interview, Officer Niemeier released Peter back into the custody of his parents, as is the norm in juvenile cases. At that point, the officer could have elected to either take Peter into detention or let him stay with his parents. Some of the factors that go into making such a decision are the serious nature of the crime, the attitude of the parents, and the attitude of the juvenile. In this particular case, Officer Niemeier opted to allow Peter to stay with his parents. He also referred Peter to the Harris County Juvenile Probation Department.

By fifth grade, Peter was consistently making B's and he did well on his required Texas Educational Assessment of Minimal Skills test, where he scored above average in everything except language.

In 1988, Peter started out in F. M. Black Middle School, but flunked out of school due to "excessive absences."

That same year, thirteen-year-old Peter got himself into even more trouble. Amber Law, a fifth-grade classmate of Peter's at Garden Oaks Elementary School, would often walk home with him and a few of his friends after school.

Amber enjoyed Peter's company, until July 25, 1988. As Peter walked Amber to the front door of her home on West Thirty-first Street, he leaned in and attempted to kiss the younger girl. Amber immediately pulled away as she had no interest in boys whatsoever. She closed the door on him and he walked away, dejected.

Peter, however, was determined to get what he wanted.

Two days later, on July 27, Peter returned to Amber's house. He walked up to her front door and knocked on it. Amber peeked outside one of the windows and saw it was Peter. She refused to answer the door. Peter knocked again, this time more insistently. Again, Amber ignored him.

"Let me in!" Peter screamed at Amber from behind the door. "I know you're in there. Let me in!"

Amber held her ground, did not respond, and refused to open the door.

Peter was furious. He began screaming obscenities at the girl and continued to bang on her front door. When that did not work, he moved to the windows of the house and began banging on them as well.

"You better let me in, you bitch!" he screamed at Amber. "You'd better open that goddamned door!"

Amber was terrified, but she would not give in. Peter continued to bang on each window of the house. He circled her home for more than ten minutes, banging on windows, on the walls, and on the front door, spewing out obscenities as he did it.

Peter started to knock on Amber's father Sherman Law's bedroom window. He banged on it so hard that the window shattered everywhere. Peter took off running, not wanting to get caught.

Once Amber realized Peter was truly gone, she rushed over to the telephone and called her father at work. The terrified girl explained what happened and begged for him to come home. There was no need for pleading, as Mr. Law rushed home to check on his daughter. Once he realized she was okay, he headed over to Peter Cantu's apartment on North Shepherd Drive. He was insistent that he would have words with Peter's father about his son's behavior.

When Mr. Law arrived at the Cantu residence on the second floor of the apartment complex, only Peter and his mother were there. Law spoke with Suzie Cantu about her son.

"My daughter told me that your son here tried to terrorize her," the flustered father spoke.

Suzie Cantu looked confused. "No, not my Peter. He's not that kind of boy."

"Ma'am, I'm sorry, but I know my daughter is telling me the truth about your son. Now, what are you going to do about it?"

"Sir, I'm sorry, but I don't believe he was over there.

He would never do anything to hurt a girl. You must be mistaken," she defended her son.

Once Sherman Law realized Mrs. Cantu was not going to be any help, he turned his attention to Peter. "I don't want you calling my house anymore, you hear me?" the angry father declared while pointing a finger at the teenager. "I don't want you harassing her and I don't want you to come anywhere near our house anymore. Do you understand me?"

"I don't have to do what you tell me," Peter sneered at Amber's father. "I can do whatever the hell I want." Suzie Cantu did nothing. She did not reprimand her son. She did not apologize to Mr. Law. She simply seemed to cower in the corner and let her son do what he wanted.

Sherman Law was furious; however, he kept his cool, turned around, and walked away. When he returned to his home, he dialed the police and reported the incident between Peter Cantu and his daughter. Houston Police Department Juvenile Division officer Johnny Kirtley showed up at the Law residence several hours later. Law explained to the officer what happened and that Peter Cantu was the one responsible. Officer Kirtley then headed over to the Cantus' apartment complex, where he spoke with the teenager as he stood on the Cantus' balcony.

"Peter, the young lady inside that house knows who you are," the officer told Peter straight up. "She knows your name. Says you go to school with her, so don't try to pull the wool over my eyes, son. We know you did it."

Peter stared at the officer and did not say a word. According to the officer, he did not look too impressed or intimidated.

"You need to just stay away from those people," the officer continued. "You don't need to be going around there anymore, all right? You break into somebody's house and they're going to shoot you and they will be in their rights to do so, so just stay away from them."

Peter continued to nod his head; however, the officer sensed what he was saying was not really sinking in.

"Think of it this way," the officer reasoned, "if you don't want something done to you, don't do it to someone else." Maybe the Golden Rule would affect the boy in some way, Kirtley thought.

"Okay, I'll stay away," Peter finally responded.

Officer Kirtley knew he had not gotten through to the kid. Kirtley left Peter Cantu with a parting thought: "You messed up this time. Don't do it again." He looked at the boy one last time and added, "Keep your life straight. Otherwise, it's going to come back and haunt you." The officer nodded at the boy and walked away. When he returned to the police station, he filed his report and referred the case over to the Harris County Juvenile Probation Department.

Unfortunately, Officer Kirtley's admonishments did not leave a lasting impression on Peter Cantu.

Just a few months after the Amber Law harassment incident, Peter found himself in trouble yet again. On November 17, 1988, at Hamilton Middle School, sixth-grade English teacher Diane Caudill was attempting to usher a few straggling students into her classroom as the bell rang. The teacher noticed one of her students, Peter Cantu, standing in the doorway, looking out into the hall. She did not really know the boy, as he recently transferred to Hamilton and had only been in her classroom for two days. Caudill was not sure why Peter did not step inside the classroom, so she walked over to see what he was doing. As she came closer to him, she noticed that he was staring at another student, a young white male, who was much bigger than Peter. The two boys were having a "stare down" contest.

Caudill described the boys as "nose to nose" with each other and not saying a word. She also noticed several more students "mobbing around in the hall," waiting to see if Peter and the larger boy were going to start a fight.

"Peter, please come in here and take your seat," Caudill asked in a calm and polite voice. Peter ignored her.

"Peter, come in and sit down, please."

Again, nothing. The showdown continued.

"Peter, I need for you to get in here now," she stated rather emphatically. She did not appreciate being ignored by one of her students.

Peter was focused solely on the larger boy.

Sensing a fight was going to break out and eager to get her class started, Caudill grabbed the back-collar area of Peter's coat and gently attempted to tug him into the classroom. "Please, Peter," Caudill pleaded, "come in the classroom and sit down."

Suddenly, without warning, Peter turned around and grabbed Caudill's hands, raised them to her chest, and pushed her away from him. Caudill was stunned. She did not say anything, because she was practically in shock that one of her students had raised a hand to her.

Peter Cantu was not done.

The teenage boy walked up to Caudill again and pushed her even harder. He knocked her backward and she stumbled a bit, but retained her footing. He then continued to push her repeatedly, until he forced her backward all the way to the back of the room.

"Get out of my way, old lady," he told her.

Caudill could not respond, nor could she fend off his advances.

Peter stopped briefly, only to grab her by both hands, spin her around, and start pushing her back in the direction they came from. "Stop touching me," the boy yelled at her, even though he was the one who had her in his grasp. "Let me go! Don't touch me!" he yelled as he pushed her back toward the hallway.

Caudill finally managed to scream, "Push the panic button!" One of the girls sprinted up to her teacher's desk and pushed an emergency button, which notified the principal something was wrong in Caudill's classroom.

Peter did not stop. He continued to shove the teacher out into the hallway and scream at her to let go of him. Once he had her out in the hallway, he continued forcefully pushing her. Caudill stumbled backward the length of two classrooms and into a group of students still standing in the hall.

In the background, the intercom to Caudill's classroom came on. "Is everything all right, Ms. Caudill?" asked the school principal.

"Ms. Caudill needs help!" one of the students yelled. "Peter is hurting her!"

Meanwhile, in the hallway, sixth-grade social studies teacher Stephen Seale saw a commotion coming toward him, but had no idea what was going on. As the cluster came closer, he could see his fellow teacher, Diane Caudill, being assaulted by a student. He saw the boy kicking at the teacher and pushing her backward. Seale took off toward the pair, moved a few students out of his pathway, came up behind Peter Cantu, and grabbed him by the back of his collar. Seale, however, was standing too close to the student and accidentally fell to the ground, taking the boy with him. Peter began to struggle and kick out at Caudill as he lay on the ground underneath Seale.

"Don't you ever put your hands on a teacher!" Seale barked at Peter.

At that point, Seale grabbed the boy and restrained him until he finally calmed down, which took three or four minutes.

"I didn't do anything," Peter lied to Seale. "I got respect for teachers."

"You sure have got a strange way of showing it," Seale replied. Once the situation appeared to be settled, Seale picked Peter up and led him to Assistant Principal Harland Maresh's office.

Maresh expelled Peter from school for the rest of the year. Diane Caudill suffered bruises on two of her fingers and sore wrists from when Peter Cantu had bent them backward while pushing her.

Diane Caudill was relieved Peter had been removed from school. She also filed a police report against the boy. Peter Cantu was arrested, charged, and let go with a warning.

Caudill's relief was short-lived, however, as the Hamilton Middle School administration allowed Peter to reenroll the following spring semester. He was back in school by January 1989. He was not placed in Caudill's class, much to her appreciation. He did, however, continue to torment her whenever he could. He would often come early in the morning into the hallway where her classroom was, even though students were not allowed in the hall at the time. He would follow Caudill approximately six to eight feet behind her as she walked down the hall. Whenever she would turn around to see what he was doing, he always had his head down as if he were not looking at her.

Stephen Seale watched Peter once as he sauntered past Caudill's classroom. He noticed the teenager looked into her classroom and gave her a facetious, disrespectful smile. It was too much for Caudill to handle any longer, so she put in a request for a transfer, which was granted.

Peter continued his reign of terror at Hamilton Middle School even after Caudill left. Assistant Principal Maresh had several consultations with Peter about his numerous discipline problems. Peter got into trouble often for cursing. He would curse several people, including teachers, other students, campus security guards, Maresh, and even the principal. He often muttered profanities under his breath; however, he would also say inappropriate things out loud as well.

Peter had also been expelled for fighting. He seemed to spend the majority of his time in Maresh's office.

"I was concerned, naturally, about Peter," Maresh later recalled. "I was hoping to turn around his behavior, try to make him a productive student, a good member of the school, but it just seemed like things only got progressively worse as time moved on." In fact, Peter's behavior steadily declined. "His attitude toward teachers and toward administrators and toward students did not improve. It got worse."

When Maresh could not reach Peter through a direct approach, he attempted to get some help from Suzie Cantu. That move did not work, as the increasingly clueless mother refused to accept that her boy could do any wrong. According to Maresh, Suzie Cantu would always side with her son against the school—no matter what.

"I didn't get any cooperation out of her," the assistant principal recalled. "Usually she came in there protecting him and she was always against the school and against us enforcing the rules that he had broken."

Peter had gotten away with assault of a teacher and had forced her to transfer. He received no punishment other than being sent home for two months. He was placed on what is known as "home base assignment," wherein a suspended student is allowed to continue to do his schoolwork, turn it in to the school, and still have it graded. Not much of a hardship for a boy who had grown to despise the educational system.

Peter also received special treatment from Hamilton Middle School in the form of extensive counseling from Maresh. Peter and his mother were also referred to an

outside counseling service for help with his disruptive behavior. The assistant principal believed Peter's behavior
was a direct result of having a poor self-image. Mrs. Cantu,
however, believed her son was never responsible for
anything bad. She blamed everyone except her own son.

"I really don't feel that Peter has a problem," Mrs.
Cantu reiterated, ignoring the many obvious signs that
stared her directly in the face. "He never acts this way at
home."

Peter was placed in a behavior class to try and help
shape up his bad attitude. That did not work, either, as
he was constantly starting arguments and provoking
fights with the other students. He was eventually removed from the behavior class and placed back in the
school's general population.

Peter Cantu was not yet done with the Caudill/Seale
situation.

Several months later, on October 19, 1989, Alicia
Seale, daughter of Stephen Seale, was in attendance at
the Hamilton Middle School versus F. M. Black Middle
School football game. The eleven-year-old girl was there
with a few of her girlfriends. Her father was also present in the stadium, but was not with her. Alicia and her
friends were having a good time gabbing with one another in the stands on the chilly evening. After the first
quarter ended, Alicia told her friends she wanted to get
something to drink from the concession stand.

Alicia arrived at the stand to find a fairly long line, so
she took her place in it. She looked down at the ground,
staring at her shoes, and did not hear the teenage boy
and his friends walk up behind her. Oblivious, she continued to look down.

"I'm gonna kill your father," Alicia thought she heard
from behind her. She looked up and back and saw Peter
Cantu with several of his buddies.

"I'm sorry?" she said.

"I'm gonna kill your father," Peter repeated.

Alicia knew Peter. They both had attended Garden Oaks Elementary School and were now at Hamilton Middle School. She was not friends with him, but knew who he was, even before the incident with her father.

"I can't believe your asshole of a father grabbed me and threw me to the ground like that. Then that fucker slapped me. Can you believe that?" Peter expressed his anger.

Alicia had no idea what to say. She began to get nervous, especially since Peter had several other boys with him.

"I hate your father! He's an asshole!" he yelled at her. "I'm gonna kill that son of a bitch. I should shoot his ass!" he growled at her.

Alicia was terrified now.

"Is your dad here?" Peter wanted to know.

Alicia finally broke her silence and lied. "No, he's not here." She hoped the lie did not show on her face.

"He better not be here," one of Peter's friends said in a loud voice. "We brought ourselves a gun."

Alicia still had no idea what to say. She simply put her head down, turned around, and walked away. She then covertly located her father and told him about the threat.

Peter was later escorted off the stadium premises. Apparently, it was for an unrelated matter that involved him and another student, which nearly escalated into a fight.

The following day, a school security guard, Marvin Lee, brought Peter into Maresh's office. The guard informed the assistant principal that Cantu had made threats against Stephen Seale at the football game the night before. Maresh had not even begun to speak to the teenager about the near fight with the other student when Peter started to cause a commotion in the administrative waiting room.

The angry youth cursed at Lee and called him "a fuckin' nigger." He also called the assistant principal's assistant, who was also black, "a goddamned nigger." He repeatedly uttered the word "nigger" and continued to taunt the pair.

Maresh contacted the school principal and told her that Peter Cantu was causing a major disruption. When she entered the waiting room, Peter lashed out at her as well.

"Fuck you, you fuckin' bitch," he yelled at the principal.

"What the fuck you looking at, nigger?" he spewed at the security guard.

Peter tried to make a run for it; however, Lee easily snatched him and placed handcuffs on his wrists. Instead of calming down, Peter's expletive-filled rants increased.

"I'll kill you, you piece of shit nigger," he screamed at the security guard. "I will kill you." He looked at Maresh and threatened him, too. "Mark my words, motherfucker. I will kill you!" Peter kicked and screamed and thrashed around, but the guard had a firm grasp on him.

"You're a fuckin' asshole goddamned nigger," he spewed at Lee. He looked at Maresh and spat out, "You're a fuckin' asshole, too!"

Peter turned his head back toward Lee and stated, "I'm going to get you back. That's not a threat. That's a promise."

Peter would not be going anywhere and he would not be killing anyone that particular day. Maresh called the police.

They arrived and placed Peter Cantu under arrest. The boy kicked out at Maresh's desk and knocked several papers and a framed photograph off it. He then attempted to make a lunge at Lee; however, the Houston police officers restrained the young boy before he could get to the guard.

It would be Peter Cantu's last day at Hamilton Middle School.

After his expulsion, however, Peter could not seem to keep away from the school. Even though Peter was not supposed to go anywhere near the campus, Maresh spotted Cantu several times loitering around the school. He and a couple of his buddies who had also been expelled would come up to school and curse at Lee.

Lee also recalled another time when the expelled Peter attempted to scare him. According to Lee, Peter and a couple of his friends came up to the campus before school started. Lee was inside the school, but he could clearly see Peter out in the school parking lot. He watched as Peter pointed at him, turned his back away, and pulled his shirt up over his head, revealing a large tattooed *Cantu* inked across his back. He then turned around and smiled at Lee, as if to say, *Look, I can withstand the pain from this. You think you can hurt me?*

Peter Cantu was eventually transferred back to F. M. Black Middle School, where he had been transferred to from Hamilton in the fall of 1988. While at Black Middle School, Peter ran into more problems, especially when it came to authority figures.

Dalton Hughes Jr., who ran security at Black Middle School, had to deal with Peter's disruptive behavior on several occasions. He was called into a classroom more than once to restrain Peter, who had verbally attacked a teacher. Peter had either been cursing or yelling at a teacher, and Hughes had to remove him from the classroom. Hughes, a large man, would grab Peter by the shoulder, and the student would jerk away and spew cusswords at him.

Hughes also spotted Peter in the hallways arguing with students. He believed the young boy was always on edge and ready to fight anyone at anytime for any reason. "He was a bully," Hughes recalled. "He was very disruptive, he didn't have respect for authority, and he was belligerent."

Finally, after too many infractions, Principal Ben Azios suspended Peter Cantu for three days. It was actually the third or fourth time Azios had suspended him—he could barely keep track, it happened so often.

But Peter would not be dissuaded. He and his friend Joe Medellin rode their bicycles up to the Black Middle School campus the day after his latest suspension. When Hughes spotted Peter, he warned him he was trespassing and needed to leave the premises or he would call the police.

Peter responded to Hughes by flipping him off.

"You no-good prick!" Peter screamed across the street at Hughes. "You can't do anything to me. I'm not on the campus."

Hughes assured him he was and that the cops would be on their way.

Peter screamed back, "I can do what I want. To hell with you."

The ranting continued for several minutes until Houston police officer M. A. Cross arrived at the scene. Officer Cross motioned for Peter and Joe to come over to him. Peter walked over to the police officer and began cursing at him.

Cross approached Peter and began to search the boy. The entire time he was being searched, Peter lit up a firestorm of expletives directed at the officer, the school, Hughes—anyone and everyone.

Officer Cross informed him he was under arrest. Before the officer could restrain the teenager, Peter picked up his bicycle, lifted it up over his head, and slammed it down on the concrete street.

Peter screamed at the officer. "I can go where I want! You can't do nothing to me, you piece of shit!"

"Dude, calm down, man." Joe tried to talk some sense into his friend.

Peter did not listen. He began to yell at Officer Cross, who grabbed him and spun him around to lead him to the squad car. As the officer pulled the teenager's arm to direct him, Peter lashed out with his feet. He began kicking wildly and continued cursing a torrent of blue phrases. The officer was able to guide him to the police car and push him up against the vehicle. Hughes helped restrain Peter so the officer could slap a pair of cuffs on him.

Peter's mother somehow got wind of what was happening with her son and she made a beeline to the school. As she pulled up, she saw her son kicking and screaming.

"Peter, stop yelling at the police officer," she warned him.

Peter ignored her as well.

"Peter, stop it," she pleaded.

Peter acted as if she were not even there. He screamed profanities as the officer forced him into the backseat of the police car. Once inside the vehicle, he started kicking at the inside of the door with his feet.

Hughes was stunned by Peter's reaction. According to the security guard, Peter was "completely out of control." He added, "He just had no regard for the police officer, the uniform, for the assistant principal out there, me. He just didn't care."

Hughes later said he should not have been surprised by Peter's reaction to the police officer. He had witnessed him bully teachers in their classrooms and pick several fights with other students. Usually these were people who were physically weaker.

"He's like a wolf to a rabbit," Hughes analogized.

Peter Cantu was arrested and released without any further charges.

* * *

The following year, Peter Cantu was transferred back to Hamilton and was given the Wechsler intelligence test by Dr. Carroll Kennedy. Neither Peter nor his parents wanted him to take the test, but the school highly recommended it. They finally realized Peter had flunked out of school three times and needed some additional help. The Cantus relented and Peter was administered the test. Dr. Kennedy discovered Peter's verbal intelligence was low, while his nonverbal intelligence was average. Based on all the other tests, she recommended he be placed in special education.

Despite the assessment, for no apparent rhyme or reason, school records indicate Peter bypassed seventh grade altogether and was sent to the eighth grade. As a fifteen-year-old eighth grader, he had the reading level of a second grader. His spelling ability was worse than a first grader's.

On September 19, 1990, Dr. Barbara Felkins gave Peter a psychiatric evaluation. She discovered he suffered from severe dysthmia, or depression, and also a severe conduct disorder. The doctor noted he was under "extreme psycho-social stressors" and had "very poor level functioning" skills. She also described him as "intensely angry" and that he "has a defensive shell built up around him."

During the evaluation, Peter confided in the doctor that "he don't trust nobody because I don't need to trust people. I have no need for help from anyone." He added he is "quick to hold a grudge" and "others do not care for" him. Also, he "must defend [himself] at all cost."

Dr. Felkins's recommendation was for Peter to be taught in a more structured environment with a lower student-to-teacher ratio.

After the evaluation, the Hamilton staff members, Dr. Felkins, and Suzie Cantu agreed it would be best to place

Peter at the Harper Alternative School, a school for troubled or emotionally disturbed students.

The goal was for him to attend Harper for one semester, hope he could get his act together, and let him return to regular ninth grade afterward.

Suzie Cantu had a completely different take on how the staff at Hamilton helped her son. She complained the principal "ignored her pleas to help her son" and instead "simply expelled him." She also claimed the staff at Hamilton "never showed me that report" in reference to Dr. Felkins's psychiatric evaluation of her son. Peter Cantu attempted to reenroll at Hamilton; however, Principal Diana Mulet would not allow him to return.

When asked why a disruptive student is usually transferred, Mulet stated it would be to hopefully provide a better environment for the student so he or she can improve his or her behavior. When asked specifically why she had requested Peter Cantu's transfer, Mulet candidly replied, "To be honest, I just felt like he didn't need to be in my school anymore."

It did not take long for Peter Cantu to have run-ins with the authority figures at Harper. According to Harper principal Paul Hanser, the school accepts students from the ages of thirteen to twenty-two. He added, "Part of getting to our school is that you have to really be out of every other school because of behavior problems." He also stated Harper is "like a school of last resort." The school's directive is to help straighten out its students so they can get back to their school with an improved outlook on life.

Harper requires its students to stay within their system for at least ninety days. If at the end of that period the student has proven that he or she can keep his or her bad behaviors in check, the school allows him or her to return to the student's previous educational institution.

According to Hanser, however, the average length of stay for a student at Harper was two years.

Hanser also stressed one of their goals is to make the student understand his actions and to take responsibility for those actions. "Our motto is, 'Together, we can,'" Hanser explained. "It's not the parents' fault that your child is this way. It's not our fault that he is not responding, but if we all work together, maybe he'll take responsibility for his actions and move ahead."

The success rate at Harper at the time was nearly 20 percent. Hanser was proud of that number. When he started eight years earlier, it was only 2 percent.

Peter was the second Cantu family member to be sent to Harper. His older brother Joe was also a student there. According to Hanser, Joe did very well at Harper and suggested to the principal they take in his brother who was getting into all sorts of trouble. The school agreed and allowed Peter to attend.

Peter Cantu's first year was "oppositional," according to Hanser, but he showed signs of improvement. This was mainly due to having only one teacher and one assistant so he was able to focus on the work at hand.

During his second year, Peter was placed into a so-called "high-school environment," where he did not function nearly as well. Mainly, he started skipping class. Other days, he would show up for his first class and then skip out the rest of the day.

Hanser noted that Peter had befriended another student, Sean O'Brien, with whom he would skip classes. Someone had informed Hanser that Peter and Sean would take off and head over to Peter's house, where the two boys would drink alcohol and do drugs. He could not confirm the information, but he had his suspicions.

Hanser did speak with Suzie Cantu about her son's potential abuse problems and encouraged her to seek drug-and-alcohol counseling for him. According to Hanser,

Mrs. Cantu seemed receptive, but he did not think she was able to follow through because she claimed she ran into too much bureaucratic red tape.

Hanser continued to work with Peter and help him through his issues. He described the young man as "belligerent" and difficult to work with. Peter would curse at Hanser if the principal said something he didn't like. He was also prone to walk away from the principal in the middle of a discussion and Hanser would end up having to chase Peter down to finish speaking to him. Peter also cursed at his teachers constantly. It was slow and not-so-steady progress dealing with Peter Cantu.

Looking at his educational records, it is readily apparent that Peter was not a good student. Not surprisingly, his mother, Suzie Cantu, had a different recollection.

"I know in school he did pretty good," Mrs. Cantu mysteriously recalled. "I know he got into trouble a little bit in school, but I know that other than that, his grades were always fair to pretty good. He got trophies for rope jumping. He also got trophies for being the Most Outstanding Student at Harper Alternative School for having the greatest improvement in his grades from the time he entered the school until the time he finished."

Mrs. Cantu also recalled some of Peter's sporting background. "He got some trophies for playing baseball. He played for three years. It would have been four years, except the third year he broke his foot going bike riding. That's when he did the rope jumping with the cast on. He did the jump rope contest at school with the cast on and he won. One of his baseball trophies was for the all-stars. He made the all-stars team and he was pretty good. He was the catcher for those years and he also played shortstop and second base, but mostly he was the catcher."

According to his mother, as Peter got older, his tastes

began to change. "While he was in Harper, he also worked on cars. He was a mechanic.

"And then one year they started to have weight lifting, so he started picking up weights and he got first place, two years straight in a row, as the one who picked up the most weight. One year he picked up six hundred seventy-five [pounds] total. The following year, he took it with six hundred ninety [pounds] total, so he was pretty good. Each year he got one medal. Each year he got first place."

When asked what her son was like growing up, Mrs. Cantu replied, "To me, he was a normal son, just like every other normal kid. He comes home with a bad grade or something, I ground him. I took the phone and TV away from him. Tell him he couldn't go out until I see that his homework is done, finished. He's grounded until his grades go up. His grades go up and then go back to his normal routine. Using the phone and using the TV."

Suzie Cantu seemed to ignore the fact that her son was not the perfect boy. Whenever he would get into trouble, and she or Rudy would ground him, he was usually nonplussed. "He would just say, 'For how long? How many days?' And I said, 'Until I get a report from school that says your grades are improving and going up. Until I feel that you are doing okay, then you are grounded.' He never complained about it, though."

Peter began to feel a bit more useful when he learned how to work on cars. "Yeah, he was pretty good on that," his mother recalled. "He'd change the oil in my car. If it needed brakes, he managed to buy the brakes and fix it and put them on. Or if it needed a jump or a tune-up, he could do it. I never had to go to a mechanic, mostly because Peter was the one who could do it all. He's very good with cars. He used to watch his grandfather on my husband's side. That's all they used to do is fix cars, so he learned how to fix them. He learned by watching."

Suzie Cantu did know her son was lazy. Whenever Peter had to go to work, "I woke him up and told him to get up and go to work. There were mornings when he said he didn't want to go to work or he was going to call in sick, but I made sure he got up."

Mrs. Cantu did notice a bit of anger in her son; however, she probably would have characterized it more as irritation. She recalled that Peter would "get mad when I got after him, he gets mad. He said, 'Gee, Mom. I know, I know.' But get violent or strike me, no."

She also mentioned it was common for Peter to get into arguments with his brothers. "They argued. They'd argue and fight and then they'd make up and go outside and play, or they'd go to McDonald's and they'd be happy."

Suzie also mentioned that Peter was nice to women and even had a steady girlfriend. When asked how he treated girls, she responded, "He treats them okay. He talks to them. There used to be a lot of girls that would call him up at home and I never heard him say anything bad on the phone or at any time." She added he was very respectful toward women.

Mrs. Cantu believed the girls liked Peter, but he was in a committed three-year relationship, so he would just be friendly with his admirers. "There was one who used to come over and stand on the porch and she would talk to him," Suzie Cantu recalled. "And they talked, but they never came inside. They always talked on the porch."

Mrs. Cantu stressed that "at that time he was settled down with one particular girl, so he didn't really used to bring them over to the house. He didn't used to say that this was his girlfriend until later on, when he found one that he went out with for about three years." According to Peter's mother, his girlfriend and her family had to move away because her father's company transferred him.

Peter and his girlfriend kept in touch mainly by writing letters and talking on the telephone. Mrs. Cantu added, "She would come down during the summer and they would see each other, or when I go up there where she's at, he comes with me and visits her there." She added that their relationship ended because they could not financially afford to keep it up. "I finally had to take the long-distance calls off my phone because the long distance was getting too high."

Mrs. Cantu also spoke of Peter's role amongst his friends. "I don't think he was a leader," she stated. "That's because whenever Joe or Efrain called him, they used to tell him to go somewhere and he said, 'Mom, I'm going to go with Joe.' I never heard him call them and say, 'We need to go somewhere' or anything like that. They would call him up and he would stop watching TV, get dressed, and wait until they came and picked him up."

On December 6, 1991, somewhere between 4:30 and 5:00 P.M., Anthony Morado received a phone call from his wife, who was working the three-to-eleven evening shift at Memorial Hermann Northwest Hospital. She was upset because she had just found out their family car had been stolen from the hospital parking lot.

Anthony rushed to the hospital, where he met his wife, who showed him the leftover passenger-side window's broken glass, which had been shattered to gain access to their car. The couple contacted the police.

Early the following morning, around 12:30 A.M., Houston police officers Kenneth Egger and James Godfrey were driving their squad car south on Antoine Drive when a vehicle sped by from the opposite direction. Officer Egger turned around, went after the vehicle, and ordered the driver to pull the car into a parking lot.

The police officer drove up behind the car and directed his spotlight on the vehicle. He noticed there were four people inside. Suddenly the driver's-side door flew open and the driver bounded out of his seat and headed back toward the police car—which does not make most police officers very happy.

Officer Godfrey spotted the driver's-side backseat passenger bend over, which usually indicates a passenger is either hiding something or retrieving something under the seat. An officer's worst fear is the person is reaching for a weapon, usually a gun.

"Get your hands up!" Officer Godfrey hollered to the backseat passenger. "Put them up, now!"

Meanwhile, the driver of the car, Peter Cantu, ran back toward the police car. Officer Egger quickly exited his vehicle to halt the driver. "Whose car is this?" the officer asked the teenager.

"It's a borrowed car," Peter replied.

Officer Godfrey also exited the cruiser, walked up to the car, and made sure the three other passengers were in a secure position so no one could attempt to hurt the officers. He walked up to the passenger side and motioned for the remaining three passengers to get out of the car. The young men sheepishly exited the vehicle. Godfrey looked at the inside of the car and noticed that the steering column had been broken, a telltale sign of a stolen car. He hollered as much to his partner.

Officer Egger walked up to Peter and placed him under arrest, handcuffed him, and stuck him in the back of the squad car.

Officer Godfrey searched under the driver's-side seat and discovered a long screwdriver, which is often used to break a steering column, thus allowing a thief to hot-wire and steal it.

Peter Cantu was arrested for automobile theft, whisked away to the Juvenile Division, and taken into custody. The passenger behind Cantu was an eighteen-year-old man named Frank Sandoval. His twin brother, Ramon, sat next to him in the backseat. Both men were charged with public intoxication.

Officers Egger and Godfrey drove Peter Cantu back to the police station. Godfrey was surprised at his attitude. Most teenagers expressed a fear of being arrested, so Godfrey would usually give them the old "don't go down the wrong path" speech. He tried with Peter, but he could tell it was worthless.

"It was no big thing that he was going to jail," Godfrey said of Peter Cantu. The boy did not care.

In April 1992, Harper principal Paul Hanser received an alert that Peter Cantu was once again out of control. One of the school's security officers had detained the student in an isolation area and needed Hanser's assistance in calming him down.

Harper had a zero-tolerance policy when it came to its students carrying beepers to class. It was Hanser's belief, as he said, "whether right or wrong," that if a student carried a beeper, it was not for "productive purposes." He instituted the "no beeper rule," and teachers were allowed to confiscate them from the students. Peter Cantu broke that policy and brought a beeper to school, which was subsequently taken away from him. He was not pleased.

While being held in the isolation room, Peter grabbed a teacher's desk made out of solid oak, picked it up, and smashed it into several pieces on the floor. Peter had been upset about having his beeper taken away and demanded that the female security guard give it back to him.

Hanser entered the room, witnessed the destruction, and watched as Peter screamed at the guard, "You better give it back to me!" He turned to Hanser and started threatening the principal. "You better give me my pager, or I'll get you!"

Hanser was nonplussed. He was used to dealing with belligerent students on a daily basis. "Peter, you need to just calm down, son," Hanser attempted to reassure him.

"I want my goddamn pager back!" Peter screamed at him.

Hanser now knew "there was no pulling back, he was going to have that beeper or else." He looked at his student and said, "It's really time for you to go home."

"I ain't leaving without my pager!" he screamed again.

"You cannot have this beeper, and if you walk out of here with it, I will call the police and you will be arrested for trespassing, because you're no longer welcome this day on campus and you'll wind up in Juvenile," Hanser informed him.

Peter finally slowed down for a moment. He began to walk toward the door, but then started up again. "Give me that goddamned pager!" he yelled at Hanser one more time.

"You're going home for the day, Peter. That's it."

"Well, I'm not coming back," Cantu barked at the principal.

"Peter, you have to, because you're seventeen."

Peter stared directly at Hanser and countered, "Well, if I come back, I'm going to kill your ass."

"That would be a mistake," Hanser calmly replied, "because you'd get locked up for that and there will just be somebody else to come in and take my place."

Peter defiantly jutted his chin out and replied, "Nothing's gonna happen to me, 'cause I'm not that old." He stormed out of the isolation room.

Hanser was not fearful of the boy's threat. He was threatened by students quite often. It came with the territory, so he did not put much credence into the claim.

Hanser did not see Peter Cantu again until the last day of school that June, when Peter came to campus to talk to one of the school's teachers out by the buses.

Peter finally got kicked out of Harper for failing to show up one too many times. In reality, he had simply stopped going.

"I guess, he just got bored, or he didn't like it," Suzie Cantu said of her son and his academic career. "What he liked the most was to run his cars. When he got this job changing oil, and then the school didn't want to give him half the day to go to work and half a day of school, he just decided to quit and to go full-time at work. They told him they needed to know a year in advance before they could do that and he said he needed to keep his job full-time, so he chose work."

Saturday, January 9, 1993—9:00 P.M.
Houston Astrodome
Monster Truck Pull Show
Kirby Drive
Houston, Texas

Seventeen-year-old Worthing High School student Mario Harkles hustled his butt over to yet another concession stand on the slick floors that encircled the mezzanine section of the Astrodome. Mario was a runner for the Harry M. Stevens concessions company, which handled all of the concession food sales in the Houston sporting facility. His job was to run from concession stand to concession stand and make sure they were fully stocked with food and drinks. He had been doing the job for two years and was good at what he did.

On this night, he was partnered up with a coworker and friend named Chris, who was checking on one of the concession stands. While Chris stocked, Mario decided to take a look at the monster truck competition roaring down below on the temporarily dirt-covered floor of the Astrodome.

"C'mon, Mario. Let's go check out the next stand," Chris said, motioning.

The two boys took off down the large hallway. Ahead of them, Mario noticed a strange commotion taking place. People who were walking were moving over to the side as if being pushed; they looked upset.

Eventually Mario saw two teenage boys, Peter Cantu and Efrain Perez, emerge from the cluster. Peter headed in his direction, just off to his side. As the two boys passed each other, Peter purposely bumped into Mario.

"Excuse me," Mario said to Peter in a very quiet voice, "why did you bump into me?"

Instead of apologizing, Peter immediately whipped around and got into Mario's face. "You got a problem with that?"

"No," said the nervous Mario.

Peter could not let it go. "You got a problem with that?" he shouted at Mario again. He moved in closer and shoved the boy in the chest with both hands.

"You bumped into me," Mario responded. "Why can't you say, 'Excuse me'?"

Peter pushed Mario again. This time, Mario pushed back and shouted, "Get off me!"

"Kick his ass, Pete," Efrain egged his friend on. "C'mon, man. Fight him. You can kick his ass."

"I'm on my job," Mario said, trying to reason with the two teenagers. "I can't fight him while I'm on the job."

"C'mon, man. Let's go." Chris tried to get Mario out of the confrontation.

"Let's go," Peter mocked Mario as he closed in to fight him. He grabbed the boy's shirt and then reached around his back and pulled out a butterfly knife and flipped the blade open. Peter swiped the blade in Mario's direction, but not before Chris saw what was happening.

He grabbed his friend and pulled him away just in time before Peter would have sliced Mario open.

The two boys began to walk away. After they put some distance between themselves and Peter and Efrain, Chris told Mario to stop.

"Let me take a look at that," Chris said. "I want to see if you are bleeding."

Mario showed his arm to his friend. His shirt had been sliced open from Cantu's knife, but there was no blood.

"Dude, you got lucky," Chris said. "You would have had to go to the hospital if he cut you."

Mario shook his head in disbelief. He was as scared as he had ever been.

"Let's go find a security guard," Chris suggested.

The two boys located Gary Leslie, an off-duty eighteen-year-veteran Houston police officer who worked security gigs for additional income. They told him what had occurred, and all three went looking for Mario Harkles's attacker.

It did not take long to locate Peter Cantu. Mario pointed him out to Officer Leslie. They watched as Peter bumped into yet another Astrodome patron and started to pick a fight. Leslie walked toward Peter and pulled him aside.

Officer Leslie took a whiff of Peter's breath, which smelled like a brewery. "You been drinking?" he asked the teenager.

Peter grinned like a Cheshire cat and did not answer.

"Did you get someone to buy some beer for you?"

Again, he kept on smiling.

"Did you pull a knife on someone?" Leslie asked.

"No, man," sneered Peter, no longer smiling.

"Do you have a knife on you?"

"No," Peter lied.

"I need to check you," the guard informed Peter.

Peter practically spat at Leslie.

The officer grabbed Peter, spun him around and up against a wall, and made him spread his legs. He then frisked the teenager and, sure enough, found the butterfly knife in Peter's right front jacket pocket. It had a six-inch-long blade with a double edge.

Peter Cantu would later be charged with a felony offense of aggravated assault with a deadly weapon. His punishment consisted of four years' probation with no jail time. He was told to avoid "injurious and vicious habits" and was placed on a curfew and not allowed to leave his home from midnight to 5:00 A.M. The final requirement for his probationary status was to get enrolled in a study program to prepare for the GED.

At Peter's second probationary meeting, and first with Probation Officer Andy Turboff, he discussed how he felt about the assault on Mario Harkles.

"I wish the cop wasn't there. I would have stabbed him," Peter stated defiantly.

Peter's bad behavior continued over the next three months despite being on probation. In February 1993, he was busted for smoking marijuana discovered via a urine test for drugs. In March, he was charged with jumping a man in a Burger King parking lot. In April, he assaulted a drunk man in a parking lot. His bad-boy behavior had only gotten worse.

In May 1993, Peter Cantu went to visit his former auto mechanics teacher, Joseph Malveaux Jr., at the Harper Alternative School campus in the auto repair shop. Peter respected his former teacher and believed he could tell him anything without being judged. Malveaux liked Peter and knew he could have a good career in auto repair if he wanted.

The two caught up with one another.

"How ya doin', Peter?" Malveaux asked his former student.

"Oh, I'm all right," Peter replied.

"Well, what have you been doing? Are you working? You got a job?"

"Nah," Peter replied nonchalantly.

"Well, are you coming back to school?" Malveaux wanted to know.

"No, I don't think so, man. School can't teach me nothing."

"Okay, man," the teacher responded.

After nearly three minutes went by, Peter Cantu looked Malveaux directly in the eyes and made a surprising revelation to his former teacher.

"You know, Malveaux, I think I'd like to kill somebody just to see what it felt like," he declared.

Malveaux paused momentarily and looked directly back at Peter, "Why? Why would you even think something like that? Do you realize what the law will do to you if you were to do something like that?"

Peter replied that he did not care.

Malveaux did not think much about what Peter Cantu had told him. He assumed his former student was simply trying to be a badass in front of him.

One condition of Peter Cantu's probationary status for the Astrodome attempted assault was to report to Probation Officer Andy Turboff twice a month. He was considered Tier 2 status, which meant he had more intense supervision requirements than the normal probationer.

Peter described himself to Turboff as "an ordinary teenager going through the '90s." He also said he liked his parents, they taught him right from wrong, and they thought he could be a good kid when he wanted to be.

He admitted they never abused him, and when they punished him, it was only with a grounding. He also added he did not like his own temper and he didn't "care too much for people except for children and older people."

Turboff encouraged Peter in his pursuit of the GED and also suggested violence counseling. Neither was required and Peter chose not to pursue either one of them.

Peter Cantu had also been required to perform a total of 240 hours of community service. As of this day, he had completed zero hours.

Thursday, June 24, 1993
Houston, Texas

Peter Cantu visited with Craig McNaughton, his latest probationary officer. As usual, he declared the meeting a total waste of time.

Chapter 8

After a couple of minutes, Peter Cantu finished up tinkering with his pickup truck and headed toward his house. He was having a good day. His parents were on vacation, and Thursday was his usual day off from work.

Efrain Perez and Raul Villarreal followed him inside. Once inside, sure enough, Cantu had plenty of beers. He opened up the refrigerator, grabbed two bottles, and handed one to Perez. He ignored Raul.

"Dude, he's cool," Perez stated again. Cantu merely smirked and walked away from the fridge. Perez instead went to it and got a cold beer for Raul. He handed it to him and the three stood silently and drank their beers.

"So what's the deal with you guys?" Raul wanted to know more about Perez, Cantu, and their other buddies.

"What do you mean by that?" Cantu snapped at him.

"No, dude, I don't mean no disrespect. I just heard

you guys do a little running together with some of your other boys," Raul said as he tried to calm Cantu down.

Cantu simply stared at the newcomer. "Why don't you tell him." Cantu glanced toward Perez.

"You mean, like Black 'n White?" Perez directed toward Raul.

"I guess, man. I just heard you guys were like in a gang or something."

Perez and Cantu stopped and looked at one another. They never did call what they had with their friends a gang. They were simply a bunch of best friends who all had one another's backs in case anything went down. They jokingly referred to themselves as the Black 'n White gang, but they knew there was no such thing.

Cantu smiled at Raul. "Yeah, we're in a gang," he told the younger boy. "But you could never be in it. You're too much of a pussy." His smile grew broader as he took another sip of beer.

Raul took his own sip of liquid courage as he shot back, "You wanna bet I can kick everyone of y'all's asses all by myself?" He drew another long sip from the beer bottle.

Cantu started to nod his head and jut out his lower lip. "We would beat your ass. Hell, I could beat your ass."

Raul, who stood a couple of inches taller than Cantu, began to size him up. He felt confident he could take him. "I bet I can kick each one of your asses." He laughed and added, "Why don't we prove it?"

"All right," Cantu agreed. "All right, my man. You got it. Only we do things differently in the Black 'n Whites."

"Yeah, what is that?" Raul asked.

"You gotta take all of us on. If you're still standing after we kick your ass, we'll let you in. If you don't"— Cantu paused and smiled at Perez, then Raul—"well, you can go home and cry to your mommy that you got your ass beat down, bitch."

"Let's do it," Raul bravely responded. He seemed a bit

more nervous as he took yet another long, hard swallow off the beer bottle. He finished his before either of the other two young men and reached into the fridge himself this time for a second beer.

"In due time, son," Cantu stated. "In due time." He then looked at Perez and said, "Let's go see what Joe's up to."

Cantu was referring to his next-door neighbor Joe Medellin.

Cantu, Perez, and Villarreal headed out of Cantu's house and walked across the lawn to Joe Medellin's garage. Cantu knew that Joe's was the place to be, since his garage was fully stocked with alcohol. The evening was still young and there were plenty of adult beverages to be consumed. Once inside the garage, everyone helped themselves to drinks. They were soon greeted by Medellin.

"What the fuck is up?" Medellin asked Cantu. He glanced over at Raul Villarreal and frowned. "Who the fuck are you?" he asked the much taller and heavier new guy.

"I'm gonna be the next Black 'n White," Raul eagerly responded.

Medellin raised his left eyebrow at the claim. He stopped, looked up at Cantu and Perez, then over at Raul. He then snorted a derisive laugh and said, "Oh, really? That's very interesting. Why the fuck would we want you in the Black 'n Whites?"

"Well, I'm bigger than all of you guys and I can fight anyone," he bragged. "I can get your back if we ever get into a big fight."

Medellin grabbed a drink, took a swig, and simply said, "We'll see about that." He looked at Cantu, winked, and headed back into his family's house.

"So what's his deal?" Raul wanted to know more about Medellin.

JOSE "JOE" ERNESTO MEDELLIN

Chapter 9

Jose Ernesto Medellin was born on March 4, 1975, in Nuevo Laredo, Mexico, to his parents, Maria Felipa Medellin and Venancio Medellin Armendariz. Maria was only fifteen years old when she gave birth to Jose.

One year later, the Medellins had another child, and also named him Jose—Jose Martin Medellin.

Two years later, on December 13, 1978, Maria Felipa Medellin gave birth to another boy, whom they named Venancio Medellin Jr. They nicknamed him "Yuni," which meant Junior.

The following year, the Medellins gave birth to their first daughter, Deanida.

That same year, 1979, Jose's father came to work in the United States. His reason for emigrating to Houston, Texas, was "to take a chance and opportunity at a brighter future." He would eventually earn a green card and become a naturalized citizen. He also landed gainful employment with a company that "made parts for petroleum."

It is unclear as to whether or not Maria Felipa Medellin came to the United States with Venancio Sr. in 1979. It is known that Joe did not come to Houston until 1984, when he was nine years old.

What is known for sure is that Maria Felipa Medellin was a stay-at-home mom who took good care of her children. Maria understood that for her children to succeed in America they would need to learn English. Eventually all of the kids would learn the language; however, only Spanish was spoken in the Medellin household. Neither Maria nor Venancio Sr. could speak English.

The Medellins also made sure their children learned the difference between right and wrong. They were taught to be respectful of others and to treat people kindly. Though the family was not wealthy with material possessions, they shared a wealth of love and support that would keep them going forward even during the most difficult times.

To confuse matters with the Jose naming debacle, his parents began to call him Ernesto. He was not happy about the name change, but he suffered through it. As he got a bit older, he wanted to be known as Joe. Not Ernesto, not Jose. Joe.

The kids tended to keep their noses clean in their younger days. His brother, Jose Martin, and his sister, Deanida, were wonderful children who never got into any trouble. His baby brother, Yuni, was also a good kid who eagerly looked up to his oldest brother.

Later in Joe's life, he would remember his early childhood as his favorite time. Apparently, however, he developed an edge at a very early age. "The last time I had a real friend was when I was five or six years old. At that time, you still have trust in everyone."

In addition, Joe's parents never walked their son through the process of becoming a naturalized citizen. Joe would, technically, be considered an illegal immigrant.

Joe showed some promise as a student early on. When he was ten years old, he was in the fourth grade at Holden Elementary School, where he displayed a particular affinity for math and science. Joe was able to show-case his intelligence at a science fair, where he worked on a crystal radio. This project was awarded top honors at Holden. Joe then advanced to the Houston Independent School District's (HISD) district-wide competition, where he took third place. Joe's success was even covered in his school's newspaper with a front-page article.

Joe's aptitude in science and success at science fair competitions allowed him to participate in several activities that most other students did not. He got to visit NASA, the San Jacinto Monument and Battleship, and the Museum of Natural Science. Usually, he was the only student on the trip, accompanied by teacher Ben Hadad, or with other fellow science fair participants from other schools.

Joe did well enough in school that he was awarded honor student accolades and maintained a 93.3 average. He was the top-ranked student in his elementary school's class.

Joe also enjoyed playing sports while in school. His favorites were football and baseball.

Joe's mother noticed something changed with her oldest son, however, when he made the transition from fifth to sixth grade. She believed part of it was because she stopped being a stay-at-home mom and took a full-time job as a supervisor for a cleaning service.

During the fall of 1990, Joe, who attended Hoffman Middle School, got suspended. He was sent to the Aldine contemporary school system, known as Drew Alternative Middle School, for misconduct and repeated misbehavior.

If he would have shown improvement while at Drew, Joe could have eventually returned to Hoffman. Joe, however, was unable to function at his new school; as a result, he was expelled from the Aldine School District.

According to Hoffman Middle School principal James

Royster, Joe "wanted to follow his own rules and did not want to conform to the rules of the district or the school. He wanted to play by Joe Medellin's rules."

Joe was eventually allowed back into school and was advanced into high school. He enrolled at Eisenhower High School, but did not stay out of trouble for very long. During his first year there, he was kicked out for cursing at teachers and making verbal threats.

During the afternoon of January 29, 1992, he continued to push his luck. A fellow Eisenhower student named Jesse Zahrask approached Assistant Principal Clarence Todd near the school's commons area. The young boy was nervous because, he claimed, another student, Joe Medellin, had threatened him. Todd listened as the boy explained what happened.

On the other side of the commons area, Joe sat on a bench in the student lounge. He was supposed to be in class. The school bell had just rung and all of the students were in their classrooms.

Joe was spotted by another assistant principal, Greg Colschen. Joe had paid several visits to Colschen's office in the past for disciplinary reasons. The two were more than familiar with one another.

Colschen walked up to Joe. "You need to get to class. You know you're not allowed in the student lounge during class time."

"I just want to be left alone." Joe ignored Colschen's request.

"C'mon, Joe. You need to get to your classroom."

A more insolent Joe Medellin glared at Colschen. "I said, leave me alone."

Colschen stepped away from the obviously angry young man.

At the exact same time, Clarence Todd and Jesse

Zahrask walked through the opposite side of the student lounge. They were startled when they heard a male voice yell out, "I'll kick your ass! I'll get you now! Piece of shit!" Joe Medellin was screaming at the boy from across the lounge.

Joe jumped up from his seat, hurling invectives at Jesse and making a dash for the small white boy.

Realizing what was unfolding before him, Colschen took off after Joe. He reached the troubled student before he was able to attack Jesse Zahrask. Colschen stepped in front of Joe and blocked his path to the other boy.

Joe was insistent and kept making advances to go through Colschen, who grabbed the student by the lapel of his shirt.

"Joe, just calm down. Stop this. Calm down," Colschen suggested.

"Don't screw with me, okay?" Joe intoned. "I'll hurt you, man."

Colschen did not respond.

"You don't know me," Joe snapped at the assistant principal. "If you don't get your hands off me, I'll fix it so you can't have babies for a while, man."

Colschen, who stood approximately five-ten and weighed 190 pounds, pushed the much smaller young man into the wall, and placed him in a full nelson wrestling hold. Joe began to buck violently against Colschen's grasp.

Assistant Principal Todd, who stood six feet tall and weighed more than three hundred pounds, grabbed Joe by his belt loop to keep him from lashing out against Colschen.

"Let go of my pants!" Joe barked at Todd. "I'll get you," he yelled at the two assistant principals.

Todd stated that Joe Medellin "became so violent that I . . . had to help restrain him with Mr. Colschen's help. He was so violent it took both of us" to restrain him.

Todd and Colschen eventually took control of Joe and marched him down to the principal's office.

"You messed up, now," Joe threatened the assistant principals. "I'm gonna pop your asses," a slang for threatening to shoot them. "I'm gonna kill you. I'll kill you both."

Colschen and Todd pulled the thrashing student to the office. He continued to yell at the men the entire time. "I'll kill you, I'm not like you. Life don't mean nothing to me."

Once they corralled Joe and got him into the office, they handcuffed him and sat him down in a chair.

"I'm gonna kill you two mothers!" he continued to shout. Finally he calmed down momentarily.

Joe sat quietly, then began to brag to the men. "Yeah, I could go to jail, man. Ain't no big deal. Jail don't scare me.

"Next time you see me, man, it'll be my picture in the papers. I'll be famous. It'll be 'cause I killed somebody." He grinned at Todd. He paused and grinned again. "Probably a cop."

"Does that mean you are planning on killing me?" asked Todd, who also volunteered as a reserve at one of the downtown jails.

Joe said nothing. He simply grinned. "I'm gonna get you."

According to Colschen, he contacted Joe's parents, and his mother came and picked him up. He was suspended from school pending an expulsion hearing.

Joe Medellin's time off from school was not productive. On July 18, 1992, Joe was sitting in the passenger seat of his friend's father's car. His friend, Peter Cantu, had stopped the car and jumped out. Joe and Peter's brother, Joe Cantu, who was sitting in the backseat of the car, watched as Peter yelled at some people in another car.

Suddenly a police cruiser pulled up on the same street. Peter jumped back into his dad's car and took off. Peter was chased by police until he pulled over at West Thirtieth Street and Yale Street, near the Heights.

Officer Paul Stavinoha shined a spotlight through the back window of the car and could see Joe Medellin "stooping over" in the passenger seat and placing something underneath it. Stavinoha decided to call backup, as such an action is often viewed as either hiding something illegal or a weapon. The officer waited until two more officers arrived.

Stavinoha ordered Peter out of the vehicle. He then ordered him to approach the officer, where he was searched, handcuffed, and placed into the patrol car.

Stavinoha ordered the front-seat passenger, Joe Medellin, out of the vehicle and over toward him. He, too, was searched, handcuffed, and placed in one of the police cars.

The passenger in the backseat, Joe Cantu, was also ordered out of the car, searched, cuffed, and detained.

After the three teenage boys were placed in vehicles, Stavinoha approached the stolen car on the passenger side where Joe Medellin had sat. The door was wide open. The officer bent down and glanced underneath the passenger seat; he spotted a gleaming silver .38-caliber pistol. He also eyed two .38 SP special live rounds of ammunition next to the gun.

The young men were taken to the police station. Peter Cantu was later charged with driving without a driver's license and other minor traffic infractions. Joe Medellin was charged with possession of a stolen gun. He would receive deferred adjudication and be placed on probation.

He would, however, be allowed to return to school.

The following October, Clarence Todd and Joe Medellin had another run-in. Todd was walking the corridors of the school when he received a report over his walkie-talkie of a fight breaking out in the commons area.

By the time Todd made it to the commons, he witnessed a melee like he had never seen before. It looked like a multiple-participant cage match out of an old-school professional-wrestling event. There were too many people involved to get an accurate count. All that could be discerned was there were a group of Hispanic kids fighting a group of black kids. It would be later learned that all of them were from the same neighborhood, the Heather Glen Subdivision.

One of those in the free-for-all was Joe Medellin. Punches were thrown, curses were screamed, and blood was spilled.

Somehow, Todd was able to contain the fight, along with the help of several teachers. Some students were shuttled off to the nurse to tend to their wounds. Others were rounded up and led to the office. Parents were called. Discipline papers were drawn up.

Joe was suspended again, pending another expulsion hearing. He was eventually expelled from school and transferred to the alternative education program at Drew Middle School for the rest of the school year.

Joe would never return to Eisenhower High School.

In a letter, Joe claimed he dropped out of school *not because I couldn't handle the work, [but] because if you give me the time of day, you'll see that I've* [sic] *quite intelligent.* Joe claimed to have different plans from the average American high-school student. His goal was to earn his GED and then head back to "the Motherland"—Mexico—and join the Mexican military. He later claimed he thought about joining the United States military, but decided against it. He did not want anyone to think he was a "traitor" to his home country.

He would join neither.

* * *

Joe Medellin went to work for a company that poured concrete foundations for homebuilders. The business was owned by a Hispanic gentleman named Sebastien Sota. He also assisted Sota's wife with her maid service by cleaning houses. The Sotas were very impressed with Joe. He always did what they asked of him and he never complained.

Joe rose early every day and clocked in at 6:00 A.M. He would usually work until 5:00 or 6:00 P.M., and sometimes as late as 8:00 P.M. He received $35 a day for his services.

Joe's family was grateful for their son's contribution. He would hand over half his paycheck without having been asked to do so. He wanted to make a difference for his family. He would spend the rest of his money buying shoes for his dad or clothes for his mother. He loved his family and only wanted the best for them.

Chapter 10

Melissa Pena smiled as she watched her daughter and her best friend laugh together. She was very happy Elizabeth had found a good friend like Jennifer Ertman, who was a good kid that never got into trouble. She felt as if the younger girl would be an excellent influence for her daughter.

Melissa drove the two girls down Thirty-fourth Street to the Silver Creek Apartments on Mangum Road so they could meet up with their friend Gina Escamilla. Melissa pulled into the apartment complex entrance and drove around to Gina's apartment. Jennifer jumped out of the vehicle and said, "Thanks, Mrs. Pena. See you later."

Elizabeth believed she was too old to give her mom a good-bye kiss, so she simply told her, "I love you, Mom. We'll see you later tonight."

"I love you, too, honey," Melissa responded, and gave

her daughter a big grin and a wave. Melissa pulled out of the parking lot, glanced up at her rearview mirror to take one more look at her lovely daughter, and then pulled back out onto the road.

The girls bounded toward Gina's apartment. They were greeted by Gina's little sister and mother. As soon as the girls exchanged pleasantries with Gina's mother, the three of them escaped to Gina's bedroom and did the things that teenage girls do—talk about boys, laugh, and act silly together.

While they were lying around Gina's room, Jennifer's pager started to beep. She looked down at the LCD read-out and saw it was her mother. Most teenagers would be annoyed to receive a page from one of their parents, but not Jennifer.

Jennifer asked Gina if she could use her phone to call her mom back. It was not unusual for the Ertmans to page their daughter three or four times a night when she was out with friends.

"Of course," Gina stated agreeably.

"Thanks," Jennifer said as she picked up the phone and dialed her parents' number. Her mother answered the telephone.

"Hi, Mom. How's it going?"

"We're good, honey. How are you doing?"

"We're good, Mom. Just hanging out over at Gina's," Jennifer responded.

"All right, honey. I just wanted to make sure you were doing all right," Mrs. Ertman said. "I love you, baby. Be good."

"I will, Mom. I love you, too."

The Ertman women hung up their respective telephones.

After gabbing for several minutes, the three girls decided to go outside and chat. They stayed outside Gina's apartment talking for the next ninety minutes.

Chapter 11

Peter Cantu picked up the telephone and dialed his friends Ramon and Frank Sandoval, nineteen-year-old twin brothers. He informed the brothers they had special plans for the evening and they needed to get ready. The brothers agreed, hung up the phone, and prepared to meet up with Cantu and the rest of his friends. They had no idea what the reason was for getting together, but they knew when Cantu told them to do something, they had better be ready to do it.

Frank Sandoval was a ninth-grade dropout. He worked at the local retail store Weiners in their warehouse moving furniture and large boxes. He was a fairly small young man, but he could handle a heavy load rather easily. He also lived at home with his parents and his twin brother, Ramon.

Ramon Sandoval had been friends with Peter Cantu since they met each other in middle school in 1989 and found out they were neighbors. Cantu lived directly next door to the Sandovals. Peter introduced Ramon to his other friend, Joe Medellin, around the same time. Medellin lived in the house on the opposite side of the Cantus. Ramon introduced Peter and Joe to Frank, but his twin brother did not hang out with the guys very much over the next few years.

The following year, Peter introduced Ramon to another friend of his named Sean O'Brien. Beginning in 1990, the four boys were a tight-knit group. They never considered themselves a gang, just a group of friends who enjoyed giving each other a hard time. This consisted of cursing at each other and ribbing one another. "Yo momma" jokes were prevalent.

The group of teenage boys used to hang out together at various locations. Sometimes it would be at T. C. Jester Park, near the railroad trestle across White Oak Bayou. Other times they would go to Cantu's house and play poker. Almost always they had alcohol with them. Usually, a forty-ounce malt liquor or some other type of beer.

The boys also decided to memorialize their friendship. They all got matching tattoos of a cross with their individual name inked across it. Ramon got his done by Cantu, who etched in the basic prison-style tattoo. Joe Medellin had *Joe* tattooed on his body. All of the boys' tattoos were created and applied by one of the other boys in the group. Ramon Sandoval later stated they "got it for the fun of it." The tattoos allegedly held no significance for him or the other boys.

At approximately 9:15 P.M., Cantu, Raul, and Yuni Medellin pulled up to the Sandovals' house in Cantu's red Ford pickup truck. They were immediately followed by Joe Medellin and Perez in Perez's gray car. All five young men hung out in the Sandoval front yard until

Cantu went inside to get the brothers. While in their house, Cantu let them know what Raul Villarreal was hoping to do. He found it funny that Raul thought they were in an official gang.

"But let's kick his ass anyway." Cantu laughed, as did the Sandoval brothers.

"Let's call Sean and do it over at his place by the Bayou," Cantu added. He made the call and they headed outside.

All seven of the young men hopped into the two cars and headed out to meet Sean O'Brien.

At approximately 9:30 P.M., the two carloads of teenagers pulled up into the tiny gravel triangular parking lot of the P-One convenience store on Thirty-fourth Street, just down the road from O'Brien's apartment complex.

They managed to purchase four 40-ounce bottles of malt liquor.

All seven young men hopped back into the two vehicles and drove less than one-eighth of a mile to the Clearbrook Apartments.

Thursday, June 24, 1993—9:45 P.M.
O'Brien residence
Clearbrook Apartments
West Thirty-fourth Street
Houston, Texas

The Clearbrook Apartments are a confusing mishmash of dwellings. There are three separate sections with three separate entrances. The buildings all look similar with their two-story blue boxes and gray-ribbed trim, like something out of a bad '70s movie. Cantu and the boys could not remember which building O'Brien lived in, so they parked the car and sent Yuni to go find it. It was only appropriate, since he was the youngest in the group.

Yuni wandered around two sections of the complex for nearly ten minutes before he finally stumbled across O'Brien's apartment. He went back to tell the guys, who were sitting on their cars and drinking the malt liquor.

"Did you find him?" Cantu asked.

"Yeah, it's all the way over there," Yuni informed them. They all walked over to O'Brien's apartment and rang his doorbell.

A rather sleepy-looking Sean O'Brien opened the door.

"What up?" he asked the assorted motley crew before him.

It was 10:00 P.M.

DERRICK SEAN O'BRIEN

Chapter 12

Derrick Sean O'Brien was actually born Eddie Wymon O'Brien Jr. on April 4, 1975, at 2:02 A.M., to nineteen-year-old Ella Louise Walker O'Brien and twenty-four-year-old Eddie Wymon O'Brien Sr., at Rosewood General Hospital in Alief, Texas.

Eddie, who worked as a hotel maintenance worker, was not at Ella's side when Eddie Jr. was born, because he had abandoned her two months earlier. According to Ella, Eddie could not handle the prospect of becoming a father, so he took off.

Ella O'Brien was worried that little Eddie Jr. would not make it into the world. Early on in her pregnancy, she had some serious complications that almost led to a "threatened spontaneous abortion," or a pre-twenty-week miscarriage.

Fortunately, Eddie Jr. was born without complications and weighed a healthy seven pounds twelve ounces. Ella headed to her tiny apartment she shared with her parents at the 5800 block of Fondren Road with her son in tow. She would never hear from Eddie O'Brien again, and Eddie Jr. would grow up without his biological father.

Ella did everything in her power to create a positive

environment for her baby boy. Since she was a single mother, Ella had to earn a living just to maintain basics for Eddie Jr. As a result, she went to work as a reception-ist at an office. Ella was lucky that her mother, Donna, gladly took care of little Eddie Jr. while she worked.

Eddie Jr.'s infancy was rather unremarkable, save for some difficulty with feeding. When he was three months old, it was determined Ella needed to put the baby on a soy formula. He tended to be "fussy," possibly with a touch of colic.

Eddie Jr. remained relatively healthy until he turned eight months old. He had some difficulty breathing and was diagnosed with asthma. The doctor prescribed Theo-Dur for his condition.

Apparently, Eddie Jr.'s asthma did not prove to be much of a hindrance to the rest of his physical develop-ment. He was walking on his own by nine months.

In 1976, Ella's divorce from Eddie O'Brien Sr. was fi-nalized. Her ex-husband readily relinquished the major-ity of his parental rights to Eddie Jr. He accepted a decree that allowed him to see his son only on the first and third Sunday of each month and then only from 1:00 until 5:00 P.M. The decree also stated he had to make child support payments to Ella. Apparently, the de-mands were too difficult for O'Brien Sr. to handle, as he saw his son only once from 1975 until 1990. According to a Houston Independent School District evaluation, Eddie Wymon O'Brien Sr. spent the majority of that time in prison for various charges, including murder.

After the divorce, Ella O'Brien changed her name to Ella Freeman.

Soon thereafter, Ella met a nice man named Harold Jones. The couple hit it off, and Jones asked Freeman to move in with him.

There was a catch: Jones lived with his parents, and he subsequently informed Ella there was not a whole lot of room available. She would have to leave Eddie Jr. with his grandmother.

Ella readily agreed and informed her mother she would be moving out. Donna did not mind one bit. She loved Eddie Jr. dearly and eagerly agreed to take care of him.

Ella Freeman eventually moved in with Harold Jones into a tiny, wooden home.

On June 23, 1976, Ella had her son's name officially changed to Derrick Sean O'Brien. There was no reason given for the new name other than she did not want to be reminded of Eddie Sr. She decided to call him Sean.

Sean O'Brien's childhood was remarkable only in its simplicity. He easily hit all of the benchmarks for infants and toddlers. He was even potty-trained by the time he was one-and-a-half years old. He never seemed to get into too much trouble and appeared to be a well-adjusted kid.

Donna, Sean's grandmother, kept a very laissez-faire attitude toward raising the boy. She did not believe in discipline or punishment. She also did not believe in giving little Sean any household chores. He also got away with a lot around the house, as Donna thought he was the most adorable thing she had ever laid eyes on.

Ella basically stayed away from her son and had no input on how he was raised during those all-important early years. Anytime Ella would question Donna about her parenting methods, she was rebuffed, or it escalated into an argument. Ella eventually gave up and let her momma call the shots in regard to Sean.

No one noticed any issues with Sean until he was around four years old. He began to act out against his grandmother, because she constantly let him walk all over her. He would talk back to her or act smart whenever he had the opportunity. Donna just let it happen and Sean's behavior went unchecked.

When Sean turned five, it became apparent he was

having difficulty learning—this development just so happened to coincide with his mother's impending nuptials with Harold Jones. The couple eventually tied the knot the following year, and the effect it had on Sean was obvious. He began acting moody, sullen, and withdrawn. He would become angry for no apparent reason. Sean later claimed he began to drink alcohol when he was five years old. How he obtained it, though, has never been ascertained, nor how he was able to hide it from his grandmother.

By the time Sean attended elementary school, he was already heading down a difficult path. He was diagnosed with a learning disability and placed in the special-ed department for children with learning deficiencies or difficulties. Unfortunately, the extra attention afforded him did not pay off, as Sean was retained for first grade after he failed too many courses.

It was the beginning of the long slide downward for Sean O'Brien.

Sean's misspent youth was filled with drama and there were signs something was not quite right with the boy.

According to the Houston Independent School District (HISD) psychological evaluation, Sean began to torture various animals. He allegedly suffocated one with a pillowcase cover. He also poked at different animals with a knife.

Until 1983, Sean's physical health had never been an issue; then the eight-year-old boy came down with a serious bout of pneumonia and missed an entire week of school. Needless to say, the absence did not help with his schooling in any way.

The following year, the biggest turning point in Sean's life took place. One day, he was playing in one of the drawers of a teakwood dresser, which belonged to his grandmother. Sean was playing too rough and broke the bottom of one of the drawers. Instead of scolding him and making him repair it, Donna fixed it herself. The older woman, however, was not quite adept on her feet and accidentally fell into the dresser and plummeted to the floor. She screamed in horror as she saw the massive teakwood dresser tilt to one side and slam down on her head. She was knocked out cold and rivulets of blood dripped from her face to the worn carpet. Sean rushed in to find his grandmother unconscious and in need of serious medical attention.

The accident was even worse than anyone could have imagined. The collision caused Sean's grandmother to suffer a traumatic brain injury. As a result, the doctors informed Sean and his mother they would have to perform an emergency craniotomy to relieve the pressure on her brain.

While Sean's grandmother came out of the operation in decent shape, the impact on her brain was substantial. She was no longer able to completely function at a high cognitive level—at least not high enough to raise a young boy. As a result, Sean was forced to move back in with his mother, with whom he had not lived for seven years, and his stepfather and their one-and-a-half-year-old daughter.

Sean was used to getting what he wanted, when he wanted it, from his grandmother. He knew he could walk all over her if need be. That would not work with his mother. She was much stricter than his grandmother; however, she was no stricter than the majority of normal, decent parents. One other issue cropped up—Sean now also had to answer to his stepfather, Harold Jones. He was in for a true culture shock.

Anytime Sean would do something wrong, his mom and stepfather were on him to stop it. They did not let much, if anything, slide. Sean would respond by clamming up and retreating or by talking back. Neither reaction was appreciated in the Jones household.

Sean felt like a fourth wheel in his new home. He always believed his mother abandoned him and wondered why she never gave him a reason for her disappearance.

Ella Jones's physical presence actually made Sean physically ill at times. He was not thrilled to have to take orders from someone he considered a deadbeat. His belief was *Why should I have to take discipline from you when you didn't even want me?*

Sean also had competition in the Jones household. His half sister, the offspring of both Ella and Harold Jones, was drenched in adoration from her parents. Sean was resentful as he watched his mother dote on the baby. It was an affection he was never privy to from his own mother. He also believed his stepfather devoted all of his attention to his daughter. Even though Harold was not his biological father, Sean wished he could have received some fatherly attention from him. Living without a father figure for the first seven years of his life led Sean to believe he was missing out on what it meant to be an honorable man. Harold Jones was not going to be that father figure for him.

Sean O'Brien was resentful of his mother, his step-father, and his half sister. It was not going to be an easy time.

Sean knew of two ways to respond to the treatment he allegedly received at home. The first reaction was to lash out. He began to get into fights in school. In fifth grade, he fought another boy and fractured two of his fingers in the process.

The second reaction was even more harmful. Again, in fifth grade, Sean tried to commit suicide by swallowing a bottle of Tylenol. He attempted it in front of his grandmother, who had stopped by to visit. Sean had gotten in trouble at home and decided to take out his anger by threatening to kill himself and then nearly going through with it.

This would be the first of several suicide attempts by Sean O'Brien.

While many psychologists consider suicide attempts to be cries for help, Sean's seemed to be legitimate attempts at killing himself.

The seemingly unpleasant environment at home and Sean's reactions to it affected every aspect of his life. The biggest hit was with his schoolwork. Sean failed fifth grade and was retained for the next school year. He had already failed first grade and now had a new albatross to wear.

The cycle of self-doubt increased.

Sean tried suicide a second time. Once again, he got into trouble at home and was disciplined by his stepfather. He lashed out this time by trying to hang himself with his own belt. As he did the first time, he waited until his grandmother came over before the attempt. His cries to her went unheeded as she was still incapable of taking care of him.

Finally, in 1985, when Sean was ten years old, Ella Jones realized her son needed serious help. She took him to the Houston Child Guidance Center to seek out psychological counseling to find out what was wrong. It did not help.

By October 1985, Ella Jones decided to take off from work as a receptionist while she was pregnant. Harold and Ella agreed they could make it work with his salary and her Aid to Families with Dependent Children (AFDC) benefits. AFDC was introduced under the Social Security Act of 1935 by President Franklin Delano Roosevelt, providing mothers with financial assistance for their needy dependent children.

The Joneses also planned to subsist off the Social Security benefits from Ella's father and her mother, who received a portion due to disabilities suffered as a result of the injuries to her head.

The following month, on November 4, 1985, Ella Jones gave birth to Torri Yvonne Jones.

Over a period of time, the tension between Sean and Harold was too much for Ella to bear. The couple argued constantly about the way he treated her son. Ella could not take it any longer and informed her husband she wanted a separation because he did not show the same affection for Sean that he showed toward Torri, and it was destroying the fabric of the household. In October 1986, Ella took both Sean and Torri and moved out of the family's apartment on Mangum and back into the house with her mother and father.

Sean O'Brien was finally one happy little boy. Not only did he get his way, he got rid of his stepfather and he got to move back in with his grandmother, who constantly spoiled him.

He could not have been happier.

By January 1987, Ella Jones filed for divorce from Harold Jones. Unfortunately, getting rid of her husband was not enough to curtail Sean's bad behavior.

Sean was tested in February 1987, as per the norm when transferring into an alternative school. He took an IQ test and scored what would be considered in the normal intelligence range; however, he was pegged for having already failed two grades. As a result, Sean was relegated back to the special education program.

Sean started off the program in a rather low-key fashion. That is, until he suffered a severe asthma attack in March, on the day he was scheduled to see his psychologist. The attack was bad enough that he missed seven days of school.

In August, Sean's grandmother returned to the hospital for the second of three surgeries on her brain. Sean could not help but feel guilty for his grandmother's condition. He believed it was his fault she had been hurt and, basically, had become disabled. It crushed him to see her after the surgeries.

On August 16, 1987, Sean snapped. While at home, he locked himself in the bathroom and threatened to commit suicide by slicing open his arms with a razorblade. His mother began to panic. She had no idea what was wrong with her son. She begged him to come out of the bathroom. She would do anything to make sure he did not hurt himself, she assured him. The showdown lasted for several minutes, until his mother finally coaxed him from the bathroom and out of harm's way. She insisted on taking him to the Hermann Hospital ER, where he checked out fine, as far as any physical injuries were concerned.

Sean's mother wanted, however, to make sure there were no mental injuries as well. Three weeks later, on September 8, 1987, she personally escorted her son to visit a psychologist to try and determine what was wrong with him. Sean later admitted to the doctor he faked the suicide attempt to get out of some punishment he was due.

The ever-downward spiral of Sean O'Brien continued.

On November 11, 1987, while at Katherine R. Smith Elementary School, Sean got into trouble for calling another young boy a bad name. To compound matters, Sean also threw a stick at the boy and hit him in the eye. Luckily, the boy was not severely injured.

Things seemed to calm down for Sean at school over the next year. That is, until he discovered his mother was pregnant again, sometime around late February/early March 1988. On November 24, 1988, Ella gave birth to another healthy son, Jonathan Eugene Jones.

Despite another intrusion into his household, things seemed to be looking up for Sean. At least until the following year, when he found out his grandparents were separating.

The separation seemed to reignite the bad fuse in Sean. On April 19, 1989, he got into trouble for harassing another student. Earlier in the day, Sean accosted young Tony Cox at school and demanded the smaller boy hand over his brand-new basketball shoes. Tony refused and Sean told him he was "gonna get him on the bus." Tony was scared to death, so he asked his teacher, Mrs. Johnson, to ride home with him to protect him from Sean and his friend Quinton Bradley.

When the final school bell rang, Tony began to tremble. He located Mrs. Johnson and together they walked toward the school bus. As they boarded the yellow tin can on wheels, the teacher saw both Sean and Quinton. She gave the young boys a look that implied, *Leave this little boy alone*. They both snickered as they saw Tony sit down next to his teacher.

As soon as the school bus pulled away, the mischief began. Sean and Quinton slowly crept forward in the bus seats, closer to Tony. Mrs. Johnson would look up occasionally and see the boys coming closer. She held her ground next to the smaller student. The bus driver hollered at Sean and Quinton to sit down.

Still, the two boys slithered forward.

Sean moved up one more seat closer to Tony. Suddenly, from the direction of Quinton, a white tennis shoe went soaring through the air and pelted Tony Cox in the mouth. Both Sean and Quinton calmly stood up as they approached the unfortunate boy.

"Sit down!" Mrs. Johnson demanded, looking at the two juvenile delinquents.

Neither boy said a thing. The corners of Sean's mouth turned slightly upward in a bit of a sheepish grin. Both boys ignored Johnson's admonition. They continued their advancement.

Mrs. Johnson leapt to her feet in the middle of the bus aisle between Tony Cox and the two other boys. She was prepared to defend Tony, but, actually, she thought they would back down.

She thought wrong.

With no compunction, Sean O'Brien forcefully tackled Mrs. Johnson and knocked her down onto the dirty bus aisle. The teacher, however, was no shrinking violet. She somehow managed to propel Sean off her with her hands. Sean glared down at the teacher and barked, "Get outta my way!" He shoved her as she stood up and she shoved right back. Johnson then attempted to push Sean down into one of the green vinyl bus seats.

He would have nothing to do with that.

Sean leg-whipped the teacher, knocked her legs out from under her, and sent her plummeting back down into the dirty bus aisle.

He was eventually expelled from school for assaulting the teacher.

Sean O'Brien was also a prolific truant who missed dozens of school days. He was written up numerous times for showing up at school, then getting up on a whim, walking out of a classroom, and heading off campus.

Sean was a middle-of-the-road student in middle school; he mostly made C's, with the occasional B slipping in every now and again.

In October 1989, fourteen-year-old Sean got in trouble off campus. He walked into a Kmart, entered the sports department, grabbed a few items off the shelf, walked into the men's restroom, stuck the items in his clothes, and attempted to walk out of the store without paying. As soon as Sean O'Brien stepped outside the front doors of the store, he was apprehended by twenty-two-year-old security guard Raymond Earl Ray.

The security guard retrieved a Crosman pellet gun from inside Sean's pants. The $39 black pistol with brown grip handles and air cartridge looked like an actual revolver and had been removed from its packaging. Sean informed Ray that he stole the gun because he could not afford it. Ray did not care and called the Houston Police Department.

Before Ray had taken over the security guard position at Kmart in 1985, the store suffered a high rate of theft from juveniles. Ray was very good at talking to the kids about the errors of their ways and encouraging them to get back on the right track. He attempted to have the same discussion with Sean O'Brien; however, it seemed to fall on deaf ears. Sean did not want to listen and did not care.

On May 19, 1990, Sean got into a heated disagreement with a security guard named Michael Mays at his new school, Harper Alternative. Once the argument ended, Sean glared at the guard and warned him he would get him.

The following day, according to another Harper security guard, Earnestine Valle, she spotted Sean in the back of the school. When she approached him, she noticed he was angry.

"I'm going to get back at Mr. Mays," Sean barked, standing less than three feet away, directly in front of Valle. He had one arm dangling by his side, the other draped behind his back. Valle raised her hands up, as if to slow Sean down. The boy's attention was distracted; however, when he spotted his current nemesis, Michael Mays, Sean calmly lifted his right arm from behind his back and swung it low in front of him.

That was the first time Valle spotted the gun.

Since the female security guard stood between Sean O'Brien and Michael Mays, the gun was pointed at her—specifically, her feet.

"Now, Sean," she reasoned, once she assessed the situation at hand, "just put the gun down. You don't want to do anything that will get you in trouble."

Sean was furious. He ignored Valle's requests and was completely focused on his target.

"Sean, you need to leave this campus right now," Valle insisted.

"I need to get that motherf - - - er Mays," Sean spat out defiantly.

"Sean, c'mon. You need to put the weapon down and leave the school grounds with me."

Sean started bouncing up and down and shaking his head. "No, no, no. I need to kill that motherf - - - er is what I need to do," he informed her. Sean began to fidget and nervously pace back and forth in front of Valle. Suddenly he stopped, pointed the gun straight up over his head, and fired. He then turned tail and bolted for the nearby railroad tracks.

Valle engaged her walkie-talkie and warned Mays that Sean O'Brien had a gun, he had just fired it, and he was coming after him.

Nothing happened to Michael Mays.

Sean attempted to change his ways once he reached high school. During the fall of 1990, he put in a request to Harper administration to transfer to the Waltrip High School ROTC program. Staffers informed him they would consider it if he behaved himself. Of course, less than two months later, he blew his chance when he left campus again without permission.

Sean later asked to transfer to Scarborough High School, where he hoped to make the varsity football squad. Sean had some speed, but he lacked in the size department. He only stood five-seven and weighed 150 pounds—not exactly Junior Seau numbers. The administration considered his request; however, he never transferred out of Harper.

When Sean turned fifteen, he ran into a young boy from school in the neighborhood named Peter Cantu. The two young men got along well and started to hang out with one another. Sean liked Peter and also liked that he had lots of friends.

According to Sean's psychological evaluation for HISD placement, he "wants to be a leader"; however, he "seldom meets the requirement." Ella Jones agreed with the assessment. As much as Sean wanted to be a badass and a leader, his mother believed he was nothing more than a follower.

Sean got into trouble again on the Harper school grounds. One morning, he was hanging outside in the designated smoking area with a few friends and another student named Alicia Siros. She claimed O'Brien pulled out a small sheet of paper and some matches. He casually lit the paper on fire, held it aloft slightly, and said, "I'd like to burn the school down." Instead, he threw the burning paper in a nearby trashcan and headed off for class.

Alicia had another unusual encounter with Sean. She was sitting at home when she heard a vehicle tearing down her road, followed by a loud crash. She jumped out of her chair to see what all the commotion was about and headed out the front door. When she got outside, she spotted a car that had run off the road. She noticed someone darting out of the car—it was Sean O'Brien. He scrambled away from the wrecked vehicle and into a waiting car. The second car took off in a flash.

The wrecked car's engine was still running.

Alicia Siros walked over to the car, peered inside the driver's-side window, and noticed that the steering column had been broken. The car had been stolen. She went back inside her home and called the police.

The following day, Alicia asked around school if anyone knew if Sean had stolen a car. Several of her classmates said that he had stolen the car. They added that he had stolen lots of cars—probably more than fifty.

Alicia described Sean's behavior as "very uncalm." She once saw the jittery teen with a knife at school. It was a large knife he stashed in a holster around his ankle. She even spotted him carrying a gun to school one day.

Alicia once witnessed Sean steal money and a pair of tennis shoes from a fellow student, Louis Colwell. Alicia, who was friends with Louis, saw Sean confront the boy and demand his tennis shoes. According to Alicia, Sean stepped in front of the skinny Louis and declared, "I like your shoes. I want them."

"You can't have them," Louis replied.

"I will get them," Sean declared.

According to Alicia Siros, Sean "got them later on that day" in a fight between the two boys. Sean O'Brien got the better end of the deal as he walked away with the shoes, and Louis Colwell walked away barefoot, with a bloody nose and split lip.

Sean O'Brien's cries for attention continued.

In 1991, he again attempted suicide—this time by swallowing an entire bottle of Triaminic, a sore throat medicine. There was no explanation given as to why he tried to kill himself.

He tried one more time that same year by slitting his wrists. He was distraught over a girlfriend.

Sean's bad behavior continued throughout the year.

He seemed to enjoy causing havoc on the bus. He was busted for fondling a girl's breasts under her clothes against her will while on the bus. He got in trouble for cursing at and picking a fight with another boy on the bus. He got in trouble another time on the bus for throwing an apple out a window at some pedestrians.

On June 25, 1991, Sean got into trouble on the bus yet again when he attempted to choke another student.

In August 1991, Sean got into an argument with his mother about his behavior at home. The yelling escalated until he got in his mother's face and pushed her away from him. Instead of cowering in fear, Ella Jones bounced right back and got in her son's face. Sean instinctively attacked and punched his mother full on in the chest. The hit was so hard Ella stumbled backward and crashed through a plate-glass window. Sean looked out the window at her bloody body as she lay on the grass. He sneered at her and walked away. The cuts were so bad, Ella had to be taken away in an ambulance and examined by a doctor.

Sean O'Brien never apologized to his mother for hitting her.

No charges were pressed against him.

Later that month, on August 26, 1991, Sean's report card from Harper Alternative failed to make it into his mother's hands. Had she seen it, she would not have been happy. Sean missed sixty-five days of school over the second half of 1990 and 125 days throughout the still-not-close-to-completed 1991 school year.

Sean's problems at school got worse. By December, he was sent to juvenile detention for assaulting a teacher.

By January 1992, Sean had had enough of school. As

his school records indicate, he "exhibited school re-fusal," which is simply a noncommittal way of saying he dropped out.

In April 1992, Sean tried to kill himself yet again. This time around, he swallowed an entire bottle of Sinutab tablets. He survived.

On June 5, 1992, Ella Jones took her son to the Harris County Mental Health and Mental Retardation Author-ity (MHMRA) services. According to Sean's MHMRA medical report, he allegedly ran away from home at least four times in the preceding six months. The report also stated he started abusing ethyl alcohol at the age of four-teen. In the report, Sean claimed he had informed his mother of his alcohol addiction.

Furthermore, according to the MHMRA report, Sean's mother claimed her son had been stealing from the family, and that he constantly lied to everyone about practically anything and everything.

Sean admitted in the report he had severe issues with his mother. He said he did not understand why his mother "rejected" him and wondered how she could then later go on to have two more children and raise and love them with no problem whatsoever.

In the report, Sean insisted his grandmother was his real "mother" and Ella Jones, his biological mother, was merely a "peer." Sean also claimed he resented it when his mother tried to "parent him." He thought she was out of line because she had basically abandoned him for seven years.

Ella Jones also stated in the report that Sean was "provocative" and "indifferent" toward his little brother and sister. She claimed her children expressed such fear to her and they worried about the "rage" Sean exhibited when he got mad. Apparently, one of the worst instances was when he threatened both children by telling them he "had access to a gun" and he "would kill them."

Ella Jones called her son "unpredictable," said she was "afraid of him," and talked about how she always "walked on eggshells" around him.

Later that month, Sean O'Brien was arrested for riding in a stolen car with one of his friends.

Wednesday, June 23, 1993—1:00 P.M.
Oak Forest Park
Judiway Street
Houston, Texas

News reporter Randy Wallace of Fox News, channel 26, spoke with a handful of young Hispanics and blacks about a double shooting that had occurred just a few days earlier. He intended to use the footage for an upcoming special on gang violence in Houston called *City Under Siege.*

Amongst the people Wallace spoke with was one young man by the name of Sean O'Brien. Bedecked in baggy pants with his white boxers spilling over the waistband, sans shirt, and donning a backward baseball cap, Sean O'Brien cut a menacing figure.

Though he was not considered a suspect in the shootings, he felt free to comment about the level of gang activity in the Houston area. Swilling from a forty-ounce bottle of malt liquor, he spoke to the reporter.

Wallace asked the young boy his thoughts on the shooting.

His response was concise and deliberate: "Life means nothing."

Chapter 13

In the parking lot stood Sean O'Brien, Peter Cantu, Joe Medellin, Yuni Medellin, Raul Villarreal, Efrain Perez, Ramon Sandoval, and Frank Sandoval. Eight young men, four with very serious problems, sharing a few 40s, and ready to engage in a bit of "the ultraviolence." They headed over to a small playground set up in the grass between the apartment parking lot and a long metal fence topped with razor wire that abutted White Oak Bayou. As the young men sat around in the small swings, they continued to throw back their beers. The outline of the railroad trestle could be seen under the moonlight.

Chapter 14

Jennifer and Elizabeth were having a blast hanging out with Gina. They were soon joined by Gina's former boyfriend, Chris, and two of his buddies, Michael and Jose. The six of them were hanging outside of Gina's apartment when Chris suggested they head over to his place at the Spring Hill apartment complex, just off West Thirty-fourth Street. He mentioned hanging out by the pool.

Another friend of the girls, Roseanne Mendoza, showed up and joined them on their way over to the Spring Hill Apartments.

Chapter 15

Thursday, June 24, 1993—10:05 P.M.
T. C. Jester Park
T. C. Jester Boulevard and West Thirty-fourth Street
Houston, Texas

"All right, man, so what's up?" Sean O'Brien wanted to know.

"We're gonna have a little fun with the newbie over there," Peter Cantu said as he gestured over to Raul Villarreal. "He thinks we're a gang and he wants to be a part of it. So we're gonna let him think it and have our way with him."

"Whatchoo wanna do with him?" O'Brien asked.

"Kick his ass! He's been talking shit all day about he can take any of us. It's time to put him to the test." Cantu smiled. "He's gotta fight each and every one of us, so he can join 'the gang.'" He started to laugh.

O'Brien started to laugh as well. "Yeah, yeah. All right. That's cool with me."

The other guys were all smiles, too.

They joked around a bit longer until O'Brien stood up and said, "C'mon, let's do this." He instigated the march through the playground and up to his secret passageway through the fence. Actually, someone had simply pulled the wire portion of it back so one could easily slip through it. All eight of them traversed into the darkness of the railroad tracks.

"Look at all the stars," Yuni said as he emerged on the other side.

On the opposite side of the fence were a cluster of trees, a small creek, and the bottom of a gravel embankment. The boys made their way up the embankment, which led to train tracks. They headed east on the tracks for a few hundred feet until they came upon the trestle, or bridge, that crossed over White Oak Bayou and led directly into T. C. Jester Park.

To the north of the train tracks and just east of the woods was a large, flattened area of grass. Frank Sandoval, Yuni Medellin, Efrain Perez, and Raul Villarreal headed for the patch of grass. The other four guys headed down toward the bayou. Everyone except Frank continued to drink their beers as they excitedly hopped down the other side of the train track embankment. Once they reached the flattened grassy circle, they stood around, drank more beer, and talked a bunch of smack.

Cantu, O'Brien, and Joe Medellin slipped off to the side for a bit as they spoke in confidence about Raul. O'Brien would later claim he had no interest in fighting. He made up an excuse about not wanting to damage his glasses. He added it was too dark and that there were too many ant beds on the ground and he did not want to get bitten.

According to O'Brien, Cantu insisted, "You're gonna fight him, Sean."

"No, I'm not," O'Brien shot him down.

"All right, you go down there later, and if it's too dark, just shake your head no, okay?" Cantu stated.

"Okay, man, I'll do that," O'Brien agreed.

After almost thirty minutes of everyone chilling,

Cantu and Joe decided Raul Villarreal's time had come. They motioned over to Ramon Sandoval, one of the twins, and whispered something to him. Ramon nodded his head and walked toward where Raul stood. O'Brien also sauntered over. O'Brien surveyed the area, looked up at Cantu, and shook his head no.

Cantu shook his head in disgust at O'Brien and turned his attention to Ramon Sandoval. "All right, Ramon, you take him."

Ramon looked up at the much larger Raul, as if sizing him up, then reared back and took a swing at the newcomer.

The fight was on.

The rest of the young men created a human ring that surrounded the two fighters. Ramon was to be the first of many opponents Raul was going to have to take on. The plan was for each boy to fight Raul for five minutes, one after the other. Raul's objective was to take them all on and still be able to stand to tell the tale. It was going to be a tough chore, as the others had every intention of knocking him out cold.

Ramon and a now-shirtless Raul went after it, hard and heavy. This was no Muhammad Ali rope-a-dope dance and shuffle routine. The two boys were standing toe-to-toe taking full-on punches to the face. They grabbed each other, placed one another in headlocks, and punched each other in the face. They grappled and wrestled each other to the ground. Ramon was cheered on by the other guys; they were yelling at Raul and cursing his name.

Ramon was supposed to test Raul to see if he could actually fight. It was obvious he could. The two fought for the entire five minutes, and Raul was still standing. According to Cantu, Raul actually seemed to get the better of Ramon Sandoval. There were no knockouts in round one.

Next up was Joe Medellin. The much smaller boy did

not miss a beat as he immediately leapt in and took over from where Ramon had ended. Again, Raul held his ground as he scrapped with the powerful Medellin. As with Ramon, Raul and Medellin stood face-to-face and pummeled each other. Joe Medellin was unable to knock out the bigger Raul Villarreal. He did, however, continue to wear the new guy down for five minutes. Once again, Raul was able to stay up.

The whoops and hollers continued. The group had no intention of letting up on their new charge.

Cantu looked over at Frank Sandoval. "Get in there, bitch," he ordered the other twin.

"Nah, man," Frank declined.

"What do you mean, no?" Cantu sounded incredulous.

"That's not how I am," stated the pacifist twin. "I don't judge others like that. Not with all this violence and stuff."

Cantu started to laugh and shook his head. "Whatever, dude."

Despite his earlier hesitancy, O'Brien decided to step into the fray. Of all the boys in the group, he was easily the strongest, although not the biggest. He did, however, lift weights and was in excellent shape. He was shorter and lighter than Raul Villarreal, but he was a much better fighter.

By the time O'Brien stepped up, Raul was moving at least one or two steps slower than when he began. O'Brien took advantage of this weakness and went straight into Raul's face, barely giving him any time to react. He landed several hard thuds into the new guy's mug.

The force of the punches began to take their toll, but Raul was not ready to throw in the towel. He recovered somehow and threw a few devastating punches in O'Brien's face, stunning his much fresher opponent.

Unfortunately for Raul Villarreal, his counterattack had the opposite intended effect. When Raul punched Sean in the face, O'Brien responded that he "liked that."

Raul's punches merely served to enrage O'Brien, who then countered with his own blow to Raul's abdomen, doubling over his opponent. O'Brien then polished him off with an uppercut to the fighter's jaw, which sent the much larger boy sprawling backward onto the dirt. The rest of the guys screamed their approval for O'Brien's skills and laughed as they saw Raul tumble to the ground.

"Get up!" O'Brien barked. "Get up, ya pussy!"

Cantu stepped into the ring to observe the aftermath. It was apparent Raul was no longer feeling combative. He lay facedown in the grass, moaning.

"That's it!" Cantu declared. "He's done."

Raul Villarreal's objective was to take on all of the guys; however, he did not even last through the first three opponents. No one knew for sure what they planned to do to him.

Everyone except Raul headed back up to the railroad track trestle to sit down. They opened up more beers and talked about what had just gone down. Raul looked on from a matted-down grassy circle. He was slow in his recovery.

"Hey, motherfucker!" Cantu yelled from atop his perch. "Get your fat ass over here, now!" Efrain Perez and Joe Medellin started to laugh.

Raul slowly lifted himself up off the ground, flicked his hands across his jeans to clear off any excess dirt, held his head up high, and slowly trudged up the railroad embankment to where the other seven guys were hanging out.

By the time he got to the bridge, Cantu told him to stop. "You know, you were talking a lot of shit today about how you could kick everyone's ass." Cantu smirked. "Well, you were supposed to take all of us on and not get your ass kicked to prove yourself." Some of the other guys muttered under their breath. "But you failed, *ése.*"

Cantu paused briefly and looked at his friends. "So

what are we gonna do with this sorry piece of shit?" he asked rhetorically. Raul stiffened up as he expected he would need to defend himself. Peter Cantu turned backward toward Raul Villarreal and asked again, "What are we gonna do with him?"

No one said a word.

Cantu took a step toward Raul and said, "You're in! Welcome aboard. You're one of us." The rest of the guys burst out laughing as they watched the new guy's expression change from anxiety to relief. "Dude, you're a badass. You're welcome to hang out with us anytime." Cantu smiled at his newest compadre. "You're in now, daddy. You're in."

Raul Villarreal finally broke out into a huge smile. He was greatly relieved he wouldn't get his ass kicked anymore. He joined the others in drinking beer and hanging out on the railroad tracks. The guys spoke of what it meant to have each other's backs and to take care of one another. They spoke of the mutual respect they must all share with one another. They also talked about having balls and being able to deal with put-downs from the other guys in the group. If someone cracked a joke about your momma, you had better take it in stride and learn how to laugh it off. They were merely fucking with you, and if you overreacted, you would be considered a pussy and not worthy of hanging out with the group. Raul informed the guys he was more than capable of doing everything they suggested. He thanked them repeatedly for letting him join the group.

"This is gonna be fun." Raul Villarreal laughed as he hoisted his beer bottle aloft.

Chapter 16

Thursday, June 24, 1993—10:05 P.M.
Spring Hill Apartments
West Thirty-fourth Street
Houston, Texas

Elizabeth, Jennifer, Gina, Roseanne, Chris, Michael, and Jose arrived at Chris's apartment complex. Despite no longer dating, Gina and Chris remained good friends, so there was no awkwardness amongst the group.

Instead of going into Chris's apartment, the group decided they would hang out by the large pool in the center of the complex. Some of the girls sat in lounge chairs that encircled the large pool, while the guys sat in chairs under the gazebo.

The friends mainly caught up with one another. There was nothing earth-shattering to discuss, they simply were glad to be in each other's company. The group sat around the pool and chatted for the next fifteen minutes.

At approximately 10:20 P.M., Jennifer leaned in toward Elizabeth and suggested they get ready to go. Elizabeth agreed and they told their friends they needed to head on back home. One thing led to another as the girls got caught up talking even more, and another ten minutes had elapsed.

At 10:30 P.M., Jennifer stood up and was bound and determined to take off. She had a great time hanging out with her friends, but she had an eleven o'clock curfew. It would take them close to thirty minutes to get back to the Pena residence.

Suddenly a beep sounded on Elizabeth's belt.

She looked down at her pager and saw that her friend Vanessa Rivera had paged her.

"Let me go call Vanessa back and see what she wants," Elizabeth told Jennifer. She asked Chris if there was a pay phone available. He pointed one out near the pool and she went to call her friend. Of course, the page was for nothing important. Vanessa merely wanted to see what Elizabeth was up to. The whole affair took up another ten minutes.

Jennifer started to get nervous. They now only had twenty minutes to get home before her curfew. Normally, they would have exited the apartment complex, taken a left onto West Thirty-fourth Street, and gone down until they took another left onto T. C. Jester Boulevard. From there, they would walk all the way down T. C. Jester Boulevard and then take a right onto Lamonte Lane, where they would have to walk another half-mile to get to Elizabeth's house.

They were not going to make it home on time. The last thing they wanted to do was get into trouble, so they came up with an alternate plan.

The two girls were joined by Gina and Roseanne at the pay phone. All four girls said their good-byes to the boys. Gina and Roseanne recalled they all four headed east on West Thirty-fourth Street until they came to the Clearbrook Apartments.

"We've got to take the shortcut through the park so we won't be late," Jennifer told Gina. She referred to a pathway that led to the train track and bridge through T. C. Jester Park and crossed over the White Oak Bayou. It would save them approximately ten minutes of walking time and would probably allow them to get home before curfew.

"All right, y'all, take it easy." Gina said good night. "Call me when you get home."

"Yes, Mom." Both girls laughed in unison.

Gina smiled at her friends, stuck her tongue out at them, and turned around with Roseanne to walk back to her apartment on Mangum Road.

Elizabeth and Jennifer made their way through the Clearbrook Apartments parking lot and up to a chain-link fence. They knew about the pulled-back fence and that they could scoot under, hit the trail to the train bridge, and they would be home in time to make Elizabeth's parents happy.

It was approximately 10:45 P.M.

They were going to have to hurry.

Chapter 17

The guys continued to drink and celebrate the addition of their newest friend, Raul Villarreal. Peter Cantu and Joe Medellin started needling one another.

"You're a pussy," Cantu slammed Joe.

"Oh, yeah? You're a pussy," Joe weakly shot back.

"Yeah, your momma's a faggot, bitch," Cantu bested Joe.

"Yeah, well, you're a faggot," Joe again weakly countered. It was their way of showing they had respect for one another. "Talking shit" was their form of male bonding.

They hung out for around ten to fifteen more minutes, when, at approximately 10:45 P.M., Frank Sandoval was hit with a feeling he could not truly describe. He knew if he and his brother hung around the train tracks any longer, they were going to be in a world of trouble. He needed to tell his brother they had to get out of there immediately.

"Ramon, c'mon, man. Let's take off," Frank requested of his twin brother.

"What for, man? Let's hang out." Ramon had no desire to leave.

Frank stood close to his brother and whispered,

"C'mon, man. These dudes have been drinking all fucking day. I don't trust them. Let's get out of here." He gave his brother a serious look he later claimed only twins could understand.

Ramon quickly acquiesced. "All right, bro. I'll be right there." He turned to the other guys and somewhat apologetically said, "Sorry, guys. Frank's being a pussy and he wants to go home. I gotta take him with me, so we're outta here."

"Pussy! Faggot!" the guys screamed at Frank, making sure to give him an extremely hard time.

Frank flipped them the finger and said, "See you douche bags later."

Raul laughed. He liked the camaraderie the guys had with one another and he was looking forward to taking part in that friendship.

Frank and Ramon's curfew was midnight but they were ready to bolt. Both boys stepped it up and began to make the trek along the railroad tracks back to the apartment complex. It was Frank's first time hanging out with O'Brien, Yuni, and Raul. He was none too impressed. He later could not give a good reason as to why he decided to hang out with the guys that night, other than to say he felt he needed to be there for his brother.

As the twins walked down the railroad tracks, the other guys stood up. Joe Medellin looked at his brother Yuni and said, "Let's go. We need to get home before Mom does." They started to walk up to the tracks and follow in the same direction as the Sandovals, but they were moving at a slower pace.

Frank and Ramon continued to walk away, when they suddenly spotted two girls several feet ahead walking up the gravel embankment to get to the railroad tracks. The girls made it up at the same time the Sandoval twins passed them. The brothers barely acknowledged the girls' presence as they slipped by. They did not warn the girls that a group of guys that had recently been drinking and fighting were just up ahead.

The Sandoval brothers went along their way and started the descent down the gravel embankment. They headed back to the path to O'Brien's apartment complex. Yuni Medellin was close behind and he also passed the two girls on the railroad tracks.

Joe Medellin looked up and saw the two girls walking toward him. "Oh, look at this!"

"Dude, hold up," O'Brien said to Joe Medellin. "They could be a couple of those dicks from the apartment complex." O'Brien, who could not see in the dark, was worried they might get jumped by some other guys.

"It's cool, Sean. It's a couple of chicks."

The girls continued to walk in the direction of Joe Medellin and Sean O'Brien. As they passed the boys, Joe Medellin reached out and pinched Elizabeth Pena on the left breast. Elizabeth swatted Joe Medellin's hand away and kept on walking.

"No, baby," Joe Medellin said to Elizabeth. "Where you going?" he asked as he grabbed her by the left hand. Elizabeth tried to shake her hand free of him; however, he had a very tight grip on her. "You ain't going nowhere, bitch!" Joe Medellin informed her as he grabbed her around the neck and placed her in a choke hold.

"Help!" Elizabeth screamed.

Frank Sandoval heard the loud scream erupt from the tracks. Before he stepped across the ditch into the woods, he looked back up to the railroad tracks. He thought he spotted Joe Medellin grab one of the girls from behind by her neck and throw her to the ground.

Instead of heading back to help the girl, Frank did nothing. He simply continued on into the woods.

"Help! Please, somebody! Help me!" the girl screamed.

According to Frank Sandoval, he stopped again to see that Jennifer Ertman had actually passed the other guys and could have escaped—had she taken off running. Instead, the fourteen-year-old girl came back to help her best friend.

As a result, Elizabeth's screams were joined in unison by Jennifer's screams. Frank Sandoval looked up and saw O'Brien and Cantu grab Jennifer by her arms and then knock her down to the ground. Jennifer attempted to scramble away, but O'Brien held a firm grasp on her legs.

"Help! Leave me alone," the girl screamed at O'Brien and Cantu. "Leave me alone." Jennifer began to kick at her tormentors and screamed in hopes that someone would come to help her and Elizabeth.

But the Sandoval brothers ignored her screams and went on. Frank Sandoval later admitted he was scared and did not know what to do. "I didn't want to get involved in none of that," he admitted.

Frank looked at his twin, Ramon, as if to say, *What do we do?* Ramon was just as confused as Frank and basically shrugged. The brothers did not go back to help the girls. Instead, they made their way to the fence behind O'Brien's apartment complex. They headed to the cars and decided they would wait for the guys to return. They would wait nearly half an hour before they realized the guys were not coming back soon. They decided they could no longer wait, so they headed home on foot. It would take them close to an hour to walk home.

When they got home, they did not contact the police.

Chapter 18

Peter Cantu was jonesing for a fight. He didn't get to take his frustrations out on Raul Villarreal and he was itching to extract some pain on someone. At that point, Cantu looked up and saw two dark silhouetted figures walking toward them. He saw the taller of the two figures and assumed it was a guy.

He still wanted that fight. Here was his opportunity.

Cantu approached one of the figures and pulled the person down to the ground. It was then he realized it was a young girl, fourteen-year-old Jennifer Ertman.

Yuni Medellin returned his gaze back toward his brother, Joe. He watched as his weight-lifting brother grabbed the taller, thinner dark-haired girl, threw her over his shoulder, and began to flee down the other side of the train embankment, almost like a caveman dragging his woman back to his lair. As Joe Medellin made his way down the gravel decline, he tripped and fell, sending Elizabeth sprawling to the ground. Joe Medellin landed on top of the girl so she was unable to get away.

Efrain Perez saw what was going on with his boy Joe, so he decided to help out. The lanky seventeen-year-old bounded down the side of the railroad track embankment and helped Joe pin Elizabeth down on the ground.

"Let me go!" she screamed again. She was not crying, but her voice was loud.

As Joe Medellin recovered from his fall, Cantu began to drag Jennifer down the same embankment to where Joe and Elizabeth were. He pulled her by her arms, with Sean O'Brien following behind, making sure she did not escape.

Joe Medellin picked up Elizabeth again and made his way toward the bald spot in the grass.

"Let me go!" Elizabeth continued to scream. The thin girl was unable to put up much resistance. But she tried to claw at his eyes and kick him with her legs. She continued screaming, "Let me go! Let me go! Please let me go!" Joe Medellin ignored her pleas and forged onward.

Yuni could hear his brother taunting Elizabeth. "Take off your clothes, bitch!" he barked. A frightened Elizabeth complied. She sobbed as she peeled off her blouse, exposing her new purple bra that she received for her sixteenth birthday just three days before. She squirmed on the ground as she lay on her back. Yuni stood thirty feet away from her on the railroad tracks. He did not lend the frightened girl a helping hand. Instead, he watched as his brother prepared to rape Elizabeth.

"Take off your pants," Joe ordered the attractive young girl.

Elizabeth did as she was told, but it was difficult for her to disrobe her pants as she lay flat on her back.

Joe Medellin leaned in closer to Elizabeth and grabbed her jeans at the waist. He ripped them down to her ankles. He then stood up, pulled his own pants down past his buttocks, and forced Elizabeth to perform fellatio on his penis.

Fourteen-year-old Yuni looked down the embankment and saw Cantu and Jennifer. Cantu had dragged the teenager down the side of the hill into the bald spot in the grass. He watched as his brother's friend tossed Jennifer to the ground. She tried to pick herself up from off her knees, but she could not muster the strength to lift herself. Cantu walked in front of the virgin, unzipped his pants, pulled out his member, and said, "Suck it, bitch!"

Jennifer never had sexual relations of any kind before. She probably had no idea how to perform oral sex other than what she had heard from some of her friends. Most likely, she did what she was told because she feared what would happen to her.

Yuni scooted down the embankment of the train tracks to where Cantu had dragged Jennifer. He gained his balance as he came to the bottom of the gravel. Five feet in front of him, he witnessed Jennifer on her knees fellating Cantu. She was fully dressed, as was Cantu. He had unzipped his pants and pulled out his penis to be serviced by the fourteen-year-old girl. Yuni watched as Cantu looked back at him and flashed a devilish grin. He grabbed the blond girl's hair and forced her head back and forth on his member. The girl looked terrified, but was doing as she was ordered.

Yuni stood in shock watching the scene unfold before him. He was mesmerized by the motion of the blond girl's head. Eventually he snapped out of his trance and turned around toward his brother. He was stunned to see his brother fucking the skinny dark-haired girl. He had mounted her in a missionary position and was thrusting into her vagina while she lay on the loose wooden railroad ties and rocks under the train tracks.

"Let me go!" Elizabeth screamed. "I'm gonna get into trouble." She was furious, but she could not fight. Elizabeth was not crying, just angry.

Yuni did not want to watch his brother rape the young girl. He had no idea where to go, but he knew he did not want to see his brother's ass flopping up and down. He turned around and stared at Cantu and Jennifer.

"Dude, let's go," Yuni pleaded.

Cantu ignored the younger Medellin and kept grabbing onto Jennifer's head. He was having too good a time to leave.

"Dude, c'mon. Let's get outta here," Yuni pleaded again. He started to freak out. He was scared and he knew this was only going to turn out bad. He wanted to get the hell out of there before anyone in the Clearbrook Apartments heard them and decided to come protect the girls.

Sean O'Brien, Raul Villarreal, and Efrain Perez walked down the embankment to watch what was going on. All three teenage boys stood directly beside Cantu and watched as Jennifer was forced to suck the boy off. None of them lifted a finger to help the young girl. Instead, they cheered on their buddy.

"Do that bitch's face," Efrain Perez hollered.

"Give it to her, brother," Sean O'Brien encouraged.

"Do it! Do it!" Raul Villarreal gleefully shouted over and over.

It was their very own private porno, and they all had front-row seats.

Yuni also watched the scene unfold before him. He stood there, almost in a daze. Not knowing what else to do, he turned to look at Cantu, who was still forcing himself on Jennifer. He stood within five feet of Cantu and Jennifer, but he did not advance. He merely watched the fourteen-year-old perform oral sex on Cantu against her will. Cantu looked back at Yuni again and smiled.

Yuni turned away, only to see his brother climbing back on top of Elizabeth. Joe had removed his penis from the girl's mouth and forcefully rammed it into her vagina.

Yuni Medellin turned away from what his brother was doing. He could not believe this all happened so quickly and was getting out of hand at such a rapid pace. He turned back toward Cantu and said in a quiet voice,

"Let's go, man." Yuni was afraid of Peter Cantu and did not want to piss the older boy off. He knew what was going down was not right, and they should all get the hell out of there before they got into even bigger trouble.

Cantu still ignored the youngest member of the group. Instead, he grabbed Jennifer by the hair and continued forcing her to orally copulate him.

Yuni was scared. No one was listening to him. He knew he should take off, but he couldn't move. He stayed put. It was his first time to ever hang with his brother and his buddies and he didn't want to come across as a pussy. He figured this incident would be over soon enough.

The only problem was, his friends were far from finished.

Yuni looked back over at Cantu and Jennifer and saw her pants had come off. He had no idea how, but they were just off. She still wore her shirt. By this time, Jennifer was lying on the ground on her back—only now, O'Brien was raping her vagina in the missionary position.

Yuni looked back over to his brother, who was still raping Elizabeth. Neither girl was crying; however, Yuni could tell that they were not enjoying themselves in any way. Instead, the girls kept begging for the boys to stop and to let them go.

The boys, on the other hand, were enjoying themselves. They were not about to let these girls go.

Joe Medellin looked up and saw that his brother was not happy. He smiled at Yuni and said, "What's the matter, bro? Don't you want some of this good pussy?" He laughed at his brother.

Joe Medellin continued to laugh as he looked at Elizabeth. He smiled and said, "What's your name, baby?"

Elizabeth began to cry softly. She lied and said, "Melissa," giving her mother's name.

"What's your phone number?" Joe Medellin asked, and cracked himself up in the process.

Elizabeth gave him a bogus phone number in an effort to keep him happy. Maybe they would leave her alone if she gave them what they wanted.

Yuni turned away from his brother, only to see O'Brien on top of the white girl. O'Brien began to rape Jennifer for at least five more minutes; then he suddenly dismounted.

"Dude, switch," he hollered over to Joe Medellin. O'Brien got up off Jennifer and casually strolled over to where Elizabeth lay. Joe Medellin did the same and went to Jennifer. The two boys grinned at one another as they passed by and gave each other "five" with a slap of their hands.

Elizabeth, humiliated from the rape she endured from Joe Medellin, was unable to get up. Suddenly she was pinned down by O'Brien. He fell on top of her and began to rape her as well. Joe Medellin began to rape Jennifer.

Yuni Medellin watched as Efrain Perez and Raul Villarreal stepped in and took turns raping the girls. Perez walked over to Jennifer and forced her to perform oral sex. Now a member of the group, Villarreal walked over to Elizabeth and pulled his pants down past his buttocks. He then forced himself into Elizabeth's unwilling mouth.

After several minutes, O'Brien hopped off Elizabeth and made his way back over to Jennifer. When he got there, the girl was being forced to suck on Cantu's penis. O'Brien jumped in and assaulted the young girl again. He then went back to Elizabeth for more forced oral sex. Apparently, O'Brien was starting to have stage fright and could not maintain an erection. After a few minutes of Elizabeth's sucking, he pulled out and zipped his pants back up. An eager Perez stepped in to take his place.

O'Brien walked back over to Jennifer and saw that Cantu was again forcing her to perform oral sex. Cantu smiled at his buddy and said, "This is some good stuff, man." Cantu pulled his penis out of the young teenager's mouth and turned toward O'Brien. "Get in there, man. Get you some more. That's some good stuff," he repeated. O'Brien unzipped his pants and pulled them back down. He stuck his flaccid penis in front of a humiliated Jennifer. The young girl was becoming exhausted.

O'Brien watched Cantu head back over to Elizabeth and resume raping her. As he looked down and saw Jennifer struggle with his penis, he noticed Villarreal moved back over to the white girl and began raping her again. O'Brien pulled his penis out of the girl's mouth and stepped away for a moment. He was quickly replaced with Villarreal, who dislodged himself from Jennifer's vagina and replaced his penis where O'Brien's had just been.

Cantu stood in front of Elizabeth, and orally raped her. He looked over at Yuni Medellin and began to egg him on.

"C'mon, dude. Get some," Cantu urged Yuni.

The younger Medellin brother simply stared and shook his head. "No, man. I don't think I can do that."

"C'mon, man. Don't be such a pussy," Cantu teased him. "Get in there and get you some."

Yuni Medellin was not sure what to do. The one thing he was afraid of was not appearing cool in front of his brother and his brother's friends. He figured to be a part of this group he needed to be doing what everyone else was doing—so he stepped toward Jennifer and unzipped his pants. By this time, the young girl was crying. She held tough for a long time, but the assault was beginning to take its toll. Yuni Medellin apparently was not too turned off by the situation, as he was able to achieve an erection despite the gruesome scene before him. Fourteen-year-old Yuni mounted fourteen-year-old Jennifer and began raping her.

O'Brien watched as Yuni raped Jennifer. O'Brien laughed as the young teen thrust into her. After about five minutes of Yuni assaulting Jennifer, O'Brien had had enough.

"Get off her, man," O'Brien ordered.

Yuni did not hear him at first and continued to rape the sophomore-to-be.

"Dude, get off her," O'Brien stated more sternly. He grabbed Yuni's shoulder and pulled him off the young girl. His gestures were not chivalrous. Instead, O'Brien masturbated himself back to an erect state and once again penetrated Jennifer against her will.

Yuni Medellin stepped back with his penis hanging out of his pants, stunned. He was not quite sure what had happened, other than he had just raped a teenage girl and his penis was hanging out of his pants in public in front of five other boys.

Once again, Yuni looked up to see what his brother was up to. By this time, Joe Medellin had returned to raping Elizabeth, and now Perez was squatting down on her neck and had his penis shoved into her mouth.

Cantu yelled over to Joe, "Hurry up. It's my turn."

"I'm gonna take my time," Joe replied. He was having way too much fun to stop what he was doing to Elizabeth. Elizabeth, however, was still not ready to give in completely. She tried to fight off the two boys by squirming and kicking her legs at Joe Medellin. Her protestations only excited the two molesters. They managed to restrain her mainly with Perez having her trapped by his crotch.

Elizabeth, exhausted, looked over at her best friend, Jennifer, who lay twenty feet away. She began to weep as she saw O'Brien and Villarreal both assaulting Jennifer. O'Brien was forcing her to suck his penis, while Villarreal raped her anally. She looked up and, at a disjointed angle, saw Cantu laughing, smiling, and cheering the other guys on.

"Dude, go get some more of that." Cantu nodded toward Elizabeth.

The next thing she knew, Cantu had pounced on her and began ripping her insides apart with his penis.

O'Brien got off Jennifer and made his way back over to Elizabeth, who was on all fours, being orally raped by Villarreal. O'Brien mounted Elizabeth from behind and proceeded to rape her doggy-style.

Just a few minutes later, Cantu barked out a command in Spanish. Suddenly everyone stopped raping the girls.

It only took a minute before they resumed the assault. By now, Joe Medellin had gone back over to Jennifer and stuck his penis in her mouth. A worn-out Jennifer began to piss Joe Medellin off as she allegedly nicked his penis with her teeth.

"Yo, bitch! You better stop biting me," he snapped at her. "You bite me again and I'm gonna kick your ass," he threatened her.

Whether it was an intentional ploy to defend herself is unknown, but Jennifer bit down on Joe Medellin's penis again. He was furious. He instantly punched Jennifer in the face so hard that she started to bleed from her nose.

"You bitch!" he screamed at her. "I told you not to bite me, you cunt!"

The rapes lasted more than an hour. Each boy, except Yuni Medellin, had nonconsensual sex with both girls at least four times. According to Yuni, "they raped them in every conceivable way." Orally, anally, two-on-one, double penetration.

Yuni Medellin stood dumbfounded between the two groups of people. Suddenly Cantu sauntered up to Yuni and whispered to him, "We're gonna have to kill them."

"What do you mean?" a frightened Yuni responded.

"They've seen our faces. We can't leave behind any witnesses. We've got to kill them."

Chapter 19

"We gotta kill 'em. They know what we look like," Peter Cantu repeated. It seemed as important to him as cleaning the cat box. Just something that had to be done, no matter how unpleasant it may get. Cantu turned away from Yuni and grabbed Elizabeth Pena. Joe Medellin and Efrain Perez walked up to Cantu and the exhausted Elizabeth. Cantu grabbed her by the arms while the other boys grabbed her long legs. She barely struggled.

The three boys ambled down the not-so-steep hill and headed toward the nearby woods just north of the bayou. A footpath had been beaten down toward a large copse of towering pine trees. They looked like a bunch of delivery men schlepping a large dog-food-sized bag filled with wet cotton. Elizabeth's body put up minimal resistance. She just undulated in an awkward motion as they carried her to the woods.

Just ahead of the foursome were Derrick Sean O'Brien, Raul Villarreal, and Jennifer Ertman. They were leading the teenager on foot past the bald spot in the dirt where Villarreal's initiation had taken place almost an hour earlier, past the open forty-ounce bottle of Schlitz Malt Liquor Bull that one of the boys had dropped during the scuffle. Jennifer, unlike Elizabeth, struggled. She resisted O'Brien and Villarreal, who were much larger, stronger, and faster, but it was to no avail. They forcefully pushed her into the copse.

O'Brien and Villarreal continued on the beaten path out into the opening in the woods. They stepped through. Jennifer kicked and tried to scream, but she was quickly silenced by Villarreal.

The threesome was followed by the foursome of Cantu, Jose Medellin, Perez, and Elizabeth. They also trudged past the fight club location, up the trail to the woods, and through the tree-shrouded hole of an entrance. Yuni followed about five to ten feet behind. He watched his brother and the others as they were enveloped by the green-by-day, pitch-black-by-night needles of the pine trees.

Not wanting to be the only one left out in the open, Yuni followed through the hole. After he entered the woods, he looked up and could barely see his brother. Eventually his eyes adjusted to the new darkness. Not only could he see his brother, he realized he was also standing next to O'Brien, who was standing next to Jennifer.

"Get down on your knees, bitch," Villarreal barked at the young girl. She hesitated. "Now!" he screamed at her.

Jennifer collapsed, spent.

Instantly Villarreal wrapped a red nylon belt around her neck, crossed the belt over with his hand for a tight fit, and began pulling with all his might from behind. Jennifer's hands instinctively thrust toward her throat as she grabbed the belt. Her elbows crooked as she attempted to pry it off her neck. Villarreal was strangling the life out of the vibrant teenage girl.

One problem for Villarreal: Jennifer was too strong. She would not give up and she continued to fight against the pressure around her throat.

O'Brien saw that the new guy wasn't cutting it, so he

moved in on the opposite side of Jennifer, grabbed one end of the belt (which belonged to him), and pulled as hard as he could, while Villarreal continued his exertions on the other end.

Yuni watched and listened as the murder unfolded.

He heard the girl begin to gasp as she was choking. He heard both Villarreal and O'Brien grunt as they gathered strength to strangle her.

Grunt—Grunt—Wheeze—Grunt—Grunt—Wheeze!

Yuni knew it did not sound good for the girl, but he did nothing.

O'Brien and Villarreal both stood behind Jennifer and pulled on the belt. Sweat began to pour down their faces. Their grunts were low and guttural.

Yuni stood transfixed at the scene for at least two minutes. Finally he could not take it anymore. He turned his back and scampered away out of the woods, back onto the open clearing, near the bald dirt patch. He could hear a gurgling sound. He did not want to see what happened to the poor young girl. Instead, he looked up into the dark moonlit sky. He spotted several stars and lost himself in the immensity of the night.

Grunt—Grunt—Wheeze!

Elizabeth had witnessed the entire nightmarish ordeal. Her friend being brutally raped and murdered before her very eyes.

Now she knew it was her turn.

Joe Medellin and Cantu grabbed one of Perez's shoelaces. They looped it around Elizabeth's neck and began to pull. Elizabeth tried to escape, but she was tackled by Cantu, who proceeded to kick her in the face with his steel-tipped boots. He kicked her so hard and so many times that he knocked out three of her front teeth. He also broke several of Elizabeth's ribs with his boots. Bloodied and exhausted, she no longer resisted.

Joe Medellin and Cantu continued the slow strangulation until she could breathe no more.

Just as Elizabeth's last gasp was sputtered, miraculously, Jennifer stirred. She was not dead.

The guys were stunned, and Villarreal, maybe still attempting to prove he was worthy, walked up to the young girl and proceeded to stand on her throat. "The bitch won't die!" He laughed.

Finally he stepped off, and O'Brien followed suit.

At that same time, two of the other boys began to stomp on Elizabeth's face and dead body. They stomped and stomped and stomped. O'Brien did the same to Jennifer's body. All of the boys stomped on the girls' bodies until they were unrecognizable masses of blood, bone, and dirt.

Yuni waited and waited. He could not escape from the horrible sounds.

More than fifteen minutes later, he looked up at the opening from the woods. His eyes had adjusted to the darkness and he could clearly see O'Brien, Villarreal, Perez, Cantu, and his brother, Joe, step out of the woods. They looked exhilarated and dirty.

The first person to break the silence was O'Brien. "Damn man, where's my belt?" he asked. He began to look around the grass for the weapon he and Villarreal used to kill Jennifer. He patted down the sun-beaten grass, but did not find it. He glanced around, but gave up after less than a minute's time.

Cantu looked up at Joe Medellin, Yuni Medellin, and Raul Villarreal. He told them to take off down the tracks. He pointed them in the direction over the trestle toward T. C. Jester Boulevard. "Why don't y'all take off over that way and wait for us on Jester?" Cantu suggested. The three boys headed down the train tracks. They crossed the bayou, crossed T. C. Jester Boulevard, and waited next to some older homes.

O'Brien walked back to his apartment with Perez and Cantu, who picked up their vehicles. O'Brien went inside and the other two took off.

Several minutes later, Cantu pulled up in his red Ford pickup truck. "C'mon, let's go." They all hopped into the truck and headed out.

The drive was short, but painfully silent. No one said a word to each other. No one looked at each other. Cantu broke the silence when he turned to Yuni and said, "Here. Take this watch." He handed him a wristwatch with Goofy adorning the center. "Take it. I don't want it."

Yuni took the watch and clasped it in his hands. He did not say anything.

Nothing more was said. Cantu drove on and eventually ended up at his house less than four miles from the murder scene.

Chapter 20

Joe Medellin, Raul Villarreal, and Efrain Perez walked up to Peter Cantu's house, which was very crowded. Cantu lived with his parents, his sister, his brother Joe, and Joe's new bride, sixteen-year-old Christina.

Joe Cantu had been trying to make the best for himself. Although he dropped out of Reagan High School his senior year without a diploma, he earned a degree from a technical institute, which allowed him to become a medical assistant. Indeed, he had recently begun working for a local blood donation center as a phlebotomist, someone who draws blood from patients.

Joe met a young girl named Christina, who was a member of a mixed-gender gang that claimed the Heights as their turf. They were mainly known for stealing cars and fencing the parts for cash. Joe wanted to be with Christina, but he couldn't stand that she was a member of a gang. He asked her to quit or he would no longer see her. She agreed, and six months later, they were married.

Christina and Joe heard a knock on the door. Joe was too tired to get up and answer it, so she got up instead. Christina unlocked the door and pulled it wide open. She was shocked to see Joe Medellin standing in front of her with blood on his clothes. She expected her brother-in-law Peter to show up, not Joe Medellin, and definitely not in such a state of disarray. She caught a glimpse of a large red scratch on his neck. His hair was mussed, he had scrapes on his knees, and he seemed a bit wild-eyed. Next to Joe Medellin stood Efrain Perez, who also wasn't looking so hot. He had blood on the lower portion of his white wife-beater undershirt near his crotch area. It looked as if he had smeared it down his shirt and into his pants. A third boy, Raul Villarreal, whom Christina did not know, stood beside Joe and Perez. He also looked worse for wear. He had dried blood caked on his right eyebrow and blood on his pants.

Christina stepped back away from the door. "What's up?" she asked.

The boys nodded toward Christina, but they did not say anything. Instead, they made a beeline for the living room like it was their own house. They seemed hopped up on adrenaline.

Joe Cantu was still in the bedroom, pulling on his jeans. Christina followed the boys into the living room.

"What happened to you guys?" Christina asked as she looked toward Joe Medellin and Perez.

Joe Medellin looked at Perez, who, in turn, looked up at Villarreal. All three of the boys began to smile as Joe responded, "Let's just say we had a lot of fun." His grin stretched from ear to ear.

Perez and Villarreal began to laugh. Indeed, all three boys were giggling. Joe Medellin joined in with loud peals of laughter.

Christina was not sure what to make of Peter's buddies. They looked as if they had been in a fight; however, they were all cracking up like they had just heard the funniest joke known to man. Of course, Christina thought, a fight was just the sort of entertainment these guys would find amusing.

Joe Cantu walked into the living room. Perez and Joe Medellin gave him a "wassup" head nod, which Joe Cantu returned.

Joe Medellin looked up at Christina, and as he looked at Villarreal, he said, "Christina, this is Raul. He's a new member of Black and White." He then glanced over at Villarreal and said, "This is Christina, Joe's wife. She's the one who cooks for us."

Villarreal and Christina exchanged nods.

Joe Medellin turned to Joe Cantu and introduced Villarreal to him as well.

Joe Cantu knew something was up. He could tell they seemed a bit too jacked-up. "What happened?" he asked, motioning toward the blood on Perez's shirt. "Who'd you squab with now?" meaning whom did they get into a fight with.

Joe Medellin responded, "Let's just say we had a lot of fun," the same thing he had told Christina. All three of the boys started to crack up again. Medellin then added, "You'll hear about it on the news." This caused the boys to burst out in laughter yet again.

Joe Cantu stood in silence. He thought the guys were full of shit.

When Christina heard Joe Medellin's boast, she only had one thought: she was standing in front of three murderers.

Joe Cantu asked Joe Medellin again, "Dude, what happened?"

Joe Medellin could not stop laughing. Finally he said

to Joe Cantu, "I'll tell you in a minute, as soon as [Perez] goes and takes a bath."

Perez looked over to Christina and asked, "Can I take a bath?"

"Hold on a minute. I gotta go to the restroom first," she declared.

Perez untucked his undershirt and pulled it off and over his head. He tossed the shirt at Christina, hitting her in the face.

"Get rid of it," Perez ordered Christina.

She was pissed. She jerked the shirt off her face and was about to throw it to the ground when she noticed even more blood. She wadded the shirt into a ball and tossed it into the trash can. She ignored Perez and headed to the bathroom.

After Christina finished up in the bathroom, she took the trash can outside and dumped Perez's bloody T-shirt. Her husband followed her, grabbed the shirt, and lit it on fire with his lighter. He made sure the entire shirt burned to a crisp.

When Christina walked back into the house, Perez had already gone into the bathroom to take a bath. He said he needed to wash the blood off his body.

Christina and Joe Cantu knew something bad had happened. They headed toward the living room and sat down on the couch next to one another. Joe Medellin began to tell them about their night. He talked about the drinking and the initiation. He talked about how they continued drinking on the railroad tracks and how they stumbled across a little surprise.

"We met these two bitches," Joe Medellin recalled as he smiled at Villarreal, "and we had a fun time with them." Villarreal nodded and smiled back at Joe Medellin.

Joe Cantu and Christina believed Joe Medellin was holding back. He would not get into any specifics. Eventually, however, his tongue began to loosen. As he relived the moment, he began to get excited. He and Villarreal laughed as they recalled the events. The more they talked about it, the more they continued to giggle, like a couple of schoolgirls.

Christina later stated they appeared as if "they were proud of what they did." She added they were "laughing and giggling and bragging about it."

Joe Medellin talked about how one of the girls begged him to spare her life. "Yeah, that one fat white bitch started begging, 'Please don't kill me. Please don't kill me' in a little whiny-white-bitch-ass voice!" he stated in a shrill, mocking tone. All three of the boys started to laugh again at the memory.

"Then we started doing those white bitches," Joe Medellin added, and slapped a high five with Villarreal. "I did that one bitch in the pussy," he bragged. "Peter was doing that other white bitch." Joe Medellin looked amazed as he continued to tell his story to Christina and Joe Cantu. "I couldn't believe it. That fat bitch that I was doing was a goddamned virgin! Dude, she bled all over me. I can't believe she was a virgin." He continued his boasting. "Man, I opened that bitch up."

Joe Medellin was on a roll. "Dude, then we all started fucking those bitches. Then I turned one of them over and started doing her in her ass. Shit was tight."

Villarreal chimed in, "Man, that skinny bitch had a nice, tight ass."

"Yeah, I made that bitch give me head," Joe Medellin countered.

"Aw, hell yeah," Villarreal hooted, and began to laugh again at the memory.

As the two teenagers recalled their exploits, Perez walked out of the bathroom. He was clean and dressed. He also seemed quieter than usual.

Joe Medellin saw Perez walk out of the bathroom, so

Elizabeth Pena, 16, was very popular in school and beloved by her family. *(School yearbook photos)*

Jennifer Ertman, 14, was a loving daughter, an excellent student, and a trusted friend who vowed to stay a virgin until she married. *(School yearbook photos)*

Raul Villarreal, 17, attended nursing school with his mother and sister before the murders but could not get a job upon graduation. *(Photo courtesy of the Houston Police Department)*

Villarreal's first night out with the boys led to the rape and murder of Elizabeth Pena and Jennifer Ertman. *(Photo courtesy of the Houston Police Department)*

Efrain Perez, Jr., 17, in an earlier mug shot for one of several juvenile crimes he committed. *(Photo courtesy of the Houston Police Department)*

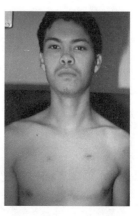

Perez cheered on his pals as they raped the two girls for over an hour. Then he jumped into the action. *(Photo courtesy of the Houston Police Department)*

Peter Cantu failed three grades by the time he finally reached sixth grade. *(School yearbook photo)*

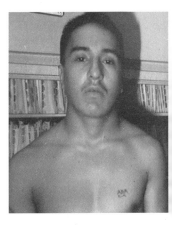

Cantu, 18, was considered to be the alleged ringleader of the group of boys. *(Photo courtesy of the Houston Police Department)*

Joe Medellin won first prize at his school science fair for his crystal radio design and was a good student throughout elementary school. *(School yearbook photo)*

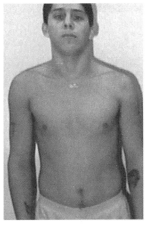

Joe Medellin, 18, later bragged about having "the blood of a virgin" on his underwear. *(Photo courtesy of the Houston Police Department)*

Venancio "Yuni" Medellin, Jr., 14, Joe Medellin's younger brother, participated in the rape of Jennifer Ertman. He would become the State of Texas's key witness against the rest of the boys. *(Photo courtesy of the Houston Police Department)*

On the day of the rapes and murders, Sean O'Brien, 18, bragged to a television reporter that "life means nothing." *(Photo courtesy of the Houston Police Department)*

The Spring Hill Apartments swimming pool where Elizabeth and Jennifer spent their last fun moments in life. *(Corey Mitchell)*

Trail from O'Brien's apartment complex, where the young men walked to the train trestle over White Oak Bayou and near the scene of the rapes and murders. *(Photo courtesy of the Houston Police Department)*

Overhead view of the crime scene. O'Brien's apartment complex parking lot, where the young men hit the trail, is bottom center. Elizabeth and Jennifer came from the complex on the left and along the train tracks. The young men encountered the girls before the bridge and raped them above the tracks near the forest on the upper left, which is where they killed them and left them to rot in the sweltering Houston heat. *(Photo courtesy of the Houston Police Department)*

Elizabeth and Jennifer walked along these railroad tracks before they met their demise. *(Corey Mitchell)*

Entrance to the forest where Elizabeth and Jennifer were murdered and left to be devoured by nature. *(Photo courtesy of the Houston Police Department)*

CSU Investigator Beverly Trumble points at evidence where the young men fought Raul Villarreal. *(Photo courtesy of the Houston Police Department)*

Jennifer's corpse was discovered just a couple of feet from her best friend, Elizabeth. Her shirt was pulled up over her face. *(Photo courtesy of the Houston Police Department)*

Elizabeth's well-manicured left foot peeks out from the pine needles in the forest. *(Photo courtesy of the Houston Police Department)*

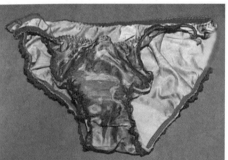

Elizabeth's jeans, purple bra, and purple panties were discovered near her body in the woods. *(Photo courtesy of the Houston Police Department)*

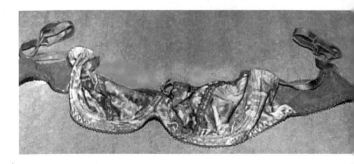

Jennifer's Goofy watch, given to her as a Christmas gift by her parents almost six months before her murder, symbolized her youth. *(Photo courtesy of the Houston Police Department)*

Jennifer enjoyed wearing lots of jewelry, which the young men stole from her and gave out as gifts. *(Photo courtesy of the Houston Police Department)*

Jennifer's purple Converse basketball sneaker had been stripped from her right foot and found near her body. *(Photo courtesy of the Houston Police Department)*

Jennifer's discarded pink panties were discovered near her partially nude body. *(Photo courtesy of the Houston Police Department)*

Portion of Sean O'Brien's red belt discovered at the murder scene. O'Brien and Villarreal pulled so hard on the belt when they strangled Jennifer that it broke. *(Photo courtesy of the Houston Police Department)*

Peter Cantu's black steel-tipped work boots were used to kick in three of Elizabeth's teeth, crack her ribs, and choke her. Note the scuffing on the right shoe while the left is pristine. *(Photo courtesy of the Houston Police Department)*

O'Brien was among the crowd that included friends of the girls and media personnel when the bodies were discovered four days after the murders. *(Photo courtesy of the Houston Police Department)*

The home of Elizabeth Pena—her hoped-for destination on that fateful night. *(Corey Mitchell)*

Residence of Peter Cantu where he, Joe Medellin, Efrain Perez, and Raul Villarreal bragged about the rapes and murders to Peter's brother Joe Cantu and his sister-in-law, Christina Cantu. *(Corey Mitchell)*

Remainder of O'Brien's red belt used to strangle Jennifer, which was discovered in his apartment complex upon his arrest.
(Photo courtesy of the Houston Police Department)

Two memorial benches were added in T.C. Jester Park across the White Oak Bayou from where the girls were murdered. *(Corey Mitchell)*

Memorial tree and plaque located at Waltrip High School, where the girls attended school. The tree and plaque were donated by Elizabeth and Jennifer's fellow students.
(Corey Mitchell)

In Loving Memory of
Jennifer Ertman
and
Elizabeth Pena

"We cannot become what we need to be
by remaining what we are."
- Max DePree

1993

Elizabeth Pena and Jennifer Ertman are buried within 200 yards of one another at the Woodlawn Garden of Memories cemetery in Houston, Texas. *(Corey Mitchell)*

he got up and proudly announced, "I'm gonna go take a bath 'cause I got virgin blood all on my underwear." He looked over to Perez and asked, "You got blood on your underwear?"

"Nah, man, I can't see none," Perez replied.

"Check it out, man," Joe Medellin said as he reached his hand into his pants. He pulled out the top of his underwear so everyone in the room could see. It was covered in blood. Joe was so proud, he looked like a fisherman showing off his biggest catch. "It's from that slut."

Christina glanced toward Joe Medellin. She saw the blood on his underwear, then turned away. She was appalled by his casual attitude, but she made sure he was unaware of her disgust. They had no idea she, too, had been raped by several guys just one year earlier.

Joe shoved his underwear back into his pants and headed toward the bathroom to take a shower. He looked back at Perez and declared, "Yo, Peter better give us some of that money and jewelry he got off them hos."

"I heard that," Perez stated.

"I want some of that money, too," Villarreal added.

Joe Medellin plodded off to the bathroom, his head held high. He went in and washed the girls' blood off his body. As he finished and stepped out of the shower, back into the living room, Peter Cantu finally arrived home. It was more than a half hour after the others had arrived. Peter walked into the living room and spotted Villarreal and Perez laughing it up while they kept talking to his brother Joe and sister-in-law Christina about the night's events. As he walked past them, Joe Medellin shouted, "Yo, where's my fuckin' money?"

Peter reached into his pants pocket and pulled out a wad of green bills. He had around $40 on him. He reached in again and pulled out some rings and jewelry, including a heart-shaped gold ring with the letter *E* on it, a gold inverted V-shaped ring, and a gold rope chain with two rings on it, a gold bracelet, and a second gold rope necklace with an *S* charm on it. He walked over to Efrain Perez, handed him a $10 bill, and said, "This is for gas." He handed some cash to Raul Villarreal and Joe Medellin as well. He pulled a ring out of his pocket and handed it to Christina. He placed the rest of the jewelry on the coffee table. Perez and Villarreal scrambled for the rings.

"Man, I want that," Perez declared, looking at one of the rings.

"Don't take it all, dick," Villarreal interjected as he pushed Perez aside. "I want some of that shit, too."

Peter gave the *E* ring to Joe Medellin because he knew his girlfriend's name was Esther. "Man, I dropped off Yuni," Peter informed Medellin, in reference to Joe's little brother. "We had to talk. He's cool."

Peter sat down on the couch next to Perez. He nodded toward Medellin and listened to the two other boys as they continued to talk about the massacre. He simply nodded his head in agreement. He did not add much to the conversation other than to back up what they were already saying.

Christina suddenly hightailed it out of the living room. She did not want to be around this group of young men anymore. She walked into her bedroom, but then reconsidered. She worried that they might get pissed at her, so she shook it off, composed herself, and returned to the living room. She sat quietly next to her husband as they continued to brag about their exploits.

Perez looked up at Joe Cantu and said, "Dude, you should have been there, man. You missed out."

Joe Cantu merely nodded his head.

Joe Medellin and Raul Villarreal started again to talk about what they did to the girls.

Finally Perez interrupted them and blurted out, "Man, y'all made her bite me! That white bitch was sucking my cock and you, fucker," he said to Joe Medellin, "you smacked that bitch on the top of her head so hard that she bit down on my cock. I had to smack the shit out of her for that one!"

Joe Medellin couldn't contain his laughter. He thought it was the funniest thing in the world.

Perez was on a roll. Through tears of laughter, he recalled that he was "doing one of the girls on the ground and I lost my balance. I think I broke my arm."

"I remember that," Peter Cantu recalled.

Medellin piped in that he, too, had "lost his balance while he was fucking one of the girls and scratched his knee." Indeed, he had white powder marks on his knees and a few scratches on them as well.

Perez, Medellin, Villarreal, and Peter Cantu were all cracking up. They were having the time of their life recalling the events. All four of the boys recounted the ways in which they violated the girls: "I did her pussy," "she sucked my dick," "I did that bitch in the ass" were some of the refrains Christina and Joe Cantu heard. After each time someone bragged about a violation, Peter Cantu would simply grin and say, "Yeah, I remember I did that, too."

Joe Medellin added, "I can't believe that bitch scratched me. I had to smack her up for that one." The boys continued cracking up until they exhausted themselves.

When the laughter subsided, Joe Cantu asked, "Well, what happened to them?" in reference to the girls.

Almost in unison, the boys said, "We had to kill them."

Christina held her breath. She also held her ground.

"Yeah, man, we had to kill those bitches," Peter declared. "We didn't want them identifying us and getting us in trouble with the cops." The others all agreed and murmured their assent.

"Yeah, we had to do it," Medellin seconded.

"Yeah, we did," Perez added, "otherwise our asses were

gonna be thrown in jail. We couldn't let those sluts turn us in."

"Yeah, man," Peter offered. "You got it, daddy."

Joe Cantu asked the group, "How'd y'all do it?"

Medellin and Villarreal began to describe how they murdered the girls.

"I took a shoelace and I pulled it around that bitch's neck," Joe Medellin said. "[Perez] grabbed the other side of the shoelace while I was tightening it around her neck. I started strangling that bitch." Medellin continued, "That bitch looked dead so I checked her pulse to see if she was breathin', and shit. I couldn't feel no pulse. That bitch was dead!"

Villarreal talked about how he and O'Brien used a red belt to strangle Jennifer. "I took that belt and wrapped it around her throat, and me and Sean pulled like a mother. We squeezed it so hard that the damn belt busted on us."

"I couldn't believe that happened." Peter Cantu cracked up.

"It would have been a hell of a lot easier if we had a gun," interjected Joe Medellin.

"After it broke," Villarreal continued, "I got on top of her neck. I started slamming her throat with my leg. Jumping on it with my feet. I wanted to kill that bitch."

Peter broke in, "We had to make sure those bitches were dead, so I kicked one of them right in the mouth." He emphasized this with a swift kick of a steel-toed boot.

"I had to do it because one of them bitches didn't want to die," Villarreal added.

"Dude, you had to do it," added Joe Medellin.

Christina and Joe Cantu continued to listen as the boys described how they took turns kicking the girls in the face and stomping on their necks. Each one of the boys did this to the girls.

"What'd y'all do with their bodies?" Joe Cantu asked.

"Once we knew they were dead," Perez answered, "we just left. They're out in the woods, man."

"Ha!" exclaimed Villarreal. "Remember, one of them bitches gave us her phone number? That's hilarious." Villarreal continued to giggle as the others joined in the laughter. "I'm gonna call it"—which elicited roars of laughter from the others—"see if they found the bodies yet." Villarreal added, "I remember when that bitch gave me her phone number, I told her, 'Yeah, this is fun. We'll have to do this again. Call me. We'll do it again.'" He burst out into even more laughter. The other three boys joined him.

The conversation lasted nearly two hours.

Christina had a difficult time listening. She would walk in and out of the room, oftentimes to go into her bedroom and cry. Finally she convinced her husband to come to bed. Once in the bedroom, she couldn't even look him in the eye. She was terrified. Joe Cantu tried to touch his wife, but she recoiled in horror, even though he had nothing to do with the rapes and murders. "I just couldn't let him touch me," Christina recalled.

She crawled into bed, worried because she was sleeping in a house with four murderers. She ignored her husband, who tried to comfort her. The couple did not say a word to one another. Christina could barely fall asleep.

Chapter 21

Friday, June 25, 1993—2:00 A.M.
O'Brien residence
Clearbrook Apartments
West Thirty-fourth Street
Houston, Texas

Sean O'Brien was restless. He had not been able to fall asleep since he returned to his apartment.

At approximately 2:00 A.M., O'Brien picked up his telephone and nervously dialed Peter Cantu's phone number. He needed to talk to somebody about what they had done.

"Hello?" said a tired voice on the other end of the line. It was Joe Cantu.

"Joe, it's Sean. Let me talk to Petè."

"Hold on, man," Joe stated in an agitated tone. He laid the phone down on the nightstand and rose out of bed to track down his brother.

After a couple of minutes, someone picked up the phone. "He doesn't want to wake up," Joe Cantu informed O'Brien.

"Did you tell him it's me?"

"Yeah, dude. He said he wanted to go back to sleep. He also said he didn't want to be bothered."

"Joe," O'Brien pleaded, "man, I think I hear one of those girls, man. I think I hear her crying." He had reached the brink and was not sure if he could come back down or if the abyss was calling him. It was eerily reminiscent of Edgar Allan Poe's "The Tell-tale Heart."

And now at the dead hour of the night, amid the dreadful silence of that old house, so strange a noise as this excited me to uncontrollable terror. Yet, for some minutes longer I refrained and stood still. But the beating grew louder, louder! I thought the heart must burst.

Joe Cantu could tell O'Brien did not sound right. "Hold on just a second, Sean." Joe returned to his younger brother's bedroom and told him that O'Brien wasn't in good shape. "Tell him to go back there and pick up those beer bottles we might have left behind and get rid of 'em." Joe went back to the phone and passed along Peter's message.

"Okay. I guess so," O'Brien replied, not thrilled with the order. The last thing he wanted to do was go back out where the girls' corpses lay. He had no idea what tricks his mind would continue to play on him.

O'Brien pulled on his pants, threw on a T-shirt and tennis shoes, and snuck out of the house one more time. He was much quieter this time as he scooted through the playground and the hole in the fence. He made his way up the trail that led to the trestle and to the area where they beat up Villarreal. The only light came from the moon, which appeared much more ominous to O'Brien now. He scanned the area for beer bottles, but he could barely see three feet in front of him.

Suddenly O'Brien heard someone call his name—

Sean—but it was barely audible as a whisper. He looked toward the woods where the two girls' mangled corpses lay.

Sean.

He heard it again. Without missing a beat, O'Brien took off in a mad dash, nearly busting an ankle as he scrambled up the gravel berm and over the railroad tracks.

O'Brien was scared to death.

He feared the girls were not dead, someone would discover them, and they would rat him out. The other side of his brain told him that, of course, they were dead.

But how did that explain the whispers?

He was not sure if he believed in ghosts.

He thought he was losing his mind.

As soon as he snuck back inside his apartment, O'Brien picked up the phone and dialed Cantu's number. Joe Cantu answered the phone. An excited and nervous O'Brien told him what had just happened.

"Dude, I heard them!" O'Brien said, wincing.

"What are you talking about?" Joe Cantu asked.

"I went back to get the beer bottles and I heard the girls say my name or something, man!"

Joe handed the phone to Peter, who told O'Brien to go back to sleep.

O'Brien was unable to rest, so he hung up and dialed the Sandoval brothers. Ramon picked up the phone fast, as it was nearly 3:00 A.M. and he did not want his parents to be woken up. Over the next ten minutes, O'Brien told Ramon what happened after the brothers took off.

Chapter 22

Sandra Ertman stirred in her bed. She was too restless to fall back asleep. As she lay on the right side of the bed, she looked at her husband, who was still asleep. She then peered out their bedroom door and to the side of the hallway into Jennifer's room. Their bedrooms were only six feet apart. Sandra always left the light on in Jennifer's bedroom, which her daughter would turn off when she got home.

The light was still shining brightly.

Jennifer was not home yet.

Sandra began to panic. Jennifer always called to make sure it was okay to spend the night at one of her friends' houses, such as Elizabeth's or Gina's. This time, however, she did not call home to verify. It was unlike Jennifer not to call her parents.

Sandra darted out of bed and headed for the telephone.

She dialed Jennifer's beeper number, then hung up the phone. After she placed the page, she realized it was a futile gesture, for Jennifer would have removed her pager and turned it off to go to sleep. Regardless, it did not stop her from dialing the pager again.

"I was a little frantic," Sandra recalled. "Panic ran over me because she hadn't verified staying over, and Jennifer had never done that before in her life."

Sandra calmed down long enough to lie back in bed. She was unable to fall asleep because she was too busy running various scenarios through her mind of what may have happened to her daughter.

At 6:30 A.M., Randy Ertman woke up from his night's slumber. When Sandra sensed her husband's stirrings, she also got out of bed. She did not want to make him nervous, so she masked her anxiety in front of him.

Randy noticed his daughter's bedroom light was still on. "Oh, did Jennifer spend the night at Gina's or Elizabeth's?" he asked his wife.

"Well," Sandra began cautiously, "she said she might spend the night."

She failed to tell her husband their daughter had not called to check in. "That was one of the laws of our house," Sandra later recalled, "I didn't say to him that she didn't call me back, because I knew it would have made him angry. So I kind of kept it to myself."

Sandra kept a lot more inside as well. Over the next several hours, she became even more worried, because she knew whenever Jennifer spent the night with a friend, she would usually wake up around 11:00 A.M. or noon and immediately call her mom to come pick her up. Whenever Jennifer slept over at a friend's house, she always slept in her jeans and shirt; as a result, she always wanted to get home and shower because she felt dirty.

Sandra was even more concerned because she knew her daughter's period would probably start on Saturday,

June 26. "She always wanted to be home and get that shower, clean up, and have her own [feminine hygiene] products that I purchased for her." Jennifer was very fastidious about her cleanliness and it was surprising she had not called to come home to take care of it. "So I was really getting worried about that."

By the time 11:00 A.M. rolled around, Sandra still had not heard from her daughter. She finally relented and told her husband. He was surprised she hadn't told him sooner and was irritated that Jennifer had not bothered to check in. "I am always used to her keeping her word," Randy noted later. In fact, she was always so good about keeping her word, he didn't even bother to wake up around her curfew hour.

He instantly reached for the telephone and dialed the phone number for Adolph Pena, Elizabeth's father. No one answered. He then dialed Gina Escamilla's phone number. Again, no one answered.

Randy looked at his wife and declared, "I'm not going to wait." He grabbed his keys and headed for the door. "I'm going over to Elizabeth's house," he said as he took off.

Randy drove four-and-a-half miles to the Pena residence. Along the way, he traveled down T. C. Jester Boulevard, alongside the park and over the train tracks that crossed over White Oak Bayou. He pulled up to the curb in front of the Penas' home, jumped out of the car, and up to the front door. Ertman knocked politely at first. After several seconds and no answer, he rapped harder with his large knuckles.

Again, no answer.

He could not hear any stirring in the house.

Randy started to worry. He continued banging on the door. When no one answered, he went around back and banged on the windows. He called out for Adolph, he called out for Elizabeth, and he called out for Jennifer—

no one answered. He could hear the phone ringing inside, but no one answered it.

After approximately fifteen minutes, Randy gave up and drove back home. The Ertmans, worried and a bit angry, decided to go about their business, at least for a little while.

That lasted for fifteen minutes.

"I've got to go back over there again," Randy exclaimed to his wife.

"Okay, honey. I'll keep calling."

Randy returned to Lamonte Lane and the Pena house. He went straight for the front window and banged on it so hard, he thought it would shatter. Still, no one answered.

Melissa Pena paged her daughter from work at noon. She did not want to do so any earlier because she knew Elizabeth and Jennifer liked to sleep late during the summer. She did not get an immediate callback, so she assumed they were still asleep.

By 2:00 P.M., Randy Ertman had become even more frantic. He jumped back into his vehicle and drove over to the Silver Creek Apartments to find Gina Escamilla. She was not home from summer school just yet, but he did speak with her mother. As Randy spoke, Gina arrived.

"Have you seen Jennifer?" Randy asked the young girl without so much as a hello.

"Not today, Mr. Ertman," she replied, a bit stunned by the tone of his voice.

"Have you talked to Jennifer or Elizabeth?" Randy barked at Gina. "Have you seen them?"

Gina had never seen Jennifer's father act this way. To Gina, Randy Ertman looked "scared, nervous, and worried." She replied she had not seen them since late the night before. "Let me page them," she suggested. She dialed the girls' pagers and left messages, but never received any callbacks. Gina then told Randy that she would call some of their mutual friends to find out if any of them had seen the girls.

None of them had seen Jennifer or Elizabeth.

Randy started to get even more visibly upset. He asked Gina to come with him to the Pena house. She agreed and they took off for the short distance. On the way over, Gina told Randy she had seen his daughter around 10:45 P.M. and that she and Elizabeth were walking home to Elizabeth's house. She assumed they were spending the night there.

Randy pulled in front of the Pena home for the third time.

"I want you to show me which room is Elizabeth's," Randy said to Gina.

She walked around to the back of the house and pointed out Elizabeth's window. "It's that one right there, Mr. Ertman."

Randy startled Gina as he banged on Elizabeth's window "like a madman." He seemed crazed. He began running around the house and banging on every window again and screaming for someone to come outside.

"Mr. Ertman, I think the neighbors are going to call the police," Gina tried to warn him. Indeed, some of them stepped outside their homes to see what all the commotion was about. They wanted to know who he was and why he was banging on the Penas' windows.

Randy ignored the neighbors and told Gina to come with him. He took her back to her apartment, dropped her off, and then drove back home to his wife.

Sandra Ertman was unable to sit still. She located her daughter's phone book. Inside were three handwritten pages with phone numbers for more than sixty friends. She began to call as many of them as she could. Many did not answer. Some went to answering machines. The people she did get through to had neither seen nor heard from Jennifer. Instead of easing her nerves, the phone calls only made her more anxious. Sandra asked Jennifer's friends to page her daughter. She also had Jennifer's aunt page her and she herself continued to page her daughter.

"I just kept paging her out of insanity," Sandra recalled.

Unfortunately, she never received a response from her daughter.

Later that afternoon, Randy met the Penas for the first time. Elizabeth's parents informed Randy they had not seen their daughter or Jennifer. Randy asked if he could use their telephone to contact the police. He spoke to a representative from the Juvenile Division and with someone in Missing Persons. He reported both his daughter and Elizabeth Pena as missing since at least eleven the night before.

Once they were made aware the girls were nowhere to be found, the Penas also began frantically paging their daughter. They never received any callbacks. They contacted Elizabeth's friends to find out if anyone had seen her or knew where she might have gone. Not one friend had any idea where she was.

Melissa and Adolph jumped in their car and drove in the direction of T. C. Jester Park, just east of their house. Melissa dropped Adolph off at the Spring Hill Apartments, where the girls were last seen. He walked through the entire complex and did not see a thing. Melissa picked him up and took him to T. C. Jester Boulevard so he could walk along the railroad tracks.

Adolph searched through the thick wooded area just south of the railroad bridge. He pulled back big branches and tore through dense underbrush. He overturned rocks and lifted up fallen trees. He found nothing.

Adolph decided he wanted to cross over the bayou on the railroad tracks. As he approached the end of the bridge, now on the north side of the bayou, he stopped. "I didn't see any need to go any farther. I assumed that if the girls took the shortcut on the train tracks and over the bridge, there would be no reason for them to be on that other side." He stopped his search and stared at the woods off to the side of the train tracks, near the flattened area in the grass, and thought, *I should probably take a look in these woods over here.*

Instead, Adolph turned around and called it off. He went away empty-handed. At the time, he thought it was a blessing.

As Adolph emerged from the railroad tracks onto T. C. Jester Boulevard, Melissa saw him, picked him up, and took him back home. They went in to call even more of Elizabeth's friends; unfortunately, the results were the same: no one knew where the girls were.

Adolph recalled speaking to Elizabeth's friend Gina Escamilla. "That poor girl. She was probably scared to death of me. I was going so ballistic."

There was one advantage to Adolph's state of mind. "They (Elizabeth's friends) were so afraid of me I knew I was getting nothing but honest answers from them. I know they weren't lying to me, for a fact, because they knew that I was not right and that the last guy they were going to lie to was me."

Adolph also called as many of his friends as he could muster up.

"As soon as my buddies knew that there was something wrong," Pena recalled, "everybody was coming over and they came by and helped put flyers out." One of those who came to help out was Adolph's brother,

Carlos, from San Antonio. "He was there with me the whole time."

"I was going crazy," Adolph vaguely recalled. "I was going ballistic. I was doing everything I possibly could to find out where those girls were. I was talking to everybody. We were trying to figure out who she might have talked to, where she might have been. We tried to do everything to find those two girls. I was going nuts."

According to Sandra Ertman, her husband was beside himself with anger. She said Randy was "lashing out at everyone" and "could not control his temper." She added that a friend of hers gave her a Valium to calm down her nerves. She said Randy chose beer as his sedative.

Each family member had his or her own way of dealing with the stress and frustration of not knowing where the girls were.

Chapter 23

Raul Villarreal and his family kept their appointment with Norberto Torres for Raul's potential drug intervention. The meeting was scheduled for 3:30 P.M., but the Villarreal family was running late. Torres, nonetheless, agreed to speak with the family.

The counselor soon realized, however, the meeting was futile. He described Raul Villarreal as "tired, lethargic, hungover, nontalkative, nonverbal, and laid-back." Torres also stated that Raul ignored the suggestions made to him concerning his drug problem.

Torres concluded he had gotten nowhere with the young man when Raul Villarreal started "chuckling" during the meeting.

Needless to say, it was not a successful intervention.

* * *

Friday, June 25, 1993—9:00 P.M.
Sandoval residence
Ashland Street
Houston, Texas

O'Brien, Cantu, and Joe Medellin arrived at Frank and Ramon Sandoval's doorstep.

"They looked like they wanted to go out and party," Frank Sandoval recalled. "You know, drink beer." However, they had no alcohol with them.

"Dude, where's your brother?" Cantu asked. "We want him to go out with us so we can go drinking."

"Um, he's asleep, dude," Frank cautiously lied to Cantu. He didn't want his brother getting mixed up in any more trouble with these guys. "He can't go out tonight, guys."

This bit of information did not please Cantu. "Get his lazy ass up," he demanded.

Just then, the Sandovals' father came to the door to see what was going on. He made it clear his son would not be going out with them. He then slammed the door on the trio.

Chapter 24

The following morning, Randy Ertman created a missing persons flyer with pictures of and information about Elizabeth and Jennifer. As he designed the flyer, Melissa Pena called around to several copying shops to see who could print them up. The owner of Texas Art Supply told them not only could he do the work for them, but he would do it at no cost. He printed up nearly three thousand copies for the families and wished them luck finding their daughters.

"We had fifteen of our closest friends come over to our house and some of the kids come and we started handing them out," Melissa recalled. The Ertmans had nearly thirteen people at their house and they began distributing the flyers as well.

The Penas posted flyers in the Heights area, the Oak Forest area, near White Oak Bayou and the train track trestle, and then branched out to a sixty-mile radius that encompassed Loop 610.

The Ertmans went to the Spring Hill apartment complex, where the girls were last seen. "We put flyers up in the laundry rooms of the complex. We made sure they were everywhere in that area," Sandra Ertman recalled. Gina Escamilla, along with four of her friends, helped the Ertmans and Penas post flyers.

Sandra ran into resistance from a few nearby store owners who did not want the flyers on their property. "The girls' friends were determined. They would stand on each other's shoulders, put them high above the buildings, above the doors." She marveled at the teenagers' tenacity. "They wanted to find their friends. They made sure those flyers got out."

Unfortunately, the flyers also brought out the worst in some people. Inevitably, the Penas and the Ertmans received several crank phone calls from people who thought it would be funny to get the families' hopes up. As soon as Randy Ertman fielded a call and received information that his daughter was alive or where she was last seen, "he would run out the door and follow up on the lead." Unfortunately, they never panned out.

Chapter 25

Christina Cantu had to get out of the house. She badgered her husband, Joe, to walk with her. He reluctantly agreed and they headed outside to nearby Love Park. At first, Christina did not talk to her husband. She merely kept to herself and kept a steady walking pace.

After several minutes of intense walking, Christina stopped next to a park bench. She reached into her pocket and pulled out the ring that Peter had given her. She laid it on top of the bench and proceeded to move on.

"I can't live with this anymore," an anguished Christina told her husband. "I can't stand knowing what they did to those girls." She was on the verge of tears. "It's not right," she said, and became more animated. "It's not right!" she screamed. "They're just a bunch of assholes!"

"They're family," Joe Cantu answered back.

"They're not *my* family!" Christina shot back. "They're your family, not mine."

Joe laid into her and the couple argued for all to see.

"I can't live knowing what they did," Christina tearfully cried. "My conscience is getting to me. I can't take it anymore."

"What the hell am I supposed to do?" Joe pleaded with his wife.

"I don't know. I mean, c'mon, what if it was your sister or even your mom?" Christina begged. "It could have been me or my sister. It could have been someone you know."

"But it wasn't," Joe responded.

"That's beside the whole point!" she screamed at her husband. "Why are you protecting them?"

"Because Peter's my brother," he told her.

"What if it was your sister? Your mom?" she asked again.

Joe did not respond. He just shook his head and glanced downward. "I can't believe this," he stated through clenched teeth.

"We gotta do something," Christina informed him.

"What? What the hell can we do?"

"I don't know. Call the cops. Isn't there one of those tip lines you can call in to report a crime?" she wondered.

"Crime Stoppers," he responded. "We gotta call Crime Stoppers. I think they even give you a reward or something." Joe stopped for a moment. "I don't know, man. I don't want anyone to know I ratted them out."

"I think those things are anonymous," she reassured her husband. "You don't have to tell them who you are. Just that you know something went down and you know where the bodies are." Christina put her hand on her husband's shoulder. "If you don't want to turn Peter in, at least tell them where the bodies are so their parents can put them to rest."

"Okay," Joe replied. "You're right."

Chapter 26

The following morning, Joe Cantu was nervous as hell. He could not stand to see his wife so upset. She had been having nightmares all weekend long about what her brother-in-law and his friends had told them.

Joe also could not fathom the idea of ratting out his brother and his friends. He knew he needed to make the call. He decided the time had come. He had to do the right thing.

Joe picked up the phone and dialed Crime Stoppers. He had not seen his brother since the night of the murders, but he was worried Peter would walk in on him while he was making the call. After two rings, a Crime Stoppers representative answered the phone.

"Crime Stoppers. How can I help you?" the representative queried.

"My name is Gonzales," he lied in a whisper. "I know where you can find those dead girls. Right off of T. C.

Jester, next to the bayou. White Oak Bayou." Joe Cantu did not know exactly where the bodies were located; he was merely going off the information that his brother had given him. He did not say who was responsible for the girls' deaths or how he knew about the killings. Just the location of the bodies.

Joe Cantu hurriedly hung up the telephone. He felt a strange mixture of guilt and relief. He knew his brother was going to be in some serious shit, but he also realized he could not live with himself if the girls' parents were unable to find their daughters' bodies.

Police officers drove over to T. C. Jester Park to check out the tip. Instead of crossing over and searching the wooded area northeast of the bridge, they stayed on the west side of the bayou. They searched the wooded areas on both sides of the train tracks, but they found nothing.

Later that night, Joe and Christina nervously watched the news to see if there was anything about the discovery of the two girls' bodies.

Nothing.

They did not know what to do.

Joe told Christina he would call back the next morning and try to give a better description of the area based on what Peter and his friends had told them.

Chapter 27

Monday, June 28, 1993—12:06 P.M.
T. C. Jester Park
T. C. Jester Boulevard and West Thirty-fourth Street
Houston, Texas

Houston police officer Mike Cromwell was cruising solo, as he always did. The twelve-year veteran did not have a partner, and he did not mind. He liked working the sprawling streets of Houston, never quite knowing what he would stumble upon next.

When the call came in, Cromwell turned his car around and headed for T. C. Jester Boulevard and West Thirty-fourth Street. It was only a few miles away from Waltrip High School. The park area was usually populated with several joggers and bicyclists who beat down a well-trodden path through the narrow grass field park. On one end of the park, approximately two miles from where the officer was being dispatched, there is a swimming pool, baseball fields, and a large playscape for children. At the other end where he was going was a jogging trail, lots of oak and pine trees, and a railroad trestle, which hovered thirty feet over the White Oak Bayou concrete floodgate.

Cromwell parked his police cruiser in a nearby apartment complex parking lot across the street from a cluster of trees located southeast of the railroad tracks and shy of the train trestle. Cromwell headed over to the woods and started to scan the area, looking for any signs of foul play. He checked the perimeter of the mini-forest and then stuck his head inside the trees, but he did not see anything.

After approximately twenty minutes of searching, Cromwell was joined by more officers at the scene. With police cars came onlookers. People in the nearby apartment complexes poured out in droves to see what was going on.

One of the officers on the scene told Cromwell he was not looking in the right area. He needed to cross the railroad bridge and look on the other side of the tracks. Cromwell headed across the bridge. As he crossed over, he noticed a path that led down the side of the embankment toward a large bald spot in the grass, approximately twenty feet from another cluster of trees. Cromwell did not head in that direction; instead he continued along the side of the railroad tracks and next to the wooded area.

Cromwell continued his search as he walked up a slight hill that graced the edge of the tree line. He walked up the hill and closer to the tree line, when something caught his eye. He paused and walked up to the trees, pulled back some branches, and looked inside. He spotted what appeared to be clothing. Cromwell then attempted to get a better look, so he pulled the thick brush to one side and tried to peer even farther inside. This time, he spotted what he believed to be a body. He attempted to enter through the wooded section; however, it was too thick, so he headed back toward the bald spot in the grass. Once there, he noticed an open entrance to the wooded area, almost like the entrance to the Bat Cave. He headed up a path that led directly to the opening.

Cromwell moved some branches to one side and stepped into the woods. The sunlight peering through the enormously tall pine trees lit up the area in a hallucinatory manner. Various particles of dust, pollen, and grass floated up in the air and passed through the sun's rays with urgency. Pine needles littered the dirt floor and felled trees lay on their sides as if taking a nap. It was a beautiful yet eerie sight.

What Cromwell saw next was far from beautiful.

Less than twenty feet from the entrance, Cromwell spotted two dead bodies lying on their backs. He immediately contacted dispatch, set up a perimeter around the crime scene, and called for assistance from Homicide.

Two of the people allowed to enter the crime scene were veterans of the Houston Police Department Brian Horowitz and Beverly Trumble. The crime scene investigators were greeted inside the wooded area of the crime scene by Sergeant Robert "Bob" Parrish. Horowitz and Trumble instantly spotted the two corpses in the enclosed area. Their first job was to make an assessment of the overall crime scene. The pair noticed various pieces of clothing strewn about the pine-covered dirt floor around the bodies. Upon closer inspection of the bodies, they could see nature had taken over. The seasoned investigators were shocked by what they saw.

Two bodies, seriously decomposed, lay within feet of one another. Both bodies were partially naked. The first body had a shirt pulled up over the head of the victim. They could not see any features of the corpse's face. The body, however, was not a pleasant sight. The genital region seemed to shimmer in the sun's rays. Investigator Horowitz thought his eyes were playing tricks on him as he swore something moved in the crotch region. He was correct. The corpse's genitalia had been decimated and infested with live maggots. Thousands of them. They were still crawling over the moist region of the victim. Their feeding frenzy did not stop.

Horowitz gained his composure and made note of the physical appearance of the rest of the body—at least of what he could see. He noted the victim's left foot was adorned in a purple Converse high-top sneaker and a white ankle sock. The right foot wore no shoe, just a sock. There was a large bloody gash on the left shin and cuts and scrapes on both legs. Maggots had dribbled down from the crotch area and were feeding on the open sores on the legs. Several more maggots had fallen to the ground between the corpse's thighs. The mass collection of maggots looked like a large pair of movable panties on the body.

Horowitz also noted large clusters of maggots on the female victim's belly button and on her left rib cage area. The victim still had a silk purple bra in place that was exposed, as her shirt was pulled up over her head. He also noted that her body was bright orange and rusty red.

The corpse lay on the ground on its back, almost as if it were a young girl sunning herself out by a swimming pool. Her arms were extended over her head and nearly crossed over each other. Both arms were rusty-orange-colored. They, too, were sprinkled with maggots. The investigators did not remove the shirt from the victim's face.

Horowitz and Trumble carefully moved up toward the second body. This one, too, was only partially clothed. It appeared to be bloated from the sweltering Texas heat, which had hovered above ninety degrees for several days in a row.

The victim's right arm was partially covered with dead pine needles, which covered up the rusty red coloring of her skin. Her right hand peered out from the needles and was pale with bright red polish on her neatly manicured fingernails. The rest of her arm did not look as good. Nature again had taken over. All of the skin and muscle had been removed, exposing only bone from the right wrist all the way to the shoulder. Her left arm had turned almost completely black.

The crime scene investigators shifted their attention to the head of the corpse. Horowitz, an eleven-year veteran in crime scene investigation, was taken aback by the gruesome display before him. What had once been a beautiful, vibrant, and young Hispanic girl now resembled a creature from a horror movie. All of the skin had been completely picked from her entire head, thereby leaving only a muddy skull. The eyes had been picked out, as had the tongue. One of the animals in the park must have been forceful with the girl's corpse, as the lower jaw was unhinged and dangling wide open beyond any human threshold of pain.

At approximately 1:00 P.M., Gina Escamilla's telephone rang. It was one of her good friends, Vanessa Rivera. She sounded as if she were on the verge of tears when she blurted out to Gina, "They found them! They found their bodies!"

"What are you talking about?" Gina tried to quiet her hysterical friend. "Calm down. Tell me what you're talking about."

"Jennifer and Elizabeth. I think they found their bodies!" Vanessa's voice trembled as she spoke.

"Oh, my God!" Gina exclaimed. "Where? Where are they?" she begged to know, while trying to stay calm.

"Right by your apartments. Over there on the bridge and the train tracks. Near the bayou. I think the police are out there right now."

"Oh, my God. How do you know it's them?" Gina asked as she held out any last vestige of hope. "How do you know it's them?"

Vanessa could not answer her. "I'm coming over right now," she declared, and simultaneously hung up the phone.

Vanessa arrived at Gina's apartment within minutes. They met up with another one of their friends, a teenage girl named Dallas Young. The three girls were afraid of what they might learn; however, they knew they needed to be there for Elizabeth and Jennifer in case they were alive.

The trio of girls hurried to the well-worn walking path just north of White Oak Bayou, which led to the train trestle. By the time they made their way around the bend, they could see there were literally dozens of people standing around and on top of the train tracks. They also saw dozens more lined up on the other side of the bayou looking toward something north of the water. The girls ventured forward.

When they made it to the train tracks, they were not allowed to go any farther. A police officer stood on the edge of the tracks that led down a gravel slope to another footpath and to a large clearing in the grass. Several police officers stood in the circle. Meanwhile, several more officers could be spotted coming in and out of a small cavelike entrance from the woods.

Gina, Vanessa, and Dallas had no idea what was going on. Gina scanned all of the gawkers at the scene until she spotted someone she knew. It was a young black boy who lived in one of the nearby apartment complexes. She recognized him from over the previous two years. They were not friends but more on a head-nodding "Hello, how are you?" basis with one another.

She had no idea his name was Sean O'Brien.

Gina stood near O'Brien and could hear the young man talking in a slightly too loud voice to a couple of black boys. Gina was not sure, but she believed he may have been babysitting them.

"I'm never gonna let y'all come back here anymore," O'Brien told the two boys. His voice turned stern as he boldly declared, "I hope that whoever did this, they get them. I hope they find the bastards."

Gina did not speak to O'Brien, because she was only concerned with whether or not the bodies that had been discovered were Elizabeth's and Jennifer's.

Sergeants Ramon "Ray" Zaragoza and Bob Parrish helped out at the crime scene. Zaragoza assisted the Crime Scene Units (CSUs) with the collection, bagging, and tagging of evidence. Parrish canvassed the crowd and questioned any potential witnesses.

More officers arrived to help control the crime scene. It was a good thing they were all in place when Randy Ertman showed up. The officers truly empathized with the grieving and hysterical father, but they had a job to do and they were going to make sure the crime scene remained uncontaminated at all costs. Luckily, they were able to calm Ertman down. They then had the misfortune of letting him know they would need copies of his daughter's dental records to determine if one of the bodies was actually hers. They managed to get him out of the crime scene area and onto his task at hand.

Not long after they were assured Randy Ertman had left the area, the medical examiners began the unpleasant but necessary task of wrapping the bodies and placing them on gurneys. They needed to be transported to the coroner's office for a full examination. Two rolling gurneys were carried back into the woods to begin the process.

Less than one hundred yards away, police spokesman John Leggio gave a brief news conference to the assembled media. Several onlookers were standing directly behind the officer, including the girls' friends Dallas

Young, Vanessa Rivera, and Gina Escamilla. As the officer spoke, he confirmed that two female bodies had been discovered. When he mentioned they were partially nude, Dallas Young broke down in a bout of hysterical tears on camera. They never mentioned Elizabeth's or Jennifer's name, but she knew. After the conference ended, the police gently asked the crowd of onlookers to clear the area.

A group of six tired-looking police officers rolled the first gurney out of the woods, over the downtrodden grass, and up the gravelly slope to the railroad tracks. On top of the gurney lay one of the two dead girls' bodies wrapped in a royal blue crushed-velvet blanket with CY-FAIR NORTHWEST printed in large white letters on its side. The officers crossed over the tracks, went down the other side of the slope, and proceeded to unsteadily remove the corpse. They transported it several hundred yards across a dirt trail that paralleled the Clearbrook Apartments until they finally came to the medical examiner's vehicle located on West Thirty-fourth Street.

The same process was repeated a second time with the second body.

Dallas Young was beside herself with shock. "They were just walking home. They were walking home. It's not that far away and somebody has to do that to them. Why?"

With the assistance of the channel 13 news cameraman, Randy Ertman returned to his home in the Heights to find the phone number of Jennifer's dentist so he could retrieve her dental records. When he arrived, he realized his wife was nowhere to be found. Another reporter stayed behind to inform Randy that his wife fainted after she heard the news of the discovery. Yet another reporter had taken her to the hospital and made sure she was okay. The reporter called back and stated that Sandy was fine, but doctors had given her a sedative to help calm her nerves. She would return home later that evening.

After all of the hubbub at the Pena residence, with so many people coming and going, things finally slowed down for a brief moment. Adolph Pena looked around his small home, which was packed to the rafters with so many loved ones who were looking for his sweet little girl. It was then, he knew, his daughter was not going to be found alive.

"I knew right away that there was something wrong," the in-tune father remembered. "She would always let us know where she was at, when she would be home, and this time she didn't.

"When we paged her and she didn't call . . . I knew exactly right then that something was very wrong."

Adolph could not remember how his brother found anything out, but stated "he heard from someone that something was going down in T. C. Jester Park, so he took off and went down there to the park. Somehow or another, Randy Ertman had also known that something was going on down at that park."

Carlos Pena returned to the Pena house. He found Adolph and told him, "Man, they don't know if it is the girls or not." His brother tried to remain optimistic.

"I know it's the girls," Adolph said in a resigned voice. "I know it's them."

Adolph Pena was furious.

He never received a call from the police in regard to the discovery of his daughter's body. He found out about it from a television newscast. He was sitting in his living room with his wife and dozens of friends when the channel 26 news broadcast came blaring over the airwaves.

"Police have discovered the bodies of fourteen-year-old Jennifer Ertman and sixteen-year-old Elizabeth Pena," the newsreader declared.

Adolph was in a state of shock and disbelief. He could not believe what he heard. He looked to his wife for confirmation. Her mouth was agape and tears were welling up in her eyes. Once Adolph saw his wife's reaction, he knew he had heard correctly.

The dead body of his firstborn child had been discovered.

Adolph was mad as hell that the media broadcast her name all over the airwaves before they even bothered to contact him. Soon after the initial airing of the discovery, the media finally started calling. Not only was he furious because the police failed to contact him first, he was also ticked off because they ignored his pleas over the weekend when there was a slim chance Elizabeth might still be alive.

This was in the days before AMBER Alerts, search teams like Texas EquuSearch, and twenty-four-hour cable-news coverage where missing girls have become a top priority. Adolph Pena and Randy Ertman tried everything they could to get help from the media, but they all refused. Some even told Pena since his daughter had run away before, she would probably be located at a friend's house in a matter of time.

Of course, as soon as the bodies were discovered, the media came slithering into the Penas' life. "These sons of bitches," Pena heatedly referred to the media, "I said, 'I tried to call you to get you to help me find my daughter and you wouldn't do it. Now that you know she's dead and you want to talk to me—get your ass out of my face.' I went ballistic."

Adolph also iterated that the police were not much better. "I don't remember who came up and told me. You know, I don't think anybody came to the house and told me that they found the girls. I don't believe anybody from HPD came and talked to us about finding Elizabeth and Jennifer."

The Penas were not the only ones upset with the way the Houston Police Department failed to respond when it became apparent the girls had not come home the previous Thursday night.

"She just had a birthday three nights ago from that night," stated an angry Vanessa Rivera. "There would be no reason for her to run away and we told them that, but no one believed us."

Randy Ertman added, "I think it's a sorry dog-damn world where the police—when I have to wait from Friday afternoon when this is put out until today, when a police officer finally shows up at my house."

Chapter 28

Despite the lack of police participation during the beginning of the ordeal, there were several officers on the case now. Two of the key lawmen involved, Ray Zaragoza and Bob Parrish, confirmed with Crime Stoppers that the tip that led to the bodies came from the residence of a Rudy Cantu Sr., despite the fact the tipster claimed his name was "Mr. Gonzales." The officers paid a visit to the house, where they discovered Joe Cantu was the caller. Joe told the officers what his brother Peter and his friends had confessed to the previous week.

The two officers then waited in their police car until they received an arrest warrant. It would be several hours before they could make their move.

* * *

Tuesday, June 29, 1993—3:30 A.M.
Cantu residence
Ashland Street
Houston, Texas

Zaragoza and Parrish finally received their arrest warrant for Peter Cantu. It was a coordinated effort amongst several officers to arrest all six young men at the same time. Cantu's arrest went down without incident, as did the arrests for Efrain Perez, Joe Medellin, and Yuni Medellin. Sean O'Brien attempted to escape when police knocked on his door, but officers were stationed outside both the front and back doors of his apartment.

The police did not know who the sixth person was because Joe Cantu had never met him before that night. They had no problem locating him, however, because when Joe and Yuni Medellin were being transported to the police station, one of the officers asked where "the other guy" lived. Joe Medellin readily gave up the name "Raul" and told the officer where he lived. The officer drove to Villarreal's house on Chapman Street and added the young man to his haul.

Once all six teenagers were brought in, they were separated into different rooms and questioned by police. It did not take long for each one of them to admit their presence at the rape and homicide of Elizabeth Pena and Jennifer Ertman. Most of the young men, however, laid blame on their supposed good friends. Everyone admitted to being there, but they begged off on specific participation. It was always: "He raped her, but I didn't touch her" or "He pulled the belt around her neck and choked her, but I only watched."

After several hours of interrogation, the police were able to create a picture of what actually occurred that night. It was obvious all six of them were directly involved in the kidnapping, rape, torture, and murder of the two girls.

Once again, the Penas heard about another major breakthrough in their daughter's case via the media. For whatever reason, no one from the HPD bothered to contact them to let them know their daughter's killers had been apprehended.

"I really didn't think they were going to find the killers," Adolph Pena exclaimed. "I had real bad feelings about that. And then to be caught that quick."

The one person who did keep in touch with the Penas as their daughter's case evolved was Harris County district attorney (DA) John B. Holmes Jr., who assured the Penas that Elizabeth's murder was his "number one priority." Holmes added, "I am going to take care of this case before I die. Believe me you, I hope to God that I'm still alive when they execute the sons of bitches. I will make it a point in my life to see these bastards fry."

The Penas were stunned when they heard the news. "I was in disbelief." Adolph shook his head. He also could not believe there were so many people involved. "I was expecting one, maybe two killers. It really freaked me out that the girls had to be gang-raped by so many individuals."

Adolph was stunned that none of the boys stopped what they were doing. "If it were that many of them, surely one of them out of the five or six would have some kind of freaking sense to say, 'Hey, let's not do this.' But you know what? There wasn't none of them that had the brains. Not one of them.

"I thanked God about a million times that day," Adolph recalled. "I kept thanking that poor little girl that turned them in, Cantu's sister-in-law. I still praise that woman every day. If it wasn't for her, they probably would have never found them."

Ertman family friend Khris Burling spoke with the local Fox television station about the Ertmans. "They're doing a lot better than they were yesterday," Burling reassured. "Especially hearing some news that they had been caught, the suspects." Burling was later interviewed and informed Fox News reporter Olga Campos that the medical examiner's office had contacted the Ertman family and stated it was definitely Jennifer who had been discovered.

Later that day, all of the suspects, except for Yuni Medellin and Raul Villarreal, were transported to the courthouse for their initial bond hearing. All four men were read their rights and had their bonds set at $100,000 each.

Afterward, the four suspects were led on a perp walk in front of television news crews outside the courthouse, located at 61 Reisner Street. Joe Medellin, dressed in a blue oxford long-sleeved shirt and white shorts, walked next to the substantially taller Efrain Perez, who was dressed in a white short-sleeved T-shirt and black jeans, and was handcuffed to Medellin. Perez's left arm was in a splint up to his elbow.

Sean O'Brien, who wore a black short-sleeved Los Angeles Raiders T-shirt, followed close behind. The three boys were not being escorted personally by any police authorities and calmly walked along the sidewalk into the building. They kept their heads bowed down so as not to have their faces appear on television. Perez, however, was grinning slightly as he bounced toward the police station.

Joe Medellin eventually looked up at one news cameraman and said, "I'm gonna mess you up, man" while he shook his head.

Behind them a local television news cameraman walked backward and filmed Peter Cantu. The alleged ringleader, who was dressed in black jeans, a short-sleeved, collared black shirt, and a pair of gleaming white low-top sneakers, was being personally escorted by two police officers, who had their arms hooked through his while his hands were handcuffed behind his back. The diminutive Cantu was not pleased to have his mug photographed and put on display for live television.

Fox News reporter Olga Campos walked directly up to Cantu and stuck her microphone in his face. The tiny reporter asked, "What happened to you? You looked pretty tough in that courtroom."

"Shut up, bitch," Cantu replied halfheartedly.

"Is that what you called Elizabeth?" Campos quickly shot back without missing a beat.

"I called your momma that," Cantu responded, like the teenager he was.

"Did you kill her?" Campos pressed.

Cantu spit on the ground and then repeated what he had said, "I called your momma that." Cantu realized he did not listen to her question, and when it finally sunk in, he immediately turned on the much older Campos. His face turned from a sarcastic badass to an anger-filled grimace; he yelled at her, "If you don't get away from me, I swear to God, man!" Cantu then kicked his right foot up and attempted to break one of the cameras. He spat out, "Get that goddamned camera out of my face."

A friend of both girls, Joey Ruiz, spoke with the CBS local television affiliate KHOU-TV about Elizabeth and Jennifer while standing on the railroad tracks near where the girls' bodies were found. "We all hung out," the young man declared. "We're all like a family. All of us. They always hung out at our apartments. We're all close. All of us."

Ruiz was aggravated with the Houston Police Department. "Why didn't they look around searching where they were missing?" the young man queried. "I feel it would have been good if they had done that when the girls had gone missing. Now they're gone, there's nothing we can do. There's nothing nobody can do. But grieve, forever."

When asked if the train tracks were a hangout for troublemakers, Ruiz angrily replied, "That's bull! That's bull! That's media. That's what they want you to believe so you will be afraid." Ruiz continued, "This was our park. It grew from generation to generation. There was no crack, none of that stuff here. If anything, they had beer, man. They come out here to kick back and talk about school."

Ruiz then spoke more about the girls and what they meant to him. "They were real sweet. Why would someone want to take away our friendship? We loved them. There's just no way I can express more grief."

Ruiz also spoke of how he hoped others remembered his friends. "I don't want them to think they were just two more girls, because they meant much too much to everybody." Ruiz did not want to hear people say, "'Oh, it's just two dead girls.'

"They didn't get to see nothing," Ruiz added about the girls. "They didn't get to graduate. Nothing. All they get to see is the harsh life and to get murdered. The least we can do is build a memorial here for them so that every time someone walks in here, they won't be forgotten."

Many more friends were frustrated with the police's handling of the missing persons reports on the girls. Dallas Young broke down in tears as she said, "No one would listen to us. No one would take us seriously. They didn't believe us. Now they're dead."

Randy Ertman also bemoaned HPD's lack of rapid response to the missing persons report. "The police over at the Shepherd Substation," Randy claimed, "were offered pictures of my daughter, but they did not take them. They took my daughter's description and that was all."

Randy was dismayed that his concerns were not taken seriously. "No one believed me," the stunned father told a Fox News reporter. "No one cared. No one."

More of Jennifer and Elizabeth's friends spoke out about the killers. "I don't know what was going on in their heads at the time they killed my friends. It's happening to us too many times," Dallas Young bemoaned to a local reporter. "It's getting sickening. You can't even walk home. You can't even walk to the store. You can't even walk to school anymore."

Dallas asserted neither Elizabeth nor Jennifer ran around with the wrong crowd. "They never messed with anybody. They never bothered anybody. They were good people. They were two good girls."

Dallas was determined to make sure her friends' killers were put away for good. "I will fight and keep fighting and keep fighting until these people have been put behind bars forever."

Dallas also expressed the sorrow she felt over the loss of two of her best friends. "Just this morning, I was walking through this hallway"—she referred to the hallways of Waltrip High School, where she and her girlfriends used to traipse up and down every day, sharing a laugh or two—"you don't know . . . how you feel when your friends are not walking there beside you."

One of Elizabeth's best friends, Vanessa Rivera, told a local TV reporter, "She called me and told me that she was at her friend's house and she never . . . she just told me she was going to go home. She never got home."

Vanessa also stated Elizabeth was very conscientious

about letting her family know where she was at all times. "Even if they were only ten minutes away, she would say, 'Pull over, I need to call my parents to let them know where I'm at.' And we did this, God only knows how many times, and we knew that when they didn't call us back, something had really gone wrong."

Word got around quickly in the Harris County Jail about the latest celebrity inductees. Of course, most of that had to do with the young men bragging about their exploits to some of the other inmates.

The bizarre honor code in jails and prisons placed the young men at the bottom of the food chain—as child rapists and murderers.

That same day, Joe Medellin, Villarreal, O'Brien, and Perez had another court hearing. The four men were escorted into the courtroom shackled with chains and decked out in beige jumpsuits. Three of the men had a little extra something on their uniforms for the court's amusement.

On the back of Perez's jumpsuit, scribbled with a Sharpie, was *I'm a baby killer.* Cantu's was *I'm a fag.* O'Brien's, *I'm a bitch.* The other inmates had gotten hold of their clothes and applied some of their own decorations.

At a police press conference the following day, outside the Harris County Courthouse Annex, Captain John Silva stressed the murders were not a part of the initiation of Villarreal. "We think that these girls happened along and that they were in positively the wrong place at the wrong time. We feel like as they happened by, these guys saw their chance to do what they did and . . . they did."

Prosecutor Denise Oncken also spoke to the media about the charges against the young men. She partially described how the girls were attacked. "Both of the complainants were sexually assaulted and we're not sure if both of them were strangled. We don't have the autopsies yet."

The media also tried to track down one of the members of the Cantu family. One news crew had a camera trained on their house. They shot footage of Suzie Cantu driving away in a small red car. She pointed at the camera as she drove off and said, "That better not be nothing, 'cause I will sue!"

An unidentified neighbor spoke to the media and expressed shock at the news of Cantu's involvement. "So far as I know, they're a quiet family," the man stated. "No trouble. I mean, we hadn't had no problems at all."

An unidentified female neighbor countered with, "There's a lot of teenagers hanging around there. A lot of them. And loud music, too. And the neighbors have been complaining about the loud music."

Chapter 29

Less than five miles away from where the bodies of Jennifer Ertman and Elizabeth Pena were discovered, friends and family gathered to mourn Jennifer's passing. Several hundred teenagers, most from Waltrip High School, clutched one another inside and outside the Heights Funeral Home. They gathered strength from their numbers and their common cause: to say good-bye to Jennifer Ertman.

The normally vibrant crowd conducted themselves in the most respectful of manners. The hush over the gathering belied their usual vivacity. Most of the kids were still in a state of shock—not only because they had lost two of their own, but several of their own had been responsible for their deaths.

"It's hard," observed sixteen-year-old Monica Alvarez, a friend of Jennifer's. "It's supposed to be a free world and you can't go out. Jennifer was innocent. She had her whole life, and dumb guys like that come and take it all away."

Most of the teenagers at the funeral home felt the same way as Monica Alvarez. Many others were in shock. Others were still seething with rage. The entire gamut of emotions, however, seemed bottled up inside the somber setting.

Jennifer's service was swift and devastatingly emotional. Her father, Randy Ertman, had written a eulogy for his beloved daughter; however, he could not bring himself to read the words. The grief was too overwhelming. He asked a family friend to read his parting words about his only child.

"Her life was short," the friend recited, *"but everyone here cared. That's a lot right there,"* he said as he acknowledged the overflowing crowd.

Dallas Young attempted to focus on the good memories of her lost companion. "The thing I'll miss the most about her," Dallas recalled as she looked directly at Jennifer's casket, which was adorned with flowers, "is the way she laughed." Warm tears streamed down the young mourner's face as she addressed the crowd.

Dallas still seemed to be in a state of shock at the murder of her friend. Denial had crept in in a big way. "I keep expecting Jennifer to come bounding out of the woods, saying that she was embarrassed by all the fuss her disappearance caused."

Longtime Ertman family friend and neighbor Earl Hatcher came to the front of the congregation next. He struggled to get out the words. "Jennifer. We love you, we need you. We miss you. We are here for you." The tears became more audible in the hushed setting.

Hatcher began to cry as well. "I watched her grow up." He smiled as he recalled how she used to flash by him as she raced her go-kart up and down the street. "Her interests changed from go-karts to cars. She was becoming a woman and, like a butterfly, I saw the transition."

More people spoke about their cherished friend they had lost. The feelings for Jennifer, for her mother and father, for those who cared for her, were palpable. The caring helped the Ertmans as they—along with the entire gathering—quietly passed their daughter's casket. The Ertmans could see the oversized photograph of their daughter next to the closed coffin. The sound of Whitney Houston's voice filled the room with the strains of "I Will Always Love You."

They would never see their daughter again.

The Ertmans were overwhelmed with the love and affection on display for their daughter. "I remember more people kissing me and hugging me than I ever thought possible."

After the relatively brisk service for Jennifer, the flock of attendees sauntered into their vehicles and headed three miles over to the Pat H. Foley Funeral Home on West Thirty-fourth Street for a prayer vigil for Elizabeth Pena. As the procession pulled up into the gravel parking lot of the funeral home, the mood seemed even more downcast than earlier.

One of Elizabeth's friends, fifteen-year-old Gillian Hemphill, seemed dumbstruck. "I won't have anyone to talk to anymore," she said to no one in particular. "I lost my best friend." Many around her nodded in agreement. They understood her anguish and pain. "I just wish she was back, that's all," the teenager wept.

* * *

Thursday, July 1, 1993
Harris County Jail—cell 6B 2-V
Sixth floor B
San Jacinto Street
Houston, Texas

Just two days after Joe Medellin's arrest, Deputy Edward Martin conducted a routine search for contraband in his one-man lockdown cell. Martin's search led to the discovery of a weapon made from a disposable Bic razor. The one-and-a-half-inch razorblade had been removed and inserted into the handle so that it was very obviously sticking out—in effect, the razor had been turned into a knife.

Upon discovery of the weapon, Medellin claimed he used it to trim his fingernails, since fingernail clippers were not allowed in Harris County Jail.

Medellin would be written up for a violation of jail rules.

Friday, July 2, 1993—10:00 A.M.
St. Rose of Lima Catholic Church
3600 Brinkman Street
Houston, Texas

Another one of Elizabeth Pena's good friends remained in shock the following morning when funeral services were held for the sixteen-year-old at the St. Rose of Lima Catholic Church. Vanessa Rivera and Elizabeth had been best friends for over a year and had made an explicit agreement to maintain their relationship for the rest of their lives. Unfortunately, Vanessa knew the agreement ceased with Elizabeth's murder.

"We were the best of friends," Vanessa declared as she

dabbed at a tear running down her cheek. "On her birthday, she said her wish was that we stay friends forever."

As with the night before, many of the same people showed up for Elizabeth's funeral. Again, the church overflowed with more than one thousand well-wishers, and those who still could not fathom the destruction wrought on the two young girls.

At the front of the church stood Rev. Steve Laliberte. The Penas thought very highly of the young priest and were pleased he would be giving the sermon. "I used to love to listen to him preach," Adolph Pena reminisced.

The reverend attempted to assuage the congregation's pain by telling the story of Jesus' crucifixion and how Mary bowed before the Cross, where her son had been executed. As she did so, Jesus' disciples ran away in fear, the reverend continued. Mary stayed.

"A mother's love for a child can only be understood by a mother," the priest explained. "Today we witness the same crucifixion over again." Laliberte paused and heard the soft whimpers. "Today we are saddened because Elizabeth Christine has gone from us," he stated, and looked at Melissa Pena, who sat next to her husband and their two surviving children. They were joined by Randy and Sandra Ertman. "But we also rejoice, because we know that she has gone with the Almighty God and we know one day we'll be reunited with her in the Kingdom of the Father."

For some, the words provided comfort. For others, they simply brought on more tears.

After Reverend Laliberte ended his sermon, Dallas Young graced the podium. She spoke of her love for her dear departed friend, but in a different tack from the night before, she also vented her anger over Elizabeth's murder. She concluded telling the friends and families, "Don't cry. She has gone on and she'll forever be our beautiful guardian angel." The room was silent except for an epidemic of sniffles.

Aware of the irony of his statement, Adolph took comfort in the fact "it was one of the best funerals I ever went to. It was just beautiful. The singers, the attendance, it was beautiful. Of course, it was the one funeral I never wanted to be at."

After the service, the mass of people headed toward their vehicles to make their way to the Woodlawn Garden of Memories Cemetery, on the west side of downtown Houston at the 1100 block of Antoine Drive. One of the members of the press stated he stopped counting cars in the procession to the cemetery after he reached three hundred. Reports indicated that the line of vehicles stretched for five miles.

The Penas were driven to the cemetery in a limousine. "They held us in the car for about thirty minutes because it took them that long to get all of the people parked and up to the grave site. We sat in that limousine for about thirty minutes and we got out and the media was everywhere." The murders of the girls had become the cause célèbre amongst the local media, and the vultures were out circling their prey.

"All my buddies were over there," Pena recalled, "blocking the cameras. Standing up on chairs and on their shoulders, making sure the press would not shoot photos of us. So we could mourn in relative peace."

Jennifer Ertman's grave can be found in the mausoleum in the center of the cemetery. Elizabeth Pena's grave is located approximately one hundred yards away. Neither family knew the other planned on burying their daughters in Woodlawn Garden of Memories.

Elizabeth is located diagonally across from Jennifer.

A sundial compass leads the way for Elizabeth, toward a giant cross.

* * *

Tuesday, July 6, 1993—evening
T. C. Jester Park
T. C. Jester Boulevard and West Thirty-fourth Street
Houston, Texas

The following week, the Penas and Ertmans gathered together with more than 125 friends and family members directly across the bayou from where their daughters had been slaughtered. As the summer evening made the transition from sweltering to bearable, the Penas and Ertmans graciously accepted the gestures of comfort from their loved ones.

The gatherers carried votive candles, which lit up the gazebo across from the murder scene. As the sun settled, the candles provided a flickering, shimmering mise-en-scène at which the parents would speak about their daughters.

Among those who came to show their support for the families were several Houston police officers who worked on the case. Adolph purposely walked toward Officer Ray Zaragoza, grasped his hands in his own palms, bowed his head slightly, and simply thanked the officer. The normally steely policeman could barely return Pena's gaze.

But Adolph was there to do more than simply grieve for his daughter in public. He wanted his neighbors to take action. He realized the ever-escalating violence in his city must be halted before it spun out of control.

"We must band together," he addressed the rapt audience, "to make our neighborhood a safer place for all." Unfortunately, he could barely get through any more of his statement as he broke down in tears. He looked toward his wife, Melissa, who stepped up and took over.

"We want everyone to know," Melissa calmly spoke, "that if any of you make any donations to the memorial fund for Elizabeth, that we are donating all of the money for the Heidi Search Center in San Antonio."

Melissa looked toward her husband and extended her hand to him. He grasped it gently and pulled toward his wife. With tears in his eyes, he nodded toward her, and she continued. "The last thing we would like to say is we hope and pray the justice system will not fail us now." Many in attendance nodded their heads in agreement; others murmured in accordance.

The seemingly docile-looking Melissa then ratcheted up the rhetoric. "We also pray that those who have deprived us of these two beautiful children," she warned as the crowd listened to her every word, "will be punished to the full extent of the law, although there is no punishment that can help with the pain we all have to live with."

Many people continued to weep; however, several felt a sense of comfort knowing the families were not going to give up on the fight they were about to embark on.

"I felt like I owed something to those kids," Adolph stated in regard to Elizabeth's friends. "I've got to do something for these kids. These poor kids are devastated. They don't know what to do."

Pena approached Elizabeth's friends and told them, "Okay, once, twice a week, whatever you want to do, I want you to come over to my house. We'll talk. We can talk about Elizabeth or we can talk about Jennifer. We can talk about your mom or your dad, whatever you want to talk about."

A few days later, Adolph and Melissa were shocked to see "all those kids had come over." The gatherings took place frequently at first and were filled to capacity. "I think I helped them out a bit, having them over for those talks. I didn't know what I was doing, but apparently it worked."

As is usual during stages of mourning, attendance began to drop. "After a while, not so many of them would come over. But I think I helped them out somewhat. They helped me out a whole lot. That's why I did it in the first place."

Once Elizabeth's friends stopped coming by, Adolph, Melissa, Michael, and Rachael would attend grief support group meetings. "We went to counseling through the Heights hospital. That helped me out a bunch. Just going there and knowing that the other people that are there have also lost a daughter or a little boy made me realize I was not alone. Man, it definitely helped me. It helped Melissa a bunch. Just being able to discuss your loss with other people who know what you are feeling, and have been there before, made a world of difference."

Chapter 30

The previous Friday, the same day as Elizabeth Pena's funeral, prosecutor Elizabeth Godwin spoke about her desire to appear before a grand jury in regard to the case of fourteen-year-old Yuni Medellin. Godwin's plan was to ask the grand jury to go along with her intention of sentencing Medellin to a forty-year sentence.

Godwin argued before state district judge Eric Andell that Yuni Medellin should be sent to a maximum-security facility known as the Giddings State School in Giddings, Texas. Under the determinate sentencing program, Medellin would spend at least the next four years in the facility. If he stayed clean during those four years, Judge Andell could conceivably free the young boy with probation. If Medellin were to find himself in trouble, or if the judge simply decided he should not receive probation, an eighteen-year-old Yuni Medellin could be transferred to an adult prison and be forced to mete out the remainder of his sentence, or thirty-six more years.

Venancio "Yuni" Medellin was officially charged with the capital murders of Jennifer Ertman and Elizabeth Pena later that same day.

* * *

One week later, the other five boys were not faring as well. Though he did not explicitly state as much, the general consensus amongst the legal minds in Texas was that Harris County district attorney John B. Holmes Jr., the rough-and-tumble cowboy with the cotton white handlebar mustache, had every intention of charging all five boys with capital murder and would seek the death penalty for each one of them.

Five death penalty charges for one case in Texas was unprecedented.

There were a myriad of permutations that Holmes could choose from. Including Yuni Medellin into the mix was out of the question, as he was a minor at the time of the murders and was therefore ineligible for the death penalty—despite the heinousness of the crime.

Another option would be to have one of the remaining five young men testify against the other four in return for a plea bargain. That individual could get lucky and escape lethal injection. That option turned out not to be necessary, since it seemed that Yuni Medellin would end up being the state's key witness.

The final option was to charge all five boys—each of whom was either seventeen or eighteen years old—with two capital murders and go for executions.

While the choice seemed obvious to the Penas, Holmes had to mull over these various scenarios, as well as the possibility that a jury might find one or more of the killers would pose no future threat to society and not convict them. There was also the possibility that not all the boys participated in the actual killings. The boys could blame each other and it might be impossible to determine who was specifically responsible for the girls' deaths.

"I don't have the foggiest idea what call I'll make on this one," Holmes informed the media.

Chapter 31

The brutal nature of the crime, as well as the age of the perpetrators, caught the eye of the national media. Conservative syndicated editorialist William F. Buckley Jr. offered an interesting spin on the murders. In his July 9, 1993, column entitled "Brutal Urban Frontier Terrifying as the Old West," Buckley opined that the girls would not have died had they been armed with revolvers. The conservative columnist blamed the murders on liberals who allegedly softened gun control laws and made acquisition of firearms more difficult for the average citizen.

Buckley briefly mentioned that the city of Houston had been paralyzed by crime. He wrote: "The answer to this reaches down to the marrow of Houston's depression. It is that nobody knows what to do about crime." Buckley asked Houstonians what exactly they were going to do about it: "Accordingly, people who live in Houston need to decide how they will comport themselves. What, as individuals, will they do?"

The reality, however, was that homicide rates in Houston had decreased dramatically in the preceding thirteen years. Despite the fact that Jennifer Ertman and Elizabeth Pena were Houston homicide victims numbers 250 and

251, at only the halfway point through the year, the overall number had dipped drastically during recent times.

Less than two weeks later, two more national media outlets stepped into the fray. The first was *Newsweek* magazine, which featured a one-page article and one-page full-sized photograph of one defendant, Sean O'Brien.

The second outlet was the NBC News national team, which came to Houston to conduct a lengthy interview with O'Brien. State district judge Donald K. Shipley, however, was having none of it. He slapped a gag order on O'Brien and his appointed counsel, Lon Harper, which prevented the news crew from conducting or airing such an interview.

According to Harris County ADA Jeannine Barr, Harper spoke very openly with the local press about his client and his case. Allegedly, Harper had been making offers to the local media for an interview, but had never committed. That is until NBC News came calling. Barr claimed she asked Harper to halt the interview. She feared the attorney was attempting to set himself up to get out of the representation by means of ineffective assistance of counsel.

Harper claimed his motives were altruistic. "A TV interview would show he's just a scared little kid," the attorney declared of his client. Harper asserted that the *Newsweek* article and the coverage by the Houston-based media had already tainted the jury pool by painting his client as a "cold-blooded killer." Harper reasoned such treatment would bias the jury pool against his client before he ever stepped foot in a Harris County courthouse.

Harper failed to mention that O'Brien had already been interviewed the day before the murders, where he clearly stated: "Life means nothing." The interview appeared on the news in the days immediately following his arrest.

* * *

The loss of life meant everything to the families of Jennifer Ertman and Elizabeth Pena. It also meant everything to President Bill Clinton, who sent personal letters to both families of the victims.

"I was deeply saddened by the news of Jennifer's death," the compassionate Arkansan wrote to the Ertmans in a letter dated July 14, 1993. "The death of a young person is especially tragic, and my heart goes out to you."

President Clinton wrote that he felt . . . "strongly that we must make America's streets safer for our children." The president suggested a proactive tact when dealing with youth violence: "Working together, as parents, neighbors, and law enforcement officials, we must dedicate ourselves to preventing senseless violence in our communities."

The president expressed his sympathies and let the Ertmans know they were in his prayers.

"This helps a lot," Randy Ertman noted, referring to the president's kindness. "I used to be a Republican," the father stated. "Now, I'm a Democrat." Randy also stated that he planned to get involved with victims' rights advocacy.

President Clinton sent a similar letter to the Penas.

"It was pretty moving," stated Adolph Pena. Even though he was excited to receive a letter from the president, he wished it were under different circumstances.

He was able to joke about the letter several years later. "I remember we got this big ol' envelope that says, 'the White House.' I said to Melissa, 'Oh, shit, something's wrong, baby. Something's gonna go all wrong with the trial. Fucking Bill Clinton sent us a letter.'

"To affect someone that high up"—Adolph Pena shook his head in disbelief—"that's pretty devastating."

Adolph also marveled at the fact that so many people around the world were moved by the deaths of Elizabeth and Jennifer. "I remember talking to my wife while opening up the mail for the day and saying, 'We got a letter from Japan,'" back in the days before widespread e-mail. "This girl is sending us condolences for losing our daughter—from a different country." Adolph looked up at his wife in amazement and said, "This has got to be a screwup. We got a letter from Japan." He turned the letter over and said, "Nope, it says 'Pena' on there bigger than shit. That just blew me away."

Monday, July 26, 1993

Efrain Perez received a completely different type of letter in regard to the murders of the two girls. A fourteen-year-old female friend of his named Beatrice "Betty" Martinez sent him a letter in jail to help lift his spirits. In the letter, Martinez wrote that she had seen him and his friends on television: "Their parents are trying to do everything they can to give you all the death penalty, even Yuni." Martinez added she and her friends would "go out and take our asses on strike" if they were given the death sentence.

Martinez ended, "All cuzz them fine ass girls you all wanted to do. Especially the white chick, she looked good, huh, Junior? Ha-ha."

She signed the letter, *Betty Perez*.

The murders of Randy Ertman and Adolph Pena's daughters led another group of people to advocate for the safety of their neighborhood. Residents of Oak Forest, led by the president of the Oak Forest Homeowners' Association, Chris Branson, rallied together to create a crime-watch program for their subdivision.

"We're scared," Branson informed the press. "We

thought that the area was a nice, serene place, and then we find out that there are murderers holding meetings in the woods. That has spooked us."

The group of residents began by clearing out the underbrush of the woods located at the southernmost tip of the park, across the bayou from where the girls were raped and murdered. Parks inspector Jeannette Rogers had doubts as to whether or not such removal would have any effect.

"That place is thick and there are all those pine trees, and leaves and needles keep falling." She shrugged. "Even if it were cleared, I don't know how much of a difference it would make."

Chapter 32

Harris County DA John B. Holmes Jr. ordered the district attorney's office to move forward with death penalty charges against the five boys. A grand jury convened, and the following Monday, August 30, official indictments were brought against Sean O'Brien, Joe Medellin, Efrain Perez, Peter Cantu, and Raul Villarreal. All five were charged with murder, rape, and robbery, except for Villarreal, who was not charged with robbery.

One of the biggest issues was how to handle the logistics of five separate trials for the same murders. One official suggested they hold one giant trial and employ five separate juries at once, one for each defendant. Judge Doug Shaver, who in 1982 allowed serial killer Coral Eugene Watts to broker a deal with the district attorney for the murder of thirteen young women and girls, which almost led to Watts's release from prison in 2006, agreed with the large-trial scenario. (See *Evil Eyes* by Corey Mitchell, Kensington/Pinnacle 2006, for more about Watts.)

"It would be a staggering savings to the taxpayers" the judge offered. He added if each defendant was to be tried separately, the trials could last for years, would cost the public millions to fund, and would be unrelenting to the victims' surviving family members, as they would have to repeatedly return to the courthouse.

The defense, of course, had another theory. O'Brien's attorney, Lon Harper, believed a megatrial would devolve into chaos and lead to the "AstroWorld of criminal justice." He referred to the onetime Houston-based amusement park known for its world-famous roller coasters.

Judge Shaver, who oversaw the administration of twenty-two Harris County felony courts, had his sights on changing the method of jury selection. Instead of individual questioning of potential jurors, Shaver desired to basically whittle jurors down to a few groups that would then be asked their stance on a single issue: the death penalty and whether or not they would be willing to enforce it.

Judge Shaver also had an idea how to deal with the witnesses for the murder trials. He suggested all of the same witnesses be used—namely, any law enforcement, doctors, medical examiners, etc., who were directly involved in the case. He did not, however, address how individual character witnesses for the defendants would be introduced, nor individual witnesses against the defendants, such as a police officer who may have arrested one of the young men in an unrelated crime before the murders.

District Judge Miron Love, however, pointed out to Shaver that a major stumbling block loomed ahead for the court. All of the defendants' attorneys would have to give consent for such a trial to take place, and he believed that such acquiescence was not fathomable. Indeed, several of the defense attorneys had already expressed their doubts about such a move.

Defense attorney Don Davis, who had been assigned by the court to represent Peter Cantu, was less than optimistic about the scenario. Davis had previously been a part of a similar experiment in Judge Jim Barr's courtroom, where the judge attempted to try seven gang members for a single rape. As far as Davis was concerned, the experiment was a failure.

"All parties," Davis believed, "including the judge and the prosecutor, decided it was completely unmanageable."

The families of the girls were skeptical as well. Even though the judge believed holding all five trials simultaneously would benefit the surviving family members, they felt different. Adolph Pena recalled that "we were there to attend all of the trials." He wanted to be sure he saw everything. "How the hell am I going to attend all of the trials if I am in one trial?" Adolph queried. "Unless you're doing them at totally different times and doing them twenty-four hours a day, it just wouldn't work." Adolph believed that the judge did not think they would want to attend every trial. "We told them, 'Hell yeah. Me and Randy and Sandy and Melissa, we're going to all the trials.'"

Just over two weeks later, Judges Shaver and Love convinced the other judges that five trials held simultaneously could be possible. Not all in the same courtroom, but at least all in the same building. Judge Shaver again focused on time and money. He believed if the cases proceeded down the usual route, they would last until the next millennium.

The breakdown would occur as follows: O'Brien's case would go before District Judge Bob Burdette, Villarreal would go before District Judge Shaver, Cantu would go before District Judge Bill Harmon, Perez would go before District Judge Ruben Guerrero, and Medellin would go before District Judge Caprice Cosper.

With everyone in agreement, it appeared as if the trials would proceed forward at a much speedier pace than normal for the Harris County court system. Indeed, Judge Shaver was eyeing February 28, 1994, as the date for the beginning of jury selection and April 4, 1994, as the starting date for testimony.

* * *

In the Harris County jurisprudence system, however, something always seems to come up to derail the best-laid plans. In the Elizabeth Pena and Jennifer Ertman murder trials, that something was the discovery that the grand jury chief, Ray Charles "R.C." Jones, who led the grand jury that brought forth the indictments of capital murder against the five young men, had problems of his own. Jones was indicted for writing a hot check to the tune of $920.12 to an auto repair shop on December 21, 1992.

As a result of Jones's indiscretion, the state district judge Lupe Salinas was forced to toss all 525 criminal cases that Jones oversaw, including the indictments of the five young men who killed Elizabeth and Jennifer. Prosecutors were furious, since they would be required to go back and dismiss each individual case and then reassign them each to a brand-new grand jury pool.

Judge John B. Holmes Jr. declared his office was not at fault for the oversight. He claimed to have purposely kept the district attorney's office out of the grand jury's hair so as not to paint any picture of impropriety between the two entities. He also stressed that background checks were conducted on all potential grand jury members, but while they did check criminal histories for potential capital murder jury members, they had never done so for members of a grand jury.

Judge Salinas had asked all of the potential grand jury members if they were a convicted felon or if they were currently under indictment, and Jones did not speak up. As a result, the judge swore in Jones as a member.

The Pena-Ertman cases would have to go back before another grand jury. It would take at least two more days to fully present the cases and to reinstate the indictments against the five young killers.

* * *

The following day was another important milestone for the Penas and Ertmans. The two families filed suit against Southern Pacific Transportation Company and a gentleman by the name of W. D. York Sr., the owner of the land where the girls were kidnapped, raped, and murdered. The suit alleged that the railroad company and York were aware of dangerous activities occurring on their property and did nothing to prevent them from continuing. Specifically, "a dangerous condition, to wit, a gang presence, gang-related activity, and consumption of intoxicating substances, existed on the premises."

Unfortunately, Andrew L. Drapkin, the attorney for both families in the civil suit, failed to conduct one basic search: find out to whom the land truly belonged.

Harding J. Rome, Southern Pacific's attorney, informed the court his clients did not own the railroad tracks referred to in the lawsuit.

"I can tell you for sure that these are not our tracks," Rome informed the court. "It's a case of mistaken identity." Rome asked the court to dismiss the case, which the judge did.

York, however, did own the land; so the lawsuit would continue forward in an amended fashion.

Adolph Pena later regretted making that call. "I don't know what the hell we were thinking. They didn't have any fault in that. We were just looking for justification, I guess." Adolph simply shook his head at the thought. "We just wanted someone to blame. I don't know what we were thinking on that issue."

On September 23, 1993, the families finally received good news. The newly formed 351st District Court grand jury quickly reindicted the five young men for capital murder. The families hoped the case had finally turned a corner and their daughters' killers would receive the punishment they were due.

The following day, September 24, 1993, Andrew L. Drapkin refiled the civil lawsuit with the correct name of the railroad company that owned the tracks near where the girls were murdered. Drapkin amended the initial complaint to drop Southern Pacific and add the Burlington Northern Railroad Holdings, Inc. W. D. York remained a party to the suit, and an additional property owner called the Maytag Corporation was added as well.

Drapkin blamed the initial error on a property search service. The attorney apologized to the legal department of Southern Pacific and agreed the suit against them had no merit and should be dropped.

The next Monday, September 27, 1993, Judge Bill Harmon made a surprise announcement. Concerned that the pretrial publicity could force Peter Cantu's trial out of Houston, he insisted the trial would begin in January, a full six weeks before the original target date set by Judge Shaver.

"I'm just not going to wait," the judge replied when asked why he would break up the original plans. "Not if I have a change of venue."

Judge Shaver, the other judges involved in the other defendants' cases, and the district attorneys were not happy with Harmon's chess move. There was a belief that if Cantu was to be tried, convicted, and given the death penalty, the media coverage would be immense, thus tainting the jury pool for the remaining four cases, which would be scheduled to commence just as Cantu's was ending. A tainted jury pool would lead to more defense filings and possibly postponements in all four of the additional cases.

Their derision, however, was not enough to stop Harmon.

Thursday afternoon, September 30, 1993, Yuni Medellin was brought before state district judge Robert Lowry in the Family Court Center in Houston. All of the families and the City of Houston Mayor's Crime Victims Assistance Office director Andy Kahan were present for a juvenile trial for Yuni's part in the murders of the two girls.

It was merely a formality, as the state, represented by ADA Robert Thomas, spent the previous two weeks negotiating with Medellin's attorneys, Esmerelda Pena-Garcia and Joel Salazar.

As expected, Lowry sentenced the juvenile to the agreed-upon forty-year sentence. The rub, however, was Yuni Medellin could be paroled by the time he turned eighteen, which was less than four years away. If Yuni behaved properly in the Texas Youth Commission (TYC), he could head back to juvenile court one month before his eighteenth birthday. At that time, a judge could possibly set him free. He could be released and placed on probation until he turned twenty-one.

Pena-Garcia was not thrilled about the deal; however, she felt it was "the best thing for the juvenile (Medellin) to do what he did today."

While pleased that the first defendant had been dealt with, the families of the victims also worried that Yuni Medellin could be back out on the streets in an incredibly short period of time. Even if he ended up being sent to adult prison at the age of eighteen, he would be eligible for parole soon after his incarceration. Most legal authorities believed he would be back out on the streets as early as 1997.

"How can anyone tell us justice is working?" asked an incredulous Adolph Pena. "I don't care if he's fourteen. He's a sick individual. He's an animal!" Adolph screamed.

Randy Ertman was in full agreement. "They should kill the little piece of shit," he emphatically added.

"It's what he deserves," Sandy Ertman proffered. "It's what they all deserve."

After the sentencing, Pena-Garcia read a prepared statement to the press on behalf of her client. "I'm very sorry for what happened," she said, reciting what were supposedly the admissions of sorrow from Yuni. "I wish I could go back and do something to help the girls. I lay awake every night and wish I had fought the others. Even my brother, to protect them."

Indeed, it appeared as if the younger Medellin would take on his brother and the rest of the young men by becoming the state's key witness against them. It was not explicitly stated, but it seemed as if Yuni Medellin would finally do the right thing on behalf of Elizabeth Pena and Jennifer Ertman.

The following week, three of the judges agreed to conduct the trials of Joe Medellin, Efrain Perez, and Raul Villarreal simultaneously, beginning on March 1, 1994. The reasoning was media coverage would be limited and, therefore, less apt to taint any future jury pools against the defendants.

Soon thereafter, Don Davis, defense attorney for Peter Cantu, filed a motion with Judge Bill Harmon for a change of venue due to excessive media coverage of the murders and his client.

Immediately after the motion was filed, on October 21, 1993, defense attorneys for Raul Villarreal and Joe

Medellin filed motions with Judge Harmon also seeking changes of venues due to the high volume of media coverage of the murders and the arrests of their clients.

It would not have been unprecedented for Harmon to relocate a high-profile murder trial out of his courtroom. He did just that in 1990 in the case of Carl Wayne Buntion, who killed a Houston motorcycle police officer. Buntion's case received an enormous amount of publicity, so Harmon shifted the trial to Fredericksburg, Texas, where Buntion received a death sentence the following year.

Harmon requested a two-hour videotape of the local news on the murders and the defendants from the defense attorneys. He also informed the lawyers he would survey the current jury pool to fully understand how much they knew about the cases, if anything.

Adolph Pena had a strong belief that none of the defendants' trials would be removed from Harris County. Members of the media and numerous attorneys assured him such a high-profile case would definitely remain within the confines of a Houston courthouse.

One week later, on October 28, defendant Peter Cantu went before Judge Harmon for a hearing on his motion to change venue. Cantu stood in between co-counsel Don Davis and Rob Morrow, but showed little interest as Judge Harmon addressed the issue of excessive media proliferation in regard to his case.

Judge Harmon summarily rejected Cantu's motion, citing a sampling he took himself of thirty-five prospective jurors. Only eight claimed to have been "irretrievably influenced" by the reports emanating from the media. Based on his informal study, Judge Harmon did not believe Cantu's arguments would be heard before a panel of biased jurors. Peter Cantu would have to face a jury of his peers in Harris County.

Chapter 33

More than one hundred Waltrip High School students and teachers gathered on the brown weathered lawn outside the school, near the entrance to the main building. They were there to remember their friends whom they had lost earlier that summer.

The group of students held hands and formed a circle around a small crepe myrtle, which was to be planted in honor of Elizabeth and Jennifer. Next to the tree stood a three-foot-high stone memorial, which also honored the girls.

The students were joined by the families of the two young girls. Adolph Pena held hands with some of his daughter's friends as two students dug into the earth to plant the tree.

Fifteen-year-old Leslie Rodriguez, the organizer of the memorial service, spoke as the tree was being settled into the earth. "I want everyone to know we will always remember them," she informed the crowd, especially the Penas and Ertmans. She then looked directly at the stone memorial and said, "It's here to ask people to change their ways and make a difference."

Rodriguez then looked at the crepe myrtle and told the crowd that that particular tree was chosen "to represent the fragility of life." At that point, Adolph began to quietly sob. The students held his hands even tighter and the group began to pray.

Meanwhile, Randy Ertman stood next to his friend Bob Carreiro. Randy met Carreiro the weekend Jennifer went missing. Carreiro had recently lost his seven-year-old daughter, Kynara Lorin Carreiro, and her ten-year-old friend, Kristin Michelle Wiley, to murder. The girls were staying at the Wileys when someone broke in and stabbed both girls to death.

The two men held hands and bowed their heads in prayer.

Rodriguez and Anne-Marie Franz, a Waltrip High School teacher who coordinated with Rodriguez on the memorial, both gave brief dedications for the memorial on behalf of Elizabeth and Jennifer. Once they completed the ceremony, the crowd slowly walked toward the tree and the plaque, many touching the memorial as if they were vicariously giving a reassuring pat on the back to the girls.

The two fathers walked away with red-rimmed eyes and hearts full of gratitude.

"All of these children did this out of their own pockets," Randy stated. "I can't ask for more than that. All I can do is thank them." He shook his head, almost in disbelief.

"I am so proud of these kids," Adolph added. "But I'm also sad that they had to do this for their friends."

Both fathers walked off with their arms draped around the other's shoulder and their heads bowed.

* * *

The following Monday, November 22, 1993, Raul Villarreal, Joe Medellin, and Sean O'Brien had their motions to change venues tossed out by Judge Doug Shaver during a consolidated hearing. All three young men's cases would be heard in a Harris County courthouse. Judge Shaver also officially set the court dates for March 1, 1994, for jury selection, and April 4, 1994, for the beginning of testimony.

The Penas dreaded the upcoming holiday season, which would be their first without Elizabeth. Patti Zapalac, Melissa Pena's sister, told them, "It's going to be real hard on us this Christmas." The Penas spent Thanksgiving with Adolph's parents and somehow managed to make it through the somber occasion.

PART II

PURE AGONY

Chapter 34

Friday, January 7, 1994
Harris County Courthouse
351st District Court
Franklin Street
Houston, Texas

State district judge Bill Harmon did indeed separate himself from the rest of the pack when he decided to move forward with the capital murder trial of Peter Cantu and not try him concurrently with the other defendants. It was less than seven months since Elizabeth Pena and Jennifer Ertman had been murdered.

Cantu was represented by Don Davis and Rob Morrow. The three men watched as a group of thirty prospective jurors were brought before Judge Harmon. As the citizens were ushered into the courtroom, Cantu flashed them a huge smile.

The judge and the attorneys proceeded to methodically go through voir dire, or jury selection. Judge Harmon guessed it would take them three weeks to determine an appropriate panel of twelve jurors plus two alternate jurors.

* * *

Wednesday, January 12, 1994
Harris County Jail—cellblock 7B2
San Jacinto Street
Houston, Texas

Less than one week after jury selection began in the Cantu trial, Raul Villarreal got himself into a whole new batch of trouble when he attacked another inmate. The teenager was housed on the seventh floor in a dorm for maximum-security inmates. This included higher-profile criminals who were usually involved in capital murder cases. Maximum-security inmates are under the most stringent restrictions of anyone in the jail.

Despite their limitations, max-security inmates were allowed to have three or four days a week of recreation time, according to Deputy Grady Castleberry. Here, they can go into a gymnasium and play basketball, spike volleyballs, lift weights, or shoot the shit with other inmates.

Castleberry and one other guard lined up the sixteen inmates from the seventh floor, ready to march them into the recreation area. The inmates stood in a single-file line with their right shoulders up against the wall. If one removed his shoulder from the wall, it was considered an act of aggression against the guards and could result in punishment. The inmates were also required to keep their mouths shut.

On this particular day, the inmates should have been happy, because they were not forced to wear shackles on their feet and handcuffs on their wrists. The main reason why they were allowed such a privilege was because there had been no incidents between any of the prisoners, or between the prisoners and the guards, in almost four months. The guards considered the lack of restraints to be an "incentive" for the prisoners. They wanted them to take full advantage of their mobility and do something positive for themselves.

Villarreal stood fourth in line. He kept his mouth shut and his right shoulder on the wall. He marched in sync through the main hall.

Castleberry followed the line of men into the gymnasium. Within seconds, twenty-four-year-old African-American prisoner Lynn Holland ran toward Castleberry.

"He's got a shank!" Holland yelled. "Stop him!"

A shank is a cell-made weapon usually fashioned out of some random item found inside the prison. One can be constructed from a toothbrush handle, a piece of wood, a spoon stolen from the commissary, anything that could be turned into a lethal weapon. They are usually used by an inmate to perform a "hit" on another inmate. They are meant to kill.

Castleberry was ready, but not sure to whom Holland was referring. The guard instantly braced himself against the wall, assuming he would be the one on the receiving end of an attack. He looked up to see Villarreal running in his direction, holding something in his right hand, which was dangling to the side of his right leg.

Castleberry could tell Villarreal was not coming after him, but rather after Holland. The much skinnier and shorter Holland was scared to death as he sprinted toward the guard. According to Castleberry, Villarreal had "a determined look on his face, a look of anger."

"Stop!" Castleberry barked. "Stop!"

Villarreal ignored the command. Instead, he continued his march through the gymnasium door, back out into the hallway, and past Castleberry. He merely glanced at the guard and continued on his way. Villarreal turned up the pace and began sprinting down the hallway after Holland. Castleberry then took off after Villarreal.

"Stop!" the guard continued to yell at Villarreal, who was four feet ahead of him. "Stop!"

Villarreal ignored him.

"I need rovers! I need rovers!" he called out. Rovers are other deputies on the floor. "Villarreal, drop the shank and stop running!"

Villarreal made it nearly two hundred feet down the hallway, rounded a corner, and stopped dead in his tracks when he saw another guard waiting for him. He pinned himself against the wall, still grasping the shank.

Castleberry followed around the corner, saw Villarreal had finally halted, and yelled, "Drop the shank! Lay it down on the ground, now."

Villarreal finally did what he was told and tossed the weapon to the floor. Holland stopped running, once he realized Villarreal could not attack him. Castleberry retrieved the shank from the ground and saw it was wrapped in a dirty sock. A sock is used as a strap to keep a shank from slipping out of an attacker's hands while doing the actual stabbing. A lack of a handle or too much blood will make the shank slippery. The sock helps keep it in place.

Castleberry pocketed the shank, which was made out of a "stinger," a tool used to heat water that could be purchased from the jail commissary. The guard looked at Villarreal and said, "What's going on?"

"I had to take care of business," Villarreal declared. He looked furious. Castleberry was not sure if it was because he was simply mad at Holland or because he wanted to kill the inmate.

Holland was taken to the jail's medical clinic. That was where Castleberry saw for the first time that the prisoner had actually been stabbed by Villarreal. It was not life-threatening, merely a puncture wound on his right side.

Castleberry later related that Villarreal had befriended two prisoners who were well-known Mexican Mafia (MM) members, one of the top gangs in the prison system. The guard believed Villarreal wanted to join the MM. One of the alleged prerequisites for membership into the MM is to murder another inmate. Villarreal denied any such desire. He stated he attacked Holland because they had a fight over whose turn it was to read the daily newspaper.

Villarreal's defense attorneys also tried to argue that Holland had attacked Villarreal way back in August and he retaliated—five months later.

Villarreal was placed in double-door lockdown in cellblock 7N, which gave all of the deputies easy access to him. (It was also the most secure cellblock in the entire jail.)

On Friday, Jaunary 14, 1994, Villarreal was charged with assault for the attack.

Chapter 35

Monday, January 31, 1994
Harris County Courthouse
178th District Court—room 7D
San Jacinto Street
Houston, Texas

Peter Cantu was ushered into the courtroom of Judge William T. "Bill" Harmon, alongside his attorneys Don Davis and Robert Morrow. He grinned as he entered the courtroom and sat down at the tiny wooden defense table. He looked back into the gallery and caught the eye of Randy Ertman, who sat in the front row of the courtroom directly behind prosecutors Donna Goode and Don Smyth, and back and to the left behind Cantu. Ertman was joined by his wife, Sandy, Melissa Pena, and Andy Kahan.

The courtroom gallery was overflowing with people, mainly supporters of the Penas and Ertmans. In addition to more family members of the girls, there were several students and teachers from Waltrip High School as well. According to Kahan, the courtroom "was packed. They even had people waiting outside in the lobby and the hallway wanting to get in." There were more than three hundred people wanting to see what would happen to the alleged ringleader of the murderers of Elizabeth Pena and Jennifer Ertman.

What most people did not know is that Randy Ertman was largely responsible for the large turnout. He personally forked over the money to have two taxis and two vans shuttle students to the courthouse.

Adolph Pena remembered the first time he walked into the large box-shaped courtroom. He noticed the long width-wise wooden pews, of which there were seven rows' worth. He also noticed four large wooden beams evenly placed throughout the courtroom, two of which caused a major obstruction for those unfortunate enough to have to sit in their pathway. To the front of the courtroom, he spotted Judge Harmon's bench. It was not overwhelmingly imposing like so many he had seen on television and in the movies. To the right of the judge was the witness stand and to the right of that was the jury box.

As Pena sidled toward the front of the courtroom, he caught sight of Peter Cantu at the defense table, not less than five feet from the judge's bench. Pena brought reinforcements with him to intimidate Cantu—namely, his cousin Joe.

"He's not a very nice guy," Adolph admitted about Joe. "Boy, he'd come in there and he's all dressed in black and wore these real dark sunglasses, and he walked in there with me." Adolph chuckled. "Peter Cantu saw him come in there with me and he put his head down on the defense table like he wanted to run and hide. Joe was just staring him down the whole time.

"Now, Joe is a pretty good guy, but he's been in and out of prison a couple of times, and all of his brothers are in prison and he knows some people in prison." Despite his cousin's less-than-savory background, Adolph was glad to have him by his side.

"He'd say to me, 'C'mon, I'm going to go with you. I'll

take care of you.'" Adolph was grateful. "It was good to have him."

Cantu sat toward the front of the table, which was positioned in a rectangular fashion with one end near the judge's bench and the other end close to the gallery's wooden rail. Defense attorneys Davis and Morrow sat opposite Cantu, closer to the people in the gallery, almost as if to act as human shields for their client.

Davis had the unfortunate distinction of resembling a taller version of the nerdy television character Steve Urkel (Jaleel White) from the sitcom *Family Matters*. Morrow, on the other hand, had the unfortunate distinction of resembling another nerd, Bill Gates—albeit, a shorter version of the Microsoft chairman. Despite their appearances, both lawyers were tough, seasoned defenders.

Adolph headed toward Cantu and the defense table, only to stop, pause, and turn left to grab a seat on the front aisle. He noticed a few teenagers shooing people away.

"You can't sit there," Adolph overheard one teenage boy tell someone who tried to snag a front-row seat. "These are for the girls' families." The seat thief quickly skittered away, embarrassed.

There were even a few Cantu supporters in attendance, mainly several attractive Hispanic teenage girls. Adolph dubbed them "the Groupies."

The state of Texas tackled the first trial of the Jennifer Ertman and Elizabeth Pena capital murder case with prosecutors Don Smyth and Donna Goode at the helm. Smyth, who resembled a smaller modern-day version of Dennis Weaver's McCloud, minus the ten-gallon hat and bolo tie, was eager to get started. Goode came in, all business. The thin, attractive prosecutor was dressed in her best business suit and had her long, curly hair pulled back with a salmon-colored barrette. She wore large, oversized glasses, as did Smyth.

Judge Harmon, a youngish, pleasant-looking fellow,

liked to maintain a sense of ease in his courtroom. He did not come engulfed in the traditional flowing black robes. Instead, he wore a simple and smart black business suit, a white oxford shirt, and a maroon tie. He looked more like an accountant for a large corporation than a formidable judge.

Harmon entered the courtroom, took his chair, and called for the jury. Soon thereafter, he asked prosecutor Smyth to read the indictment against Cantu.

After reading the formalities, Smyth then stated, "Peter Anthony Cantu, heretofore on or about June 24, 1993, did then and there unlawfully while in the course of committing and attempting to commit the kidnapping of Jennifer Ertman, hereinafter called the complainant, intentionally cause the death of complainant by strangling the complainant with a deadly weapon, namely hands, and by strangling the complainant with a deadly weapon, namely a belt, and by strangling the complainant with a deadly weapon, namely a foot, and by strangling the complainant with a deadly weapon, namely an object unknown to the jury."

Smyth added the charge of robbery of Jennifer by Cantu, in addition to her murder. The prosecutor also added the murder of Elizabeth Pena, along with an added deadly weapon of a shoestring.

Smyth finished reading the indictment and quickly moved on to his opening statement. He asserted the evidence would show what happened that night, how it happened, and that it was Cantu and his friends who were responsible for the murders of Elizabeth and Jennifer. Smyth detailed, point by point, what Cantu and the others did to the girls. He also stressed it was Cantu who instructed the other boys to execute them.

Though logical and practical, Smyth had an annoying habit of starting each and every paragraph with: "I anticipate the evidence will show that . . ." Even though his opening was brief, the repetition of the phrase—thirty-two times—was tiresome.

The state's first three witnesses were Gina Escamilla, the friend of the girls whom they were out with the night they were murdered, and the Sandoval twins. They laid out the timeline for what happened from when the girls left their parents' houses until they walked past the Sandoval brothers and into the den of hell.

Defense attorney Don Davis spent much of his cross-examination of the Sandoval brothers attempting to disprove the theory that the boys were part of some organized high-end Houston gang. Frank Sandoval basically agreed and stated they were more a tight-knit group of misfits, outcasts, and friends who looked out for one another.

Davis asked Frank why he left the scene after he witnessed Joe Medellin drag Elizabeth by her neck and heard her screaming. "You said at that point when you saw that, you decided to leave. Is that correct?" Davis asked.

"Yes, sir," Frank replied.

"Why did you decide to leave then?"

"'Cause I knew that was wrong," Frank added.

"You knew what was wrong?"

"Getting the girl and throwing her to the ground and forcing her, forcing her . . ."

"What did you think Joe was going to do at that time? What did you think Joe was about to do?" Davis queried.

"I thought they were going to rape her. Rape them."

"So at that point," Davis continued, "what do you decide to do then? You think Joe is going to rape this girl, so what do you do at that point?"

"Turned to my brother, told him it was time to leave," Frank responded, nonplussed. "At the same time, too, he turned to me and told me [it was time to leave], so we started walking."

Frank also testified Cantu went after him and told him to "get some." Frank declined and continued on walking with his brother. Neither boy went back to help. Davis did not bother to go after the teenager any further as to why he did not help the two young girls. The look on Adolph's face indicated he would like to have known why the boy did not do anything to help his daughter.

Frank did claim he was afraid of the other boys, because "they had the Devil in them." He claimed that is why he did not even bother to call the police. When asked if it bothered him that he did not seek help, Frank Sandoval simply responded, "No, it did not bother me."

Adolph would later express his opinions on the Sandoval brothers. "Those two sons of bitches, I wish I could run across them." His disgust was palpable. "They could have saved the girls. All they had to do was call 911 as an anonymous caller and say, 'Hey, people over here are beating on these girls.' Cops would have been over there in about thirty seconds. But they never did. I believe they're just as guilty as the other guys and they didn't get shit. I hope to God they have nightmares every night."

The next witness for the prosecution was also their key witness: Yuni Medellin, Joe Medellin's little brother. Yuni gave a graphic description of what happened that night. His testimony was difficult for many in the gallery to hear, especially the girls' parents. The youngest participant in the attacks also seemed to express remorse—not for the girls, but rather for getting caught.

"Why did this have to happen to me the first time?" Yuni wondered aloud in reference to the night of the murders being the first time he ever went out with his brother and his brother's friends.

Yuni Medellin spoke of how Cantu took him aside after they had sexually savaged the two girls and told them they would have to kill the girls. "He talked low to me," Yuni said, "'We're going to have to kill them.'"

Adolph later discussed how difficult it was to watch one of the six boys responsible for the rape and murder of his daughter on the witness stand. "It was so hard to not want to jump up out of my seat and over that rail and just strangle him. You had to control yourself." It was a constant test of will for Adolph to keep that pain within himself. "The anger—you just have to talk your way through it. You have to calm down. You hope they will get what they deserve, and hopefully, justice will prevail."

The first day's testimony ended with Christina Cantu, Peter Cantu's sister-in-law, testifying against her husband's younger brother. She recalled how the boys bragged about the killings later that night. She testified that some of them had blood on their bodies and clothes. She also mentioned how they were all giggling like a bunch of schoolgirls. She finished by describing how she convinced her husband to call Crime Stoppers and turn them in.

The following morning, February 1, the key witness for the day was Joe Cantu, Peter's older brother. Joe testified for nearly an hour about the lifestyle that he, his brother, and their friends lived. While many attempted to paint them as a bona fide street gang, he described them as a group of friends, more like a family, who had each other's backs, but rarely, if ever, resorted to violence.

Peter Cantu could not bring himself to look at his older brother on the witness stand. He spent the entire hour of Joe's testimony either fiddling with papers on the defendant's table or leaning over and whispering into Davis's ear. He made it a point not to acknowledge his brother's presence.

Joe Cantu recalled the boys' description of the killings of the two girls, again, in explicit detail. He claimed the reason he called Crime Stoppers was to protect his wife,

Christina, who suffered nightmares ever since the encounter with Peter and the guys.

"I couldn't stand to see my wife that way," Joe Cantu testified.

The other key moment of that day's testimony came when defense attorney Don Davis argued about the nature of the crime scene and autopsy photos of the victims. He argued that the large quantity of the photos ventured into prejudicial territory due to their gruesome nature. The prosecution successfully argued that were it not for Davis's client and his client's actions, such photos would not exist and would not need to be presented to a jury.

Adolph Pena recalled the difficulty of having to listen for the first time to the details of his daughter's murder. "They (the prosecutors) had tried to prepare us for what we were to expect with the gory details. We thought we were prepared, but it was really tough.

"You really didn't know what the girls went through until you sit there and listen to all the gory details. In fine print, it's detailed like nobody's business. Which way their hair was and all that stuff.

"That first trial liked to kick my ass the first few days of it."

Adolph was upset with the defense attorneys in the case because he believed they purposefully left out graphic photographs of his daughter's crime scene on the defense table just in the line of sight of the Penas and Ertmans, who sat in the front row every day directly behind the prosecution. "They had these big ol' photos of these girls that are half-mutilated. A couple of times, I'd seen the photos." Adolph approached prosecutor Donna Goode.

"Donna, do me a favor," Adolph asked.

"Anything, babe," Goode responded.

"Tell them that when they flash those pictures that they flash them away from us. Nobody on this side of the bench needs to see those photos." Adolph added, "Make sure the jurors see them, but not me. I want them to look at what happened, not me."

Goode gladly did as she was asked, and the defense complied and made a point to be more discreet with the crime scene photos.

The remainder of the day's testimony focused on the various police officers and crime scene investigators who worked the scene, also, details of Cantu's arrest, the search of his home for evidence, and his subsequent confession to the rapes and murders. Cantu's written statement was also read aloud for the record.

The third day of Cantu's trial, February 2, was the grimmest. The focus was on more police officer testimony and medical testimony from dentists and a medical examiner (ME).

Several photos of the girls' decomposed bodies at the crime scene were shown to the jury by the medical examiner. Some members of the jury were repulsed at the sight of Jennifer's desiccated vagina, which had been devoured by maggots. Furthermore, the photo of Elizabeth's detached skull as it lay on the autopsy table caused several jurors to turn away. One male juror simply put his face in his hands after he witnessed the photographic carnage. Another male juror quietly cried after viewing the atrocities.

Peter Cantu could not be bothered to look up to catch the jurors' reactions. He merely continued scribbling in his notebook.

The testimony, however, was too much to bear for the families of the girls. Both Adolph Pena and Randy Ertman rushed out of their pews and into the hallway. Each man clutched the other around the shoulder and shielded their faces from the cameras that followed. Sobs were easily audible as the two men headed for the elevator.

After the day's testimony ended, Andy Kahan spoke to the press about the horrors witnessed inside the courtroom. "That was some of the most gruesome testimony ever heard in a Harris County courthouse. Today, you are seeing the real, sheer savagery. The sexual assaults, the brutality. It just makes you want to wring their necks," he stated of Peter Cantu and his cohorts.

Several members of the gallery were in tears by the end of the day's testimony. Most of them had no idea just how much the girls were made to suffer. One spectator, Teresa Castillo, a friend of both girls, cried outside the courtroom. "I just can't understand why he would do such horrible things to them. It's disgusting."

The fourth day of Cantu's trial, Thursday, February 3, found the courtroom packed to the gills. Filled to capacity with more than three hundred onlookers, including nearly one hundred Waltrip High School students, with dozens lined up against the back wall of the courtroom, the anticipation hung over the gallery like pollution on a hot Houston summer sky. It was inevitable that a verdict for Peter Cantu would come this day.

Even more police officers took their place on the witness stand to lay out the minute details of the crime and arrest of Cantu. To conclude, Smyth read the entirety of Cantu's confession.

The state rested and Judge Harmon turned to Don Davis, Rob Morrow, and the defendant. Davis informed the court the defendant had no witnesses to testify on his behalf. Davis later admitted he had difficulty finding anyone who was willing to do so. The defense also rested.

* * *

Prosecutor Donna Goode led off the closing arguments for the state. She first apologized to the jury for having to view so many gruesome photos of the victims; however, she explained to them that it was the handiwork of the defendant, not the state of Texas. Goode then proceeded to plow through all the charges and attempted to clarify the legal mumbo jumbo for the jurors. She narrowed it down that Cantu could be convicted for his direct actions, for his participation with others from the group, or for his encouragement or ordering of others to do his bidding.

Goode also described the actions of Cantu and his buddies as "much like a pack of dogs feeding on its prey or a frenzy of sharks going after something."

Don Davis's argument for Peter Cantu basically consisted of claiming, since his client did not have any blood on his boots or clothes four days later, he could not have killed the girls.

Prosecutor Don Smyth gave the final argument and asked the jurors to simply go back and read Cantu's own words from his confession. Smyth also praised the jury for undertaking such a difficult task.

"You have had to hear about a part of society that you never believed existed," Smyth consoled them. "Nobody could do that. Nobody. But I submit to you, ladies and gentlemen, if you take a careful look at the evidence, you know that it does happen. Unfortunately, it did happen, and because of that you are now a different person." Smyth continued looking directly into the eyes of all members of the jury panel. "Your mood is as gray as the sky outside. You'll never look at your own kids the same way. When you hug them, you will hug them a little tighter, a little longer, because of people like this defendant, because you never know when you are going to see them again."

Smyth paused and turned around to look at Cantu. "Because of what he did," Smyth declared as he pointed at the defendant, "the Penas and the Ertmans never got to hug their daughters again." The parents of the girls were fighting back tears. The audience in the gallery hinged on Smyth's every word.

The prosecutor closed out the state's case by adding, "This defendant is guilty of the capital murder of Jennifer Ertman. There is only one true and fair verdict to render—guilty of capital murder."

Smyth again turned his attention to the defendant and directly addressed him. "Peter Cantu, you did it. You're responsible for it."

The silence was overwhelming.

Judge Harmon instructed the jury to deliberate Cantu's fate.

Less than half an hour later, his fate was sealed.

The jury returned to the courtroom. Judge Harmon had already admonished the gallery to keep its collective voices down and warned that any outbursts would lead to jail time.

Jury foreman Stephen Profitt read the verdict to the courtroom.

"We, the jury, find the defendant, Peter Anthony Cantu, guilty of capital murder as charged in the indictment." Cantu had a combination look of surprise and a smile on his face as the guilty verdict was read. He scratched his right cheek with his right hand. Davis placed his hand on Cantu's right shoulder and the now-convicted Peter Cantu sat down in his chair. He continued to look bemused at the verdict.

As the verdict was read, the reaction in the gallery was drastically different. Nearly everyone was on the edge of their seats. One very noticeable sight occurred at the front of the wooden railing that separated Randy Ertman from Cantu by less than ten feet. Randy's large body could be seen slightly bouncing up and down in a staccato motion.

His movements were accentuated by quick bursts of sobs. He kept his head down so most people could not see the rivulets of tears streaming down his cheeks into his sandy blond beard.

When the word "guilty" was uttered by the foreman, it seemed as if the entire room exhaled. The tension quickly released as the spectators realized the first defendant had gone down. Randy, however, did not appear relieved. He continued to convulsively sob.

After the verdict was read and the jurors were polled, Judge Harmon informed the court the penalty phase of Cantu's trial would begin the following morning, at ten.

After several minutes, everyone was ushered out of the courtroom into the hallway of the courthouse. Randy and Adolph clutched each other in a manly embrace and both began to sob. They buried their heads into the other's neck and wept openly and loudly.

Randy appeared befuddled, as if he were not quite sure that he heard a verdict of guilty. He pulled back from Adolph, with his friend's head cradled in his large hand, and half-stated, half-asked, "We got it. We got it. We got it. Right?"

Adolph simply nodded his head. He was speechless.

Several of the girls' friends were not speechless, nor were they shy about their opinions of Peter Cantu. Nikole Martinez, a girlfriend of Elizabeth's, stated, "I wish everything that happened to her would happen to him."

Jennifer and Elizabeth's friend, Anthony Calleo, added, "He got what he deserved. I hope he gets the death penalty. He should fry."

Adolph spoke about what it was like having to look at the alleged ringleader who was responsible for killing his daughter: "It was hard for me to sit there in control."

Randy Ertman added in an interview with the *National Enquirer* that he looked forward to the day Cantu would be executed.

Chapter 36

Friday, February 4, 1994—10:00 A.M.
Harris County Courthouse
178th District Court—room 7D
San Jacinto Street
Houston, Texas

The prosecution brought in several witnesses to paint a picture of Peter Cantu as a less than savory character who had been that way for a while. He was described as a thug, a bully, and a stalker.

Many people from his past were brought in to lay out a timeline from the beginning of the downfall of Cantu. A grown-up Darren McElroy and his mother testified about the bicycle theft Cantu engaged in when he was eleven years old.

Cantu's former sixth-grade teacher, Diane Caudill, testified how he bullied her in her own classroom. The petite young woman expressed how terrified of him she was back then, and that she has been in fear of him ever since.

As more and more witnesses filed in, it became

increasingly clear that Peter Cantu had been heading in a more violent direction with each day.

The prosecution also brought in Melissa Pena and Randy Ertman to talk about their daughters. Many people in the gallery wept as the parents recalled their daughters and the things they enjoyed doing with them. They cried even more when the parents were asked to describe the pain and misery they experienced ever since the murders of their daughters.

After the first day of punishment testimony had ended, several girls gathered in the hallway to discuss the loss of two of their best friends. They also spoke of how the murders of Elizabeth and Jennifer had changed their lives.

"I listen to my parents more," Elina Figueroa admitted. "I don't like going out so much anymore, and I definitely won't go anywhere without a big group of people."

Yet another, smaller group of girls also congregated in the hallway away from the other group. These were also pretty Hispanic high-school girls. They were friends of Cantu's.

"They're just showing the bad side of Peter," stated one girl. "He was always real nice to me. He is not like they are portraying him in court."

Another attractive girl, with big hair and ultra-red lipstick, added, "He was a nice guy. They're bringing all the bad points up, but he really wasn't a bad person."

The following day, even more witnesses were paraded in front of the jury to map out the downward trajectory of Peter Cantu's life.

Prosecutor Don Smyth stated the issue very clearly: "Peter wrote this story. We're just reading it."

The defense brought in Peter's mother, Suzie Cantu. The mother testified for almost ninety minutes. She came across as devoted, if somewhat delusional, toward her son. She tried to show he was a normal kid who tended not to listen to his mother. She expressed how much she loved her son and how surprised she was he would be involved in such a heinous crime.

Cantu's father could not make it to his son's trial because he suffered from epilepsy.

Things were not looking good for Peter Cantu.

At the end of the defense testimony, at 4:30 P.M., Judge Harmon instructed the jury to begin deliberations.

In the halls of the courthouse after the day's testimony, Cantu's lead defense attorney made a startling proclamation. "Peter Cantu is innocent." Don Davis shocked members of the hardened press with his statement. Davis stated his client admitted to participating in the rapes, but did not participate in the actual murders of the girls. "He feels remorse for not stopping the murders," Davis declared.

Prosecutor Don Smyth reacted to Davis's eleventh-hour claim: "I'd take issue with that. The only thing he probably regrets is that he got caught, because it turns out the cops know what they can do, and that's catch people."

Four hours later, the jury returned. Unfortunately, Judge Harmon was nowhere to be found. After several minutes, he was finally located.

Before he returned to courtroom 7D, Judge Harmon came across victims' rights advocate Andy Kahan.

"Andy, let me ask you something." Judge Harmon stopped the much taller Kahan.

"Sure, Judge. What do you need?"

"What would you think about me letting the parents speak to Cantu after the sentence is read?"

Kahan was elated. "I think that would be fantastic. It should really help them on the road to healing."

"You might mention it to them." Harmon referred to the families. He nodded and entered the courtroom through his back entrance.

Judge Harmon asked for the jurors to be admitted into the overflowing courtroom. Despite the late hour, the room was again packed to the rafters.

"Mr. Foreman, has the jury reached a verdict?" Judge Harmon inquired.

"Yes, we have," replied jury foreman Stephen Profitt.

The judge asked Profitt to hand the sentence to the bailiff, who, in turn, handed it to Judge Harmon. The judge unfolded the document, read it carefully, and looked up at Cantu.

"Special issue one," Harmon began to read the verdict. "Is there probability that the defendant, Peter Anthony Cantu, would commit criminal acts of violence that would constitute a continuing threat to society?"

Cantu merely shuffled his feet and looked down.

"The answer: we find and determine beyond a reasonable doubt the answer to special issue one is yes.

"Special issue two," Judge Harmon continued. "Do you find from the evidence beyond a reasonable doubt that Peter Anthony Cantu, the defendant himself, actually caused the death of Jennifer Ertman, the deceased, on the occasion in question, or if he did not actually cause Jennifer Ertman's death, that he intended to kill Jennifer Ertman or another, or that he anticipated that human life would be taken? Answer is yes.

"Special issue number three: Taking into consideration all of the evidence, including the circumstances of the offense, the defendant's character and background, and the personal moral culpability of the defendant, do you find that there is a sufficient mitigating circumstance or circumstances to warrant that a sentence of life imprisonment rather than a death sentence be imposed?"

The judge paused. The spectators practically stopped breathing. Peter Cantu grimaced.

"We, the jury," Judge Harmon continued, "unanimously find and determine that the answer to this special issue is no.

"Verdict: We, the jury, return in open court the above answers to the special issues submitted to us, and the same as our verdict in this case.

"So say you all?" the judge asked the jurors.

"Yes, sir," they all replied in unison. Not a single jury member was crying.

The tears were flowing in the gallery, though. Young girls were walking up to Sandra Ertman and giving her hugs in her seat. She seemed to be doing more consoling of the kids than anything.

Judge Harmon again looked directly at the defendant. "Mr. Cantu, would you please rise?"

The bored-looking Cantu stood up to face the judge.

"Based upon the answers to the special issues by the jury . . . I'm now going to assess your punishment in accordance with the laws of death."

For the first time, Peter Cantu showed a look of despair. He grimaced at the pronunciation of the word "death."

"Do you have any reason to say, Mr. Cantu, why I should not go ahead and pronounce sentence against you today?"

"Nah" was Cantu's unenthusiastic reply. He then scooted back to his chair and sat down in it.

"Having nothing further to say," Harmon continued before he noticed Cantu had taken his seat. "Please rise, Mr. Cantu." Cantu hesitantly stood up. "It is the order of the court that you, Peter Anthony Cantu, adjudged to be guilty of the offense of capital murder, whose punishment has been assessed by the verdict of the jury, the judgment of the court at death.

"That concludes the trial," Judge Harmon declared. "It is now over."

But not really.

Judge Bill Harmon allowed Randy Ertman to confront his daughter's killer in court through a then-little-known law on the Texas books known as the Victim Impact Statement, which is a part of the Crime Victims' Bill of Rights. At the time, no one in the state of Texas had ever used it before.

There is a first time for everything.

"Mr. Ertman?" Judge Harmon asked as he looked toward Jennifer Ertman's father.

"Yes, sir, Your Honor?" Randy Ertman said as he raised his six-foot-plus, 245-pound frame toward the wooden railing that separated him from one of the killers of his only daughter. He was nicely dressed in a gray wool jacket.

"You have anything you wish to say to the defendant?" the judge asked.

People in the courtroom were taken aback. Nothing like this had ever occurred in a Harris County courthouse. Even Cantu's attorneys, Davis and Morrow, were caught off-guard.

"Yes, sir, I do," Randy clearly replied. He had been quietly sobbing during the reading of Cantu's sentence. He stopped as soon as the judge spoke to him.

Randy stood behind the wooden railing, placed his hands on it, and began to talk to Peter Cantu.

"I'm not going to put you down and get on your level. I'm not going to call you 'sir.' I am not going to call you a thing."

Cantu, with his hands shoved deep down inside his pockets, kept his back turned to Randy, instead facing toward Judge Harmon.

"You can look at me if you want." Peter Cantu did not take Randy up on his offer.

"Look at me!" Randy yelled at Cantu.

Still nothing.

"Look!" Randy hollered so loud, two grown women sitting behind him began to cry.

Finally Cantu deigned to turn his head toward the father of the young girl he murdered. He kept the lower portion of his body facing the judge so only his head craned back over his left shoulder to look at Randy Ertman.

Peter Cantu sneered at the father.

"You're not even an animal." Randy spit the words out of his mouth. "I have cats that kill animals. They kill an animal, they eat it. You're worse than that. You're a piece of shit!" he yelled at Cantu.

The defendant continued to look at the man who stood more than a half-foot taller and weighed nearly a hundred pounds more. He was partially blocked by his attorney Don Davis, who refused to look back at Randy.

"Excuse me," Randy apologized to the court and to the spectators in the gallery. He returned his attentions to Cantu, who had turned his head back toward the front of the courtroom.

"Look at me!" Randy yelled again. "Look at me!" Cantu looked back again.

"My cats eat something. That's the way they were brought up, they eat it. You didn't eat nothing. You destroyed a life. You destroyed my life. You destroyed my wife's life. You destroyed the Penas' life." All of the family members in the crowd were either crying or on the verge.

"I haven't seen any remorse from you," Randy chided Cantu.

"You're worse than anything I've seen in my life and I hope that . . ." Randy paused. "I hope that you rot in hell!" At that point, Justice for All founder and crime victims' advocate Pam Lychner stood up and grasped Randy's left forearm to provide him some comfort.

"Do you understand that? Just nod your head if you can even think about talking, boy." Cantu continued to sneer at Randy Ertman. "Can you say 'boy'?"

Randy was exhausted. He sat down.

That was the end of the first Victim Impact Statement in the state of Texas.

The judge had Peter Cantu removed and asked for the court to be cleared.

Before Randy stood up to confront Cantu, Adolph Pena said, "it felt like everyone in that courtroom was on edge. The tension was almost unbearable."

Andy Kahan recalled a telling anecdote provided by one of the court's bailiffs. Apparently, the young man leaned over and said to Kahan, "If he goes over the railing, we're going to give him a few minutes and then we're gonna pull him off."

Afterward, Adolph discussed Randy's confrontation with Peter Cantu. "He was steaming. But, hell, it made him feel better. It made me feel better. I told him more power to him and give him hell." Adolph added, "I think everybody in there felt better after he said something to that bastard."

Some critics, mainly defense lawyers not involved in the case, decried Judge Harmon's decision to allow Randy Ertman to give a Victim Impact Statement to Peter Cantu. One critic called the entire event "a circus."

Randy responded by asking, "You ever go to a circus and see two girls get killed like that?"

Adolph Pena said of Peter Cantu, "I look forward to seeing all of them being executed, but he's the one I am looking forward to the most. I bet there will be two hundred people there in Huntsville outside those walls when they execute that son of a bitch."

Adolph was constantly appalled by Cantu's behavior and total lack of remorse. "He acts like, *Yeah, so I killed these girls. So what? What's the big deal?*"

Both families of the girls gathered in the hallway of the courthouse. Soon thereafter, the members of the jury spilled out of the courtroom into the hallway. They were standing just feet away from the families of the girls when one of the jurors opened up her arms to embrace the families. Several jurors joined in the embrace and the tears finally came for the jurors.

The scene was so moving that local Fox News reporter Andrea Watkins began to tear up as she recalled the events. When told by her in-studio counterpart that it had been a long day, Watkins replied, "Yes, it has" as she practically ripped her earpiece out and tossed down her handheld microphone.

Adding to the emotional day, Bob Carreiro found out the man who had recently been captured in connection with his daughter's murder, Rex Warren Mays, was being arraigned in the same courthouse.

As a result of the extensive media coverage of Randy Ertman's confrontation with Peter Cantu, lawyers for Sean O'Brien and Raul Villarreal requested changes of venues. Their motions were denied. Both young men would also be tried in Houston.

Chapter 37

Wednesday, March 30, 1994
Law Office of Connie Williams
Houston, Texas

As Connie Williams, the newly appointed defense attorney for Sean O'Brien, looked over his client's case files, he shook his head at the enormity of the case. A jury had just been impaneled and he was supposed to begin the trial the following Tuesday. The nearly twenty-year-veteran attorney had plenty of experience handling death penalty cases.

But despite Williams's experience, it would not prepare him for what was about to happen next. He received a call from a detective in the Houston Police Department Homicide Division in regard to O'Brien. The detective informed Williams that the police would need to pick up his client, bring him down to the police station, and collect fresh new samples of blood and tissue. Apparently, O'Brien, Joe Medellin, and Peter Cantu were considered suspects in an additional murder prior to the deaths of Elizabeth Pena and Jennifer Ertman.

Williams was beside himself.

"Who are they suspected of killing?" the attorney asked.

"Sir, I'm sorry, but I'm not at liberty to discuss that information with you at this time," the detective replied.

"What *can* you tell me, Officer?"

"Just that we received another tip from a caller." It was reminiscent of Joe Cantu's phone call that led detectives to where the bodies of the girls were located. "The caller wanted to be reasonably certain that those three men were not going to get out anytime soon and come after the caller."

"I understand," Williams conceded. "Thanks for the heads-up."

Williams hung up the phone. Despite having put several dozens of hours into preparing for O'Brien's trial, he believed this might actually help his cause. If word got out about the suspected murder, then the current jury pool could be considered tainted if they were exposed to any of the media coverage.

"The first thing we are going to do is probably ask this panel to be excused," Williams confirmed. Frankly, he was surprised the judge moved forward with the jury selection earlier, because of the more than two hundred potential jury members in the pool, the overwhelming majority had heard of the case. Several had stated they had already formed opinions of the guilt or innocence of the defendants—based on what they had heard. Nonetheless, the court was able to whittle the pool down to twelve jurors and one alternate.

Williams was not sure which way was up. "I don't know where it leaves us."

On Thursday, the following day, police met with Sean O'Brien, Joe Medellin, and Peter Cantu. They drew the samples they required without incident.

* * *

Williams gleaned a bit more information by Friday, April 1, April Fools' Day, 1994. It turned out the person who telephoned in the tip was none other than Joe Cantu, Peter Cantu's older brother. He claimed that his younger brother, Peter, bragged in January 1993 about raping and killing a young woman in Melrose Park, at 400 Carby Road, after she had run out of gas. The victim, twenty-seven-year-old Lourdes "Patricia" Lopez, was a mother of a young boy and girl. She also had a drug problem.

According to Cathy Lopez, Patricia's mother-in-law, Patricia was last seen on New Year's Eve, December 31, 1992, when she stopped by her mother-in-law's house on Warwick Road. Patricia wanted to have a word with her soon-to-be ex-husband, Joe Lopez, and to see her two children. Joe Lopez, who lived with his mother, took care of the couple's two children, Joe Jr., nine, and Tiffany, ten.

According to Alfredo Ballestros, his brother was dating Patricia and they all three lived together at Ballestros's home. Ballestros claimed the last time he saw Patricia was on Sunday, January 3, 1993. It was an easy day for him to remember because the hometown Houston Oilers professional football team blew a 32-point lead in the playoffs against the Buffalo Bills in what turned out to be the greatest comeback in playoff history.

Ballestros recalled that around 6:00 P.M., his brother and Patricia got into an argument. "She was my friend and he's my brother, so I didn't want to get in the middle of that, so I went to shoot some pool."

Ballestros returned home a couple of hours later. Patricia was not there. Another hour passed, when the phone rang. Ballestros picked it up and heard a weary Patricia Lopez on the other line.

"Alfredo, it's me," Patricia informed him.

"Where are you?" the concerned friend asked.

"I'm at a pay phone over at Gulf Bank and Airline."

"Is everything all right?" he asked.

"Not really. I'm over here at the Smart Stop convenience store. I ran out of gas and I don't have any money," she declared, exasperated. "Can you please come get me?"

"Yeah, no problem," he offered. "What happened between you two?"

"Just come get me," she pleaded.

Ballestros had been to the Smart Stop numerous times, so he drove there as if on autopilot. It only took him a few minutes to arrive at the store. He parked his car and got out to look around. He did not see Patricia or her car anywhere.

Ballestros's son was coming in that same night from Denver, Colorado, to visit, and he needed to pick him up at the bus station. He jumped back into his car and picked up his son. The two returned to the Smart Stop, but still, there was no Patricia. He gave up and drove home.

Alfredo Ballestros never heard from Lourdes or saw "Patricia" Lopez again.

At 1:50 A.M. on January 4, 1993, eighteen-year-veteran Houston police officer T. E. Westerman was making his usual rounds on the north side of Houston in his patrol car. His shift was from 10:00 P.M. until 6:00 A.M. His patrol area included Melrose Park, a small community park with benches and large oak trees. It has a tiny triangular-shaped gravel parking lot and a metal fence with a turnstile entrance.

Officer Westerman pulled his cruiser into the parking lot and began to check it out. It was not uncommon for stragglers to be populating the area late at night; usually, teenagers up too late getting into trouble or a homeless person looking for a semiwarm place to curl up in the frigid Houston winter. It was also a haven for gang activity and a drop-off point for stolen cars, according to the officer. He was there to enforce the 11:00 P.M. closing rule.

As the officer cruised around the parking lot, sure enough, he spotted the hand of someone lying down on the grass. He pulled up his vehicle next to the person and shined the lights in his or her general direction. He found the person's position to be a bit unusual, however, between the chain-link fence that surrounded the park and one of the rounded wooden-log parking obstacles. It appeared as if the person was passed out as well.

Officer Westerman stepped out of his vehicle to get a closer look. He could tell it was a female and she was lying flat on her back. He noticed something on her belly region, but he could not make it out at first. Westerman immediately summoned for backup and an ambulance; he began to search the parking lot for any potential suspects.

It did not look good for the woman on the ground.

Westerman was unable to locate any suspects, so he secured what was an obvious crime scene.

The backup police officers showed up in just a few minutes, as did the ambulance. The CSU showed up more than an hour later and Westerman was asked to remove his vehicle so they could work the scene collecting any potential evidence that may have been left behind.

CSU detective Keith Webb took over for Westerman. Webb, a twenty-one-year veteran of the HPD, had been involved with CSU for the previous five years. The veteran spoke with the officers at the scene, then began to photograph the area. What he witnessed was not a pretty sight.

A young woman lay on her back without any pants or underwear. Her legs were splayed out and pulled back with her knees up, and her genitalia exposed. She wore a white sock on her left foot and none on her right. The victim's white button-down blouse was covered in blood and was open so her breasts were exposed. She had been wearing a bra, which had been removed and discarded near the body. It had been severed by a knife or some type of sharp instrument. Just below the victim's breasts lay her intestines on top of her stomach. The young woman had been sliced open and her insides expelled.

Webb made an interesting discovery. He noticed the victim's shirt was unbuttoned, not ripped open. The implication being the victim may have willingly disrobed or was forced to do so under duress.

Webb also noted she wore a black leather jacket over her white shirt, which had been unzipped. It, too, had been pulled back.

Once Webb took photographs of the crime scene in the dark environs, he brought out a one-thousand-watt searchlight. With the scene illuminated, he was able to shoot more pictures of any additional evidence he could not spot in the dark. He noticed a pair of black hiking boots on the other side of the fence in the direction of the woman's body. He also spotted a pair of white panties to the left of her body, as well as a woman's belt. Interestingly, the belt had been broken on the side with the holes. It appeared to Webb as if the "belt had been broken while it was buckled, with the little buckle pin still inside the hole."

Webb eventually discovered a pair of medium-size Lee denim blue jeans, which presumably belonged to the woman. The blue jeans were located behind another fence, dozens of yards away from the body, behind some shrubs and trees in some brush. The left leg of the blue jeans had been turned inside out and there appeared to be bloodstains on them.

Webb also discovered two forms of identification that confirmed who lay on the ground next to the parking lot in Melrose Park. One was a Texas driver's license and the other was a Texas identification card. There were also several other items located next to the identification cards, including slips of paper, lottery tickets, and some brand-new tampons. They appeared to come from the victim's purse and were strewn about near her body.

As Webb continued to document the murder scene, he spotted something next to the fence. It was a used tampon, which had been removed from the victim and tossed aside.

Webb also noticed five Budweiser beer cans clustered next to the corpse, including one directly under her right knee. The crime scene technician bagged and tagged the cans in hopes they might contain usable fingerprints.

All of the crime scene evidence was collected and sent off to Homicide for inspection and testing.

Officials then removed the body of the victim. When her corpse was lifted up, Webb spotted a belt underneath, located where her neck had been. He gathered this, too.

Webb took a look at the Texas driver's license. The victim was Lourdes Patricia Lopez.

The corpse had a name.

Upon later inspection, Lopez's white shirt was found to have three large holes in the back. It appeared as if she had been stabbed at least three times in the back. Furthermore, her bra had definitely been sliced in the front. The bra had still been latched in the back so her attacker must have been straddling her and slit it from the front or the attacker may have stood in front of her and sliced it.

Lopez's leather jacket also had three holes in the back. She had been stabbed through both her jacket and shirt.

The belt found under Lopez's neck matched the belt used to strangle Jennifer Ertman less than six months later.

Webb returned to the crime scene eight hours later to photograph the location in the daylight for better reference points.

Nearly four hours later, Webb was ordered to photograph the area where Patricia Lopez's automobile had been discovered. The detective drove two blocks north-east to Hopper Road, at the corner of Foxridge Drive.

Webb documented the 1986 gray Chevrolet Cavalier driven by Patricia Lopez the night before. It appeared as if it had been pulled off to the side of the road. Webb photographed the location of the abandoned vehicle, as well as the interior and exterior of the car.

A police officer contacted Joe Lopez, Patricia's estranged husband. He and his mother took off for the park as soon as they heard. They lived right down the street and were there in no time at all.

"There was so much blood," Cathy Lopez reported. "Blood on the ground, on a post to keep cars out. And there were beer cans everywhere. Budweiser beer cans were all over, like it was some kind of big party."

Joe Lopez spoke with some of the detectives at the scene. They asked him to go downtown with them to discuss what happened with his wife. He agreed and met with detectives at the Houston Police Department headquarters. He was shocked when detectives began to question him about his whereabouts and about his relationship with his wife. Officers kept Joe Lopez at the station for several hours.

Cathy Lopez began to worry about her son. When she later found out police had suspected him in the murder of Patricia Lopez, she was shocked. "He had no idea they would think he had done it," the concerned mother recalled. "They kept him for hours, and the kids were so upset and needed him here."

Eventually the police determined Joe Lopez had no involvement in the murder of his former wife. He was released, and they suggested he be available for them. "After that," his mother stated, "we kept in touch with the police for a while, but there just didn't seem to be any clues."

When the Lopez family was informed by the police that three of the confessed killers from the Elizabeth

Pena and Jennifer Ertman murders were involved, they were flabbergasted. "Oh, my God! Cantu? That animal?" Cathy Lopez uttered in disbelief when she heard Peter Cantu's name mentioned.

"We always felt more than one person killed her," Patricia Lopez's mother-in-law stated. "She was very strong. She would have fought."

A good friend of Patricia's, Rebecca Delgado, bemoaned her friend's fate, as well as her last several months alive. "Patricia was lost. She and her mother had a real bad relationship," she sadly recalled. "She had a hard life and she never really seemed to get past it." Delgado dabbed away tears as she said, "She was human. Sometimes she'd feel real bad about herself and her kids and she'd decide to straighten up and do right."

According to Cathy Lopez, Patricia had been on drugs for quite some time. It was the reason why she and her husband, Joe, were estranged and why he had custody of their two children. "Most of her problems stemmed from drugs, but she could be a sweet person when she wasn't using them. She liked to do things for people. She wanted to be liked."

Delgado added that her friend would no longer have that chance. "She may have, someday. But they didn't give her that chance, did they?"

Cathy Lopez shed tears as she added, "What it comes down to is, nobody deserves what she and those other girls got, do they? Do they?"

According to the Harris County Medical Examiner's Office, Patricia Lopez was not a large woman. She stood only five feet three-and-a-half inches tall and weighed around 130 pounds. She wore her black hair long down the back.

Lopez had been stabbed three times deep in her

back. The wounds measured more than four inches in length.

Also, her throat had been slit from the right side to the left. There was also a single stab wound to the neck. It was determined from the depth of the wounds that the instrument used was probably a knife at least four inches long. The stab wound was considered fatal, as it penetrated Lopez's larynx, or voice box, "through and through," or all the way through, the left common carotid artery, and the jugular vein located on her left side. It measured one-and-one-sixteenth inches in length and had gaped open to approximately three-sixteenth of an inch.

The throat slice only cut soft tissue and muscle and, therefore, was not considered to be fatal. It did, however, measure three inches in length and had a gap of one inch in width. The depth of the slice was three-sixteenth of an inch.

More glaringly, Lopez had also been stabbed at least four-and-one-half inches deep on the left side of her stomach. The stab wound pierced the abdomen and a portion of her small intestine. The stab was so deep that it severed the psoas muscle, or the back muscle. The abdomen stabbing also pierced the mesentery, which is vital because it carries several blood vessels inside. The wound was three inches long and one-and-a-half inches wide. The blow would have been considered fatal as well, as it could bleed excessively.

Harris County medical examiner Dr. Vladimir Parungao explained that it was not unusual for a person's intestines to spill out of a person's body after they have suffered a large stab wound to the abdomen. "If the wound is big enough, because there is a tendency for the inside, the gut, to produce some air when people die, even when they get stabbed," the medical examiner explained. "Some people at the time they are stabbed, their belly comes out and they try to put it back inside while still alive. That is not so unusual."

As for the three stab wounds to Lopez's back, Dr. Parungao determined two of the inflictions were considered fatal "because they involved vital organs inside the body." The organs that were struck and pierced were the left and right lungs and the spleen. The killer stabbed her so hard that the weapon sliced through her seventh rib bone. Each stab wound was approximately four-and-a-half inches deep and the spleen had been stabbed "through and through." According to Dr. Parungao, the wounds "varied from one to one-and-a-half inches in length and gaped up to three-sixteenth to one-quarter inch in width."

The third stab wound was not fatal because "it had struck bone."

Dr. Parungao was able to determine the direction of the stab wounds as "back to front, downward, slightly to the left, backward down toward." He stated that it was consistent with a person standing over the victim and stabbing her.

Dr. Parungao also discovered needle track marks on Patricia Lopez's arms. According to the doctor, the deceased had been shooting up methadone, a drug commonly used to combat addiction to heroin. The doctor located the drug within her bloodstream and measured the amount at 0.8 milligrams per liter. He did not find any fresh needle marks. He did, however, measure her blood alcohol content level at 0.133 percent, or approximately .033 percent over the legal limit of .10 percent (it was lowered to .08 percent in 1999) for being considered intoxicated in the state of Texas.

The victim's hands were also marred with red contusions, usually a sign of defensive wounds. Patricia Lopez fought for her life.

Chapter 38

Connie Williams, who resembled a younger version of the Reverend Jesse Jackson, stood before his client, Sean O'Brien, and also before Judge Bob Burdette. Next to him at the defense table sat the nattily dressed Steven Greenlee. Across the aisle at the prosecution table were assistant district attorneys Steve Baldassano and Jeannine Barr, both young, thin, dark-haired go-getters.

Williams was pleading with Judge Burdette to have his client's trial relocated due to what he believed to be excessive media saturation.

"Judge, at this time we ask the court to excuse this jury panel for the reasons we believe that this community, as well as the panel, has become saturated with the facts in and surrounding this case," Williams requested.

The attorney proceeded to present research to the judge

that he believed would back up his claim. After speaking with 212 individuals in voir dire, the defense stated that 98 percent of them had heard of the murders of Elizabeth Pena and Jennifer Ertman. Of those 212, seventy-five of them were disqualified due to their predetermined opinions on the guilt or innocence of the defendant.

Williams also introduced four new newspaper articles from the *Houston Chronicle* that had been published since the selection of the jury. Two of the articles contained a photograph of Sean O'Brien. Williams also pointed out twelve of the thirteen jurors that had been selected were familiar with Peter Cantu's case. He also mentioned five of the thirteen jurors knew of the name Sean O'Brien. Williams believed he had a strong case for change of venue.

Williams also argued he heard information that one of the jurors saw or read something about the case either on television or in the newspaper. This was enough to force Judge Burdette to question each juror as to whether or not the individual had been exposed to coverage of the O'Brien trial.

The first ten jurors had not been exposed to anything about O'Brien's case.

The eleventh juror, Claude Brister, informed the judge he did have some exposure. He claimed he came home to a message a friend left on his answering machine stating he read O'Brien might be involved in the murder of Patricia Lopez.

The final two jurors reported they had no exposure to the case.

Williams reiterated to the judge the entire panel should be tossed due to Brister's exposure. The corpulent, white-haired, black-robed judge agreed to dismiss Brister; however, he would not remove the entire panel.

The trial of the *State of Texas* versus *Sean O'Brien* began one hour later.

After the reading of the charges, the state opened up with ADA Steve Baldassano. The prosecutor spoke in a reverent tone. "This case is about the story of the untimely death of two young girls. It's a story about their last hour of life. It is also the story about the defendant and his friends and about how they had a good time for an hour."

Baldassano recalled the scene of the two groups of friends: the girls by the swimming pool and the boys at their own party on the railroad tracks. He laid out the various routes one could travel to cross over White Oak Bayou. He detailed how the two girls unwittingly chose the route where the boys were hanging out.

Baldassano briefly described the attack. Adolph and Melissa Pena cringed as they heard the descriptions one more time. The members of the gallery seemed to flinch as the prosecutor described, in grim detail, what O'Brien and the other boys did to Elizabeth and Jennifer.

He spoke of how the girls screamed and pleaded for their lives.

He described how O'Brien participated in the strangling of Jennifer.

Baldassano summed up his opening by explaining, "The judge said that those who do the blamin' have to do the provin'. We are fixin' to do the provin' right now."

Judge Burdette acknowledged the prosecutor, "Thank you, sir." He then glanced over to the defense table and Connie Williams. "Mr. Williams, anything from you?"

"Nothing at this time, Your Honor," the attorney declined.

Instead of allowing the state to begin its case, Judge Burdette broke for lunch. A rather anticlimactic beginning to the second trial in one of Houston's most brutal homicide cases. The judge, however, had a reason for the move. He asked the jury members and attorneys to stay seated and informed them that because there were no longer any more alternate jurors, he was going to sequester the jury during the entire trial. Burdette informed the jurors they could eat lunch, make phone calls to arrange to have someone bring them several days' worth of clothes, and be prepared to stick around.

"If we lose one more juror," Burdette reasoned, "all of this work and all of this time will be for naught."

The jurors did not seem particularly pleased to hear the news.

Judge Burdette added the jurors needed to return, take care of their clothing situation, and be prepared to be shipped off in a van together to a nearby hotel. The judge then informed them that the evidence portion of the case would not begin until the following day.

At that point, the prosecutors did not look so thrilled, either.

Tuesday, April 5, 1994—10:00 A.M.
Harris County Courthouse Annex
184th District Court—room 514
Preston Street
Houston, Texas

Judge Burdette's courtroom was substantially smaller than Judge Harmon's courtroom, where Peter Cantu was tried and convicted in February. While Harmon's courtroom held over three hundred spectators, Judge Burdette's courtroom listed a maximum occupancy on the courtroom door at 108 people.

Needless to say, the courtroom was packed.

The courtroom itself was rather antiseptic: white walls, brown pew seats, four large windows with black venetian blinds drawn.

The judge's bench was located in the back right

corner of the courtroom. The jury box was across the small room to the judge's right-hand side.

In front of Judge Burdette resided the defendant.

Sean O'Brien, dressed in black slacks, a royal blue sweater over a white oxford, and wearing studious-looking glasses, sat at the right end of the horizontal-lengthwise wooden defense table. He absentmindedly tugged at his miniature goatee, which had recently sprouted.

Directly behind him, in between O'Brien and the gallery, sat defense attorney Connie Williams. Steven Greenlee sat next to Williams and to O'Brien's left.

To the defense's left sat prosecutors Steve Baldassano and Jeannine Barr.

The state's attorneys decided to kick off the testimony from an emotional angle. The first witness for the state was Sandra Ertman. Mrs. Ertman, dressed in an aquamarine business suit, recalled her daughter growing up, how she was modest, and that her daughter had never had sex. She also described exactly what clothes her daughter was wearing the night she was murdered. She spoke of how she and her husband became worried when they could not reach the Penas, and how none of the girls' friends knew where they were. A distraught Sandra also recalled how much pain her husband suffered during the days of Jennifer's suspected disappearance.

The state also called up Gina Escamilla, Jennifer and Elizabeth's good friend. The teenager spoke of how the girls' spent their time together the night they went missing. She also spoke of the last time she saw her two friends alive.

Next up for the prosecution was Houston patrol officer Mike Cromwell, who was the first officer at the scene. He was followed by crime scene investigator Brian Horowitz. Both witnesses laid out the gruesome details of the murder scene for the jury. The descriptions were illustrated by several crime scene photos of the two girls. Some of the jurors were taken aback by the grim nature of the discovery.

The afternoon session of the trial started off with Houston police officer Todd Miller, who described his arrest of O'Brien, as well as detailing the youth's confession to the double rape and murder.

Miller's testimony was followed by Frank Sandoval and then Yuni Medellin.

Sandoval appeared nervous on the stand as he contradicted himself repeatedly and went back and forth on whether or not he believed Peter Cantu was the leader of the group. The defense's strategy was to try and convince the jury that the boys belonged to a gang, with Cantu as their leader, and that their client, O'Brien, was merely following Cantu's orders—thereby alleviating some of his responsibilities in the rapes and murders.

Yuni Medellin appeared in court, again represented by his own attorney, Esmerelda Pena-Garcia, who had been appointed by the 113th District Court to represent him in juvenile court. Pena-Garcia informed the court her client was under his own free will to testify or not. She also reiterated no deals had been struck to benefit her client and he was simply there to do the right thing.

Judge Burdette, Pena-Garcia, and Yuni Medellin held a conference outside of the presence of the jury. Judge Burdette simply wanted to make sure Medellin understood the potential consequences of his testimony in the case against O'Brien.

"I am sure that Ms. Garcia has explained those potential problems to you," the judge inquired of the now-fifteen-year-old boy.

"Yes, sir," Yuni obediently replied.

"And understanding what she has told you," Burdette continued, "and the advice of counsel she has given you regarding your circumstances, you decline, and still having some of these matters ahead of you in several years—that is, the other aspect of sentencing—it is your desire to—nevertheless, understanding what those pitfalls may be, is it your desire to go ahead, give up whatever rights you might have, and go ahead and testify in this case freely, voluntarily, and willingly?"

"Yes, sir," Yuni Medellin answered without hesitation.

Medellin took the stand with Pena-Garcia standing directly behind him. Judge Burdette introduced the witness and his attorney to the jurors so there would be no confusion as to why she was hovering over Yuni.

Prosecutor Baldassano had Yuni Medellin explain to the court that he had also been arrested for aggravated sexual assault of Jennifer in the same case, he had pleaded guilty, and he was serving time in juvenile detention for his participation in the crime. He also explained he received a forty-year determinate sentence and had made no deals with the district attorney's office to come and testify against the defendant, O'Brien.

Yuni proceeded to tell the story of what happened that night and how O'Brien had willingly taken part in all of it. He described O'Brien as being the toughest one in the bunch. He made it clear to the jury that O'Brien was neither drunk at the time they picked him up nor high on drugs. In other words, he had a clear head and was under no duress from anyone else in the group to do something against his will.

Yuni described the initiation of Raul Villarreal and talked about the aftermath when the guys were on the trestle, drinking beer, and talking about sticking up for one another. He stressed the guys were not "like a regular gang that goes out and starts fights. They were more like brothers that were always there for one another, who helped each other out."

At the end of the day's testimony, victims' rights advocate Andy Kahan spoke on behalf of the victims. He commented on how the proceedings were much calmer this time around than in Cantu's trial.

"I give the families of the girls all the credit in the world." Kahan praised the Penas and Ertmans. "I think they're showing true character. In my opinion, they are true American heroes." Kahan paused and added, "They're here because their daughters couldn't be here."

Thursday, April 7, 1994—9:30 A.M.
Harris County Courthouse Annex
184th District Court—room 514
Preston Street
Houston, Texas

Prosecutor Steve Baldassano read through the lengthy list of charges for the jurors to start off his closing argument. He then turned his attention to the two girls who were the reason why everyone had gathered in the courthouse.

"You have to think of the defendant's rights," the handsome prosecutor intoned. "But I also think you could remember the victims' rights. In fact, it is your committed duty to do so. These two little girls certainly have the right to be on the beach in Galveston in their bikinis instead of being rotted corpses in a cemetery."

The prosecutor was not holding back.

"They have the right to walk down the streets of their own town," he declared. "To go through a park in their own city. They have those rights. Think of those girls. They have rights, not just the defendant."

Baldassano also warned the jury not to focus on Peter Cantu being the alleged ringleader of the group. "I think it's real easy to pick on Peter Cantu because most of the city probably hates him. He's a fall guy, but he's not the only guy out there. One person doesn't make everybody do a sexual assault." The prosecutor brought it back around to Sean O'Brien. "The defendant lived right there. He didn't leave. So you know that Peter Cantu isn't the mastermind that makes everybody do everything."

Next up was Connie Williams, who represented O'Brien. "I know it's been a difficult case for you," the impeccably smooth defense attorney informed the jury. "It's been a difficult case for Houston, Texas, period."

Williams reiterated his client did have rights, just like each one of the jury members had rights in the event they were ever to get into trouble. Rights established long before even their grandparents were born.

Williams closed with, "I am a parent. I am a citizen of the community just like you are. I agree with everything Mr. Baldassano said about these beautiful young girls and what they have been reduced to, but here we are and it's your task."

Prosecutor Jeannine Barr ended up the closing statements. "The thing that struck me," she addressed the jury, "was this defendant's own words to Ramon Sandoval—'We had to do it. We had to do it.'"

Barr looked directly at one of the jury members in the front row. "That's a lie. He didn't have to do it. They didn't have to do anything," she sneered as she looked back at O'Brien.

"He's here charged with this crime because of his choices, because of his desires, and because of his own personal rules.

"He chose to associate with these guys.

"He chose to go out that night.

"He chose to go to the tracks.

"He chose to get involved in the fight.

"He chose to have sex with Jennifer Ertman.

"He chose to have sex and to rape her over and over again.

"Those were his choices," Barr emphasized.

"He then chose to take off his belt and he chose to take that belt and to strangle Jennifer Ertman, and he chose to kill her."

Barr closed by asking the jury to give O'Brien his proper label. "Label him what he is. A capital murderer. Nothing else will suffice."

The jury returned from deliberations after only ninety minutes, led by jury foreman Bryan Beck.

"Mr. Beck, has your jury arrived at a verdict?" Judge Burdette asked.

"Yes, we have, Your Honor," the foreman replied.

The verdict was handed to the judge. "We, the jury, find the defendant, Derrick Sean O'Brien, guilty of capital murder, as charged in the indictment."

O'Brien did not flinch. He did not smirk. He did not cry. He simply stood there in silence.

Judge Burdette informed the jury they would be allowed to go to lunch, but they were required to return by 2:00 P.M. to begin the penalty phase of O'Brien's trial.

Outside in the courthouse hallway, the families were happy yet restrained. Adolph Pena attributed his calmer mood to his wife.

"During the Cantu trial, I was a complete wreck," Adolph admitted. "I couldn't handle the graphic testimony."

Andy Kahan, once again, handled the media for the families. "Derrick Sean O'Brien has been held accountable for his actions. In the families' opinions, he should be given the same sentence as Peter Cantu. There's plenty of room on death row for people like O'Brien."

Thursday, April 7, 1994—2:00 P.M.
Harris County Courthouse Annex
184th District Court—room 514
Preston Street
Houston, Texas

During his sentencing, a videotaped confession by Sean O'Brien where he admitted he was at the scene of Patricia Lopez's murder was played for the jury. The prosecution popped in the videocassette and a hush fell over the courtroom. O'Brien's face appeared on the screen. He claimed he was involved in Lopez's murder and was joined by Peter Cantu and Joe Medellin.

O'Brien claimed the three young men were walking along the road when a car stopped just ahead of them. As they approached the car, they saw a woman, older than they were, but still young. She exited her vehicle at almost the same time they walked past. She asked the young men if they could help her out. She stated she had run out of gas and needed a push to a nearby convenience store. The guys, eager to purchase some alcohol, agreed as long as she would buy them beer for their troubles. The motorist agreed, got back in her car, and the three boys pushed it all the way to the store.

When they arrived, the grateful Lopez got out of her car, removed the gas cap, and pumped gas into the tank. She smiled at the boys, walked inside, and returned with a twelve-pack of Budweiser beer cans.

O'Brien claimed they asked Patricia Lopez to party with

them; however, he "was too drunk to know who did what."
He denied on videotape that he killed Patricia Lopez.

Jose Martin Medellin, brother of Yuni Medellin and
Jose "Joe" Ernesto Medellin, claimed, however, that
O'Brien, Cantu, and Medellin's brother Joe bragged
about killing the young lady.

After the videotape, several witnesses were brought
in to testify about the bad things O'Brien had done to
them during his short life. One included a friend who
overheard O'Brien say he would kill his own girlfriend.
The other was a cellmate who testified O'Brien said he
didn't care if the girls died because "they were whores
anyway."

The punishment-phase testimony lasted for two days.

On April 9, both sides laid out their closing arguments.
Judge Burdette sent the jury off yet again to deliberate.

This time, they returned in less than half an hour.

Their verdict was guilty. Sean O'Brien would be the
second defendant in the case to receive a sentence of
death by lethal injection.

Outside in the hallway, the family members once again
congregated to celebrate. Sandra Ertman, comfortably
dressed in a white T-shirt and blue jeans, spoke to the
local media. "I'm just glad he's off the streets of Houston," she said of O'Brien, "so he can't do this to any other
children, and so no adults or families have to suffer what
we're going through . . ." Her voice trailed upward into a
higher register as she fought back even more tears. She
quietly stepped away from the microphone and began to
softly sob. She was soon comforted by one of her many
supporters.

Her husband, Randy Ertman, was nearly speechless.
He simply wanted to thank the many people who came

to the courthouse every day and packed it to the rafters in support of his daughter and Elizabeth Pena.

"God Bless y'all," he stated in a teary voice. "Thank you very much. That's all I can say." He turned around and walked away while wiping yet another tear from his weary eyes.

The Penas, who were very quiet during Peter Cantu's trial, were less than thrilled with the outcome.

Melissa Pena was shaking as she stated, "I don't think it's good enough," referring to O'Brien's punishment of the death sentence. "Our daughters don't have an extra day to live." Tears began welling in her eyes. "He'll live ten more years before he dies."

Adolph Pena, who stood next to his wife, was equally incensed. "Why can't they put a belt around his neck? Why can't they stomp them down with their feet? Stomp them into the ground until they are dead. . . ."

No one standing near him was about to disagree.

Andy Kahan recalled, "The thing I remember the most about that trial was how quick that jury came back with a death sentence. I think they were out fifteen minutes. They went in to deliberate his sentence, and within fifteen to twenty minutes, they came back with death. I had never seen anything that fast in my life."

Adolph spoke about Derrick Sean O'Brien. "Even in the courtroom," he recalled, "he really looked like he felt bad for what he did. Out of all those guys, I think he was the only one who felt any remorse for his actions. I think it was because of the way he was brought up by his grandmother. Real respectful, and that's the way his grandmother brought him up. Why he ended up killing two or more girls? You got me."

Chapter 39

While waiting for his trial, Joe Medellin was found to be a DNA match for blood found on Patricia Lopez.

Meanwhile, Efrain Perez was analyzed by a psychologist named Wendell Lee Dickerson. The doctor diagnosed Perez with a "character disturbance," or a "personality trait disorder," and declared he was basically a "follower and not a leader."

Apparently, Perez relayed to Dickerson that he was a very jealous kid. He got "frustrated watching all the other kids in school who owned cars, because he didn't own one" himself. He added, it "caused him to get bored with school" and "turn to a life of crime."

Perez also found God while behind bars.

A different type of divine intervention took place along the shores of the White Oak Bayou in T. C. Jester Park, where the girls were murdered. Randy Ertman met with Houston officials about erecting memorial crosses in the park on behalf of his daughter and Elizabeth Pena. The crosses were constructed by friends of the girls from Waltrip High School. The city officials agreed to allow the crosses to be raised.

A local atheist warned that he would file a lawsuit against the city, but he eventually conceded. The crosses went up on the one-year anniversary of the girls' murders. They would, however, be taken down after another atheist threatened to go forward with a lawsuit. The crosses were subsequently taken down and two memorial benches were installed in their place.

Chapter 40

It was agreed upon by the courts that the three remaining defendants—Jose "Joe" Medellin, Efrain Perez, and Raul Villarreal—would all be tried at the same time in the same courthouse, but in three separate courtrooms with three separate judges and juries. It was an unprecedented move by the courts to accommodate the families of the victims, as well as several witnesses who would have to give repeat testimony in all three cases.

Before the trials of Efrain Perez, Joe Medellin, and Raul Villarreal had even begun, advocates who were anti–death penalty were up in arms. In addition to the three trials conducted simultaneously in the Elizabeth Pena and Jennifer Ertman murders, three more cases that were capital murder/death penalty–eligible were to be tried in Harris County courts at the same time. An unprecedented number of six cases—more than some death penalty states have in a given year—were to be tried at once.

Victims' rights advocate Andy Kahan had no problem with the anomaly. "Nobody forced these defendants to be participants in a capital murder trial," he stated in reference to Perez, Medellin, and Villarreal. "Nobody forced the defendants to do what they did. I'm just pleased that Harris County has enough guts and gumption to try these cases like they should be tried."

The first trial of the trio to kick off was Efrain Perez's in Judge Ruben Guerrero's courtroom. It was located right across the hall, and just slightly to the left, from Judge Caprice Cosper's 339th District courtroom. The walk from one door to the other was less than fifteen feet.

To successfully coordinate the shuffling of witnesses from one courtroom to the next, the judges agreed that Raul Villarreal's trial would not begin until the following day. It, too, would take place on the same floor in Judge Doug Shaver's courtroom, just down the hall from Judges Guerrero and Cosper's courtrooms.

Perez's trial began around 9:00 A.M. Judge Guerrero's courtroom was substantially smaller than the courtroom used for Peter Cantu's trial earlier in the year. The layout was plain. One would simply walk into the courtroom, turn left, and see several yellowish brown wooden pews, which made up the gallery for any spectators. As with Cantu's trial and then Sean O'Brien's trial, each inch of each pew was filled with a person, usually a supporter of the Penas and/or Ertmans.

After the four rows of pews, and on the other side of the wooden railing used to separate the gallery from the legal teams, Perez was seated at the defense table, which was positioned perpendicular in between the gallery and the judge. Perez was dressed in khaki pants, a long-sleeved white oxford shirt, and a black tie. He was flanked by three attorneys, Will Gray to his right, Terrence Gaiser and Jill Wallace to his left.

Seated directly across from the defendant at their own perpendicularly positioned table were prosecutors Marie Munier and Don Smyth. Oddly enough, the prosecution's table was positioned so their backs were to the jury. A lectern between the tables and the judge, however, would be used to address the members of the jury directly.

At the head of the brightly lit room sat Judge Ruben Guerrero, who resembled Pugsley from *The Addams Family* television series. He was rather heavyset, with a shock of thick black hair, expansive jowls, and bedecked in his flowing black robe. He made a fairly ominous presence in the courtroom as he loomed high over the defendant.

Perez spent the majority of the beginning of his trial with his head buried in his hands and on the table.

Monday, September 12, 1994—10:00 A.M.
Harris County Courthouse Annex
339th District Court
Preston Street
Houston, Texas

One hour later, the trial of Joe Medellin began. The families of the victims were helped along by Andy Kahan, Joseph DeBruyn, and Joan Taliaferro. They would make sure that someone from the Ertman and Pena families was situated in a courtroom of both defendants at all given times.

Joe Medellin was brought into Judge Caprice Cosper's 339th District courtroom. It appeared to be the exact same layout as the courtroom Sean O'Brien had been tried and convicted in five months earlier. Judge Cosper

was situated in the back right corner of the room.
Medellin and his defense attorneys, Jack Millin and
Linda Mazzagatti, were seated around a rectangular
table that was positioned parallel to the wooden railing
that separated the defense teams from the gallery. To
the side of the defense team was the prosecution, led by
the handsome, well-dressed African-American Mark
Vinson. There were five rows of smaller wooden pews
where the spectators could sit. Again, as with the previous trials, the gallery was overflowing.

The intense crowds made traveling to and from each
courtroom physically difficult for the families; however,
it all went off without a hitch.

Inside Judge Cosper's courtroom, Joe Medellin
looked pensive and stoic. He was dressed in black slacks
and a dark blue sweater pulled over his long-sleeved
white oxford. He rarely looked back into the gallery. He
knew he would not have anyone there to support him,
and it appeared as if he had no interest in making eye
contact with Randy Ertman or Adolph Pena. Instead, he
looked forward at the judge and fiddled with a yellow
legal pad.

Though it was expected the vast majority of witnesses
who testified in the Cantu and O'Brien trials would be
testifying in the three remaining defendants' trials, there
were a few new twists on the horizon.

The first involved Joe Cantu's testimony against Efrain
Perez. First, Cantu testified when Perez and the rest of
the boys came over to his house on the night of the murders, he witnessed their disheveled appearance and
knew something bad had gone down. Cantu asked
Perez, "Who'd y'all kill now?"

The implication was they were involved in a previous

killing that Joe Cantu was allegedly aware of, and they were capable of participating in similar behavior again.

Joe Cantu also testified that he witnessed Perez shooting Gary Ford so he could steal his leather Raiders jacket.

Perez became visibly upset as he listened to Joe Cantu's testimony. He kept his head bowed down and actually began to cry.

In the courthouse hallway during a break from Perez's trial, Andy Kahan spoke with the press about Joe Cantu's surprise testimony.

"This was really a twist right here," Kahan stated on behalf of the families. "We are all stunned. The family members never heard this from previous testimony from Mr. Cantu. This certainly was a revelation." Kahan added, "This shows that this was not onetime behavior."

Testimony continued in both courtrooms as coordinators Joseph DeBruyn and Joan Taliaferro worked beyond the call of duty, shuffling witnesses back and forth between the two courtrooms. The testimony inside was as grim as it was in the Cantu and O'Brien trials; however, the families of the girls were becoming slightly more numb to the descriptions of what had happened to their daughters. Not that the testimony wasn't heartbreaking, they just understood they had to keep it together to make it through three simultaneous trials. Dwelling on the details of their daughters' deaths yet again was going to make it near impossible.

"It's really a Catch-22 for them," Kahan declared, "because this is the last chapter of their daughters' lives that will be visible to them."

Despite all the medication and the self-perpetuated wall of numbness, Adolph Pena was not completely invulnerable. When he listened to one of the police officers describe how Perez smiled at him while confessing to Elizabeth's murder, Adolph excused himself from the courtroom and stepped out into the hallway.

Adolph walked down the hall, until he came to rest against a nearby wall. His arm raised up against the wall, he buried his head in the crook of his arm and began to sob. His weeping was controlled at first, but it became more violent. Suddenly his sister-in-law Patti Zapalac came up to him and placed a reassuring hand on his back. The sobbing lessened and Adolph regained his composure. Eventually Adolph made it back into the courtroom.

He was glad he did, because he got to see Yuni Medellin, Joe Medellin's brother, testify against Perez. Yuni wore the prototypical slacker grunge outfit that was worn by several Seattle-based rock groups such as the Melvins, Screaming Trees, and Nirvana. It was a long-sleeved blue flannel shirt over a white T-shirt.

As in the previous trials, Yuni Medellin was flanked to his left by his own attorney, Esmerelda Pena-Garcia. The short, hefty Hispanic woman, with dark unkempt hair, wore a lime green dress and sat next to her client. She was prepared to represent his best interests.

Yuni Medellin had no problem going over the details of the rapes and murders of the girls and of his and Perez's participation in the tragic events.

He would, however, have a problem telling the same story in the 339th District courtroom. Yuni Medellin had no intention of ratting out his brother, Joe—despite a threat of contempt of court from Judge Caprice Cosper. The prosecution went through their entire list of questions for Yuni, but he pleaded the Fifth with every single one. The judge warned him there would be severe consequences in regard to his own sentence if he refused to answer the district attorney's questions, but he held true to his word. Despite the fact that Yuni Medellin had no Fifth Amendment privilege to invoke, he refused to speak.

Prosecutor Mark Vinson was not pleased with the developments in the courtroom. Vinson had made an earlier agreement with Yuni Medellin that Yuni would testify in court—as long as the prosecution did not ask him any questions in regard to his brother.

Yuni Medellin reneged on his promise.

"Do you understand that if you continue to not answer my questions," Vinson asked, "I'm going to ask the judge to hold you in contempt and that may result in a citation or a sentence of up to six months and a fine not to exceed five hundred dollars? And that I will also request that [your refusal] be considered by the juvenile court in determining whether or not you shall have to fulfill the forty-year determinate sentence that has been assessed in your case?"

"I understand, sir," Yuni Medellin responded.

"So you realize you're playing with your future life?"

"Yes, sir."

Vinson continued to ask the youth more questions, but he refused to answer.

"I would ask the court to require him to answer those questions," Vinson asked Judge Cosper.

"Mr. Medellin," Cosper addressed the young boy, "the court is specifically ordering you to answer the questions posed to you by Mr. Vinson."

"With respect, Your Honor," Yuni addressed the judge, "I refuse to answer the questions."

"Do you understand the possible consequences of failing and refusal to answer Mr. Vinson's questions, now that I have ordered you to?"

"Yes, ma'am."

Vinson asked the judge to rule that Yuni Medellin violated a direct court order by his refusal to answer any questions and that he should be found in contempt.

Yuni's attorney, Pena-Garcia, claimed her client struck a deal with another district attorney that in exchange for testifying before the grand jury against the other four defendants, he would not have to testify against his brother.

"Not only did we not make such a deal," countered Vinson, "the record of his testimony before the grand jury reflects he did testify before that body against this defendant, Joe Medellin."

"The court has heard nothing that speaks to an agreement," Judge Cosper ruled, "concerning not testifying in the criminal courts against [his brother]. As a result, the court finds that you, Venancio Medellin, are guilty of misbehavior in the immediate view and presence of this court."

The judge fined Yuni Medellin $500 and added six months' jail time to his sentence as punishment.

After Yuni Medellin's testimony, Pena-Garcia spoke about her client's refusal to testify against his own brother. "They can't force words out of anyone's mouth, but the judge can say you have no Fifth Amendment right," Pena-Garcia explained. The judge could hold Pena-Garcia's client in contempt, but "What is contempt when you are already serving forty years in TYC?"

After the first day of testimony ended, Andy Kahan again spoke on behalf of the families. He let the press know that the courtroom-hopping was difficult for the families, "and it's hard for them not to be with each other" through each trial.

Kahan also alluded to the earlier complaint about the number of death row cases being tried in Harris County at the same time. After hearing the medical examiner describe how Elizabeth Pena's head was almost decapitated, Kahan declared, "They committed offenses that are worthy of death penalty punishment."

Tuesday, September 13, 1994—9:00 A.M.
Harris County Courthouse Annex—courtroom 5
262nd District Court
Preston Street
Houston, Texas

The following morning, Raul Villarreal was brought into the courtroom of Judge Doug Shaver. It was similar in its makeup to Judge Guerrero's courtroom, where Efrain Perez was being tried. The main difference was that the defense team for Villarreal had their table set up parallel to the gallery and placed directly in front of Judge Shaver's perch, and the jury was located on the opposite side of the defense table and to the judge's left.

Villarreal came into the room looking extremely well-kempt. His previous long-haired mullet was gone. The hair on the sides of his temples was shorn and stylishly long on the top of his head. He was dressed in a blue suit with a white oxford and blue tie. He sat down at the far end of the defense table in the direct line of sight of the jury.

All three trials were now running simultaneously. The courtroom coordinators had one day under their belts and felt more confident about the logistics—despite having the additional trial to contend with. The families were all evenly dispersed throughout the various courtrooms. Each courtroom was packed with spectators, and the victims' rights advocates were there to shield the victims' families and to handle the press.

Most of the trial witnesses who passed through the doors of the Medellin and Perez trials from the previous day were now testifying in the Villarreal case. As with the other two defendants, the prosecution read Villarreal's confession, which attempted to exonerate himself.

After the day's testimony ended, Andy Kahan spoke about the defendants' confessions. He said they were "textbook-style confessions where they absolve themselves and claim they were just hanging around and not doing anything. All of the others were the ones who were sexually assaulting and murdering the girls." Kahan sneered as he added, "Then you go into the other trials and you hear the reverse from the other defendants."

Thankfully, the trials ran smoothly and there were no

major disruptions in any of the courtrooms or inside the courthouse.

That was about to change.

After only a few days of testimony in each trial, everyone was just about ready to wrap up their cases. Attorneys in the Perez and Villarreal courtrooms were prepared to give closing arguments, while the Medellin trial looked as if it would probably go on for one more day.

In Judge Shaver's courtroom, an unwelcome guest made his way inside. Jimmy Dunne, an advocate from the Texas Coalition to Abolish the Death Penalty, was somehow allowed into the courtroom with a box of flyers promoting an anti–death penalty rally the following day. When word got out that Dunne was passing around flyers to members of the gallery, he was quietly escorted from Judge Shaver's courtroom.

Once out in the hallway, the local television crews pounced on Dunne to find out what he was up to. "We don't believe the state should be trying to execute boys that commit their crimes under the age of eighteen, for one thing," Dunne declared. "This is like an assembly-line death machine down here."

Andy Kahan got wind of Dunne's misplaced civil disobedience. "I am just incensed that they would have the chutzpah to do something like that," Kahan castigated Dunne and the two or three supporters he had in tow. "It is just unbelievable that they can come up here and do that and cause these families more pain and misery. This is the wrong place for him to be picking his fights for this type of issue."

Kahan returned to the courtroom to hear closing arguments. The judge sent the jury members off to deliberate the fate of Raul Villarreal. In Judge Guerrero's court-room, he did the same thing with the jury members for Efrain Perez.

Less than three hours later, the jury members for the Villarreal case returned with a verdict. Even though Villarreal's trial was the last of the final three to start, it was the first one completed. Just like with Sean O'Brien and Peter Cantu, the jury wasted little time in reaching a guilty verdict. Villarreal showed absolutely no emotion as the verdict was read.

One hour later, the jury returned on behalf of the trial for Efrain Perez. The end result was the same: guilty.

Unlike Villarreal, Perez openly sobbed in court at the reading of the verdict. He bowed his head down in his hand and laid it on the defense table. The tears flowed down his face and he had one lone droplet trickle to the end of his nose, and the tear hung there the entire time.

Adolph was rather disgusted by the display of tears from Perez.

"That damn Perez. He was always wanting to cry. I said, 'Bite the bullet, you piece of shit. You're up there. You killed someone. You gonna have to be tougher than that.'"

Adolph began to mock Perez's sobbing. "Just shut the you-know-what up and take it like a man.

"Now, if you are a tough guy and you can go out there and kill somebody, then you better stand up there like you got a pair. Man up, dude."

The families also had tears in their eyes as they left the courtroom. They had kept their emotions under wraps during the two trials—unlike the Cantu trial.

Unfortunately for them, the ordeal was not quite over. Joe Medellin still had to go through closing arguments, and deliberations would not take place until the next day.

"Two down, one to go," Andy Kahan summarized the

day. "Three more death sentences on the way, shortly." He added, "Hopefully."

But even before that last stressful situation, the families found unrest outside the courtroom. A handful of anti–death penalty protestors lined the sidewalks outside the courthouse holding placards and yelling at the victims' families as they walked out of the courthouse.

The Penas and Ertmans kept their distance. Randy Ertman's friend Bob Carreiro, however, decided to take a closer look. The gray-haired ponytailed father of a murdered daughter walked directly up to the loudest protestor, a gray-haired woman in her mid-to-late fifties, who literally had spit dripping off her lips as she hollered invectives.

"Don't kill for me!" she chanted. "Don't kill for me!"

The woman was armed with two signs—one that repeated DON'T KILL FOR ME! while the other was a juvenile drawing of a bloody knife, a gun, and a bullet, with splashes of blood across the canvas. It said DON'T EXECUTE—DEATH IS NO WAY TO TEACH SOMEBODY A LESSON!!! GET THE PICTURE!

The protestor brandished her placards and yelled at Carreiro that what was happening inside the courthouse was a travesty. He just stood inches away listening and not letting her get under his skin.

Several minutes later, on another portion of the sidewalk, Jimmy Dunne, the man tossed out of the Perez trial for distributing anti–death penalty flyers in the courtroom, was surrounded by an angry mob of at least fifteen to twenty people, most of them family members of the girls. Bob Carreiro made his way over to Dunne as well and stood directly in front of him. Elizabeth's aunt Patti Zapalac stood behind and to the left of Carreiro, and just to the right in front of Dunne.

"We're for the maximum," Dunne stated rather hesitantly, knowing he faced the toughest crowd possible.

Nonetheless, he forged on, some would say rather foolishly. "We like the way the law is now, where it has a forty-year minimum sentence for anybody that—"

"How many years does my niece have?" screamed Zapalac in Dunne's face. She thrust the index finger on her left hand in Dunne's direction. The protestor seemed visibly shaken. There was no doubt Zapalac was shaken. "She turned sixteen three days before they brutally murdered her. You tell me, how many years does she have left?"

Dunne continued to talk, oblivious to the pain he was causing the throng gathered around him. Eventually he was encouraged to remove himself from the family members without incident.

The following morning, Joe Medellin's defense team and the prosecution presented their final arguments. Judge Cosper sent the jury on its way to deliberate the young man's fate.

Several people in the gallery decided to leave the courtroom to stretch their legs, grab a cigarette, and to simply mill about.

Only thirteen minutes later, they would all come rushing back into the courthouse. The jury had already made its decision. Like all the other defendants, Joe Medellin was found guilty. He showed no emotion throughout the reading of the verdict, just as he had shown no emotion throughout his entire trial.

Outside the courtroom in the packed hallway, Andy Kahan spoke with the press about the decision and the expediency with which the jury returned a guilty verdict. "I think that probably startled everybody, but that shows how strong the case was against the defendant. That shows that we have jurors in Harris County that believe in swift and extreme justice."

Unfortunately, the families of the girls were not able to relax and contemplate what a fifth jury had just done on behalf of their daughters. Instead, the Penas and Ertmans once again walked outside into the sunshine, only to be berated by a small group of anti–death penalty protestors.

The most insistent person was a man, slightly younger than the two fathers, by the name of Ronald Carlson. His sister, Deborah Thornton, was brutally murdered with a pickax several years earlier by Karla Faye Tucker.

Carlson was there to spread the word that he did not believe in executions. Apparently, he was a little too vocal for Randy Ertman and Adolph Pena. Having had enough of his demonstration, the two fathers hooked themselves together, arm in arm, and were joined by Bob Carreiro. Together, the three men turned their backs away from Carlson and moved slowly back toward him until they literally had him pinned up against the redbrick wall of the Harris County Courthouse building. They were not being forceful or violent. They had merely created a human barrier against Carlson, who was unable to escape.

Carlson was determined, though. "Killing anybody ain't gonna bring your daughter back, sir," Carlson said to the three fathers. "It ain't gonna bring my sister back."

The three fathers kept their composure and chose to ignore Carlson. Eventually he slithered out from behind the impromptu grieving-father prison and joined up with Jimmy Dunne.

In a scene reminiscent to the one from the day before, Dunne was again surrounded by nearly two dozen grieving family members who lost loved ones to killers. Dunne, dressed in a white sweatshirt with DON'T KILL FOR ME printed on the front, stood before Bob Carreiro, who once again moved over to the scene of the fracas.

"All I know is that we are against the death penalty in

all cases," Dunne barked out at the hostile crowd. "We don't think it helps things." The murmurs of the family members and pro–death penalty supporters began to rise. They were tolerating Dunne's speech, but their patience was being tested.

"It makes things worse," Dunne continued as he placed his left hand on Carreiro's right shoulder. "It continues a cycle of violence." Carreiro showed great restraint as Dunne condescendingly addressed the crowd.

Suddenly the mood changed.

Dunne prattled on. "If my daughter was murdered," he said to Carreiro, "I'd feel the same way."

A roar from the crowd rose above the din. They were no longer willing to tolerate this man's insensitivity.

"*If* your daughter were murdered?" one woman asked incredulously.

Finally the composed Bob Carreiro began to lash out at Dunne. He stepped closer to the much taller Dunne and put the fear of God into the man with a stare that spoke volumes. "You! Don't! Know!" Carreiro snapped back at him. "Why don't you go back to where you came from, because you don't know!" He was joined by a chorus of yelling and screaming.

Once again, however, the assembly was broken up without any physical incidents—though no one would have blamed Carreiro had he taken out his frustrations on Dunne. Many, in fact, would have applauded such behavior.

"My wife would sit in one, I'd sit in another," Adolph Pena recalled of the triple trials. "My sister-in-law Patti Zapalac would sit in one, and my brother, Carlos, and his wife would sit in one. My cousin Joe, the guy with the dark sunglasses. He would sit in one." In other words, there was a Pena family representative in each courtroom during the three simultaneous trials. Adolph was also grateful for the people who ran interference for his family.

Andy Kahan was arm in arm with the Penas and the Ertmans. He was there to make sure they were able to get to the separate courtrooms and had someone in each trial at all times. He also ran interference between the families and the media. Any question directed to the families was redirected to Kahan. Not once did they have to stand in front of the hot klieg lights and cameras with microphones shoved in their faces to answer questions about the murders of their daughters or the "how they felt?" level of questions, which are normally associated with local television news reporting.

Pam Lychner, from the crime victims' advocate group Justice for All, also helped the families out with the coordination of the chaos in the courtrooms. She would come early each day, gather the families of the victims together, and inform them of the day's activities in the court. She presented an additional calm face for the families and helped Kahan with keeping the media away from them.

Every member of the girls' families considered Kahan and Lychner to be invaluable resources. They allowed the families the opportunity to sit and watch the trials in peace.

As far as the crimes that the three defendants committed before they killed Elizabeth and Jennifer, Adolph was not surprised in the least. "It was just the norm for those guys, because they were the most evil thing I ever thought would be on the face of this earth. I wouldn't put nothing past them."

Omar and Louisa Villarreal testified on behalf of their son, Raul. For Adolph, these were moments of sheer "frustration. You didn't want to share the air that they were breathing. Your son is just as evil as the other ones. Why would you try to find any innocence in this guy who just killed innocent little girls?"

Thursday, September 22, 1994
Harris County Courthouse Annex
Preston Street
Houston, Texas

Joe Medellin, Efrain Perez, and Raul Villarreal—all three went through the punishment phase. They had some people testify on their behalf, but the majority of witnesses were against them. So were the juries.

All three young men were sentenced to death.

It only took the jury ten minutes to deliberate Perez's fate.

Chapter 41

Tuesday, October 11, 1994
Harris County Courthouse
177th District Court
Houston, Texas

Nearly three weeks later, all three defendants—Joe Medellin, Efrain Perez, and Raul Villarreal—were shackled together and escorted to the courthouse. The judges agreed to wait such a long period of time so tempers would lessen.

Instead of wearing their Sunday finest, as they had throughout their respective trials, the three defendants were now dressed in Harris County–issued orange jumpsuits. They took their places around a long rectangular table right next to the gallery and several feet below the elevated riser where the judges hovered overhead.

The three judges—Caprice Cosper, Ruben Guerrero, and Doug Shaver—gathered together at the head of the giant makeshift judge's bench. The purpose of the gathering was to read out the sentences that had been handed down to the boys.

The standing-room-only crowd in one of the largest

courtrooms in the county listened intently as each judge read off each sentence for each defendant.

Three death sentences.

After all three death punishments were handed down, the judges turned to the families of the girls. Once again, they would be allowed their Victim Impact Statements. Many in the much larger auditorium-sized courtroom were nervous. They remembered how Randy Ertman blew up and seemingly wanted to strangle Peter Cantu back in February during the first-ever Victim Impact Statement in Texas. This time, however, he kept his cool.

Randy stood up behind the wooden railing that separated him and the three defendants by less than ten feet. This time, he was joined by his wife, Sandra, who placed a reassuring hand on his lower back. Randy pulled out a piece of paper, unfolded it, and began to speak.

"Thank you, Your Honor, for allowing me to speak. I appreciate it, sir." Randy addressed the defendants. "You have no excuse and you have no remorse. Ever. In sixteen months, I have never seen any of you show any remorse whatsoever. You're worse than spit!"

At that point, one of Joe Medellin's attorneys stood up to object.

Joe Medellin looked bored. He never once looked toward Randy Ertman and he never smiled, grimaced, or cared.

"I hope you rot in hell. I honest to God mean that, sir," Randy closed. He remained calm throughout the entire ordeal.

Unlike in the Cantu trial, this time around, Adolph Pena was allowed to give a statement as well.

Adolph remembered, "They had three of those sons of bitches in one court and they wouldn't let us say anything to them directly. They brought us all in there together and we could address the court then, but not the defendants. So I thought I would write something down. Well, by the time I got in there, I just decided I was going to say something from the heart. Then I started addressing the individual, I don't remember who, and the court immediately stopped me. They told me I could give the impact statement, but that I couldn't address them."

Adolph spoke passionately about how the three boys not only murdered his daughter, but also his two other children, his wife, and himself.

"The way they are going to be executed," Adolph lamented, "is not fair to us. It's gonna be real simple for them to get a needle in their arm. Just lie there and die.

"I wish these guys would get executed the way my daughter did. And just be left there on the ground to die." He started getting angry.

"And they don't even have the nerve to look at me when I'm talking to you," he addressed the three defendants directly. "Yeah! I'm talking about you!" he said as he pointed at Perez, "and you!" at Medellin, "and you!" to Villarreal.

"You didn't even know these girls," he yelled at the defendants. This time, it was one of Villarreal's defense attorneys who stood up to object.

After the statements were completed, the judges informed the defendants they were to be removed to holding before being transferred to prison. Joe Medellin was the first person at the defense table to jump out of his seat and head for the exit. He could not get out of there soon enough.

The families of Elizabeth and Jennifer were relieved. All five murderers had received the death penalty. The trials were finally over and they could resume grieving for their daughters. They all stepped out of the courtroom and into the hallway to make their way outside.

Like proverbial sardines in a can, the hallway was packed with courtroom spectators, reporters, cameramen, victims' rights advocates, family members and friends of the girls, and some family members of the convicted defendants.

A member of the media who spoke Spanish walked up to Adolph and whispered in his ear, "Perez's dad just said that it was your fault that the girls were killed."

Adolph looked at the reporter and said, "You guys are just looking for a story." Adolph seemed as if he would not take the bait, but the tempers were flaring after the impact statements in the courtroom.

"I'm not making it up, Mr. Pena. He really said that."

"Where's that son of a bitch at?" Adolph sternly asked the reporter.

The reporter dutifully pointed out a man who was actually Efrain Perez's stepfather, Ismael Castillo.

Adolph looked back at the reporter and said, "You're going to get your story, right now!" He thrust his way through the overcrowded hallway in Castillo's direction. Television cameras whipped around in a frenzy toward the maelstrom. Lights flashed on, like someone just restored the power during a blackout.

Once Adolph spotted the man, he glared at him and inched his way toward him.

"*Es culpa tuya!*" Castillo yelled at Adolph, which means, "It's your fault!"

Adolph was livid. He went ballistic and charged after the smaller man. The cameras were trained on the two fathers, waiting for fists to fly and spit to spew.

"How in the hell do you figure it's my fault that *your* son killed *my* daughter?" Adolph screamed at Castillo as someone amidst the throng held him back by his jacket. "She didn't do nothing to him. What makes you think you have the right to tell me it's *my* fault?"

Castillo responded by thrusting a finger in Adolph's

face and repeating it was his fault for not raising his daughter properly. A middle-aged woman wearing a bright red dress, who was a member of the Perez family, grabbed Castillo's finger as he defiantly thrust it toward Pena. She was trying to scoot Castillo away from the conversation.

The very short Castillo, however, who apparently suffered from an overdose of Napoleonic machismo, kept at it. He began cursing in Spanish at Adolph.

Adolph responded by simply telling him, "That's your son!"

Castillo seemed even more enraged.

At that point, Randy Ertman had heard enough. The 245-pound grieving father maintained his composure throughout the triple trials, and even during the Victim Impact Statement. He had finally had enough.

Randy charged through the crowd, past Adolph, in Castillo's direction. Castillo looked like a deer caught in headlights, scared out of his wits. Once he saw several of Randy's friends and family members were restraining the angry father, however, he got up his nerve and started cussing and wagging his finger at Randy.

The throng turned into a melee that looked like a rugby scrum, with bodies pushing and people screaming at each other.

Adolph scooted in front of Randy and placed his hand on the bigger man's chest to push him away from Castillo. "C'mon, Randy. Don't listen to the guy," Adolph begged his friend. Randy backed up, all the while glaring at Perez's stepfather.

Castillo kept screaming and the small woman in red continued to try to get him out of the way. Another woman, holding a toddler less than ten inches away from Castillo, tried to move, but he continued cursing and taunting Randy, regardless of the safety of the child. Cameramen swarmed in on Randy, trying once more to snap a "furious dad" photo they so relished from the Cantu trial.

Patti Zapalac placed herself directly in the line of fire. She wedged herself in between Randy and the cameramen. She began screaming at the cameramen just as much as she was screaming at Castillo: "Get out of here! Get out of here! Leave them alone!" At that point, she grabbed one of the media member's cameras and shoved it out of the way. Suddenly several cops swooped in and bulldogged the cameraman through the crowd and up against the wall.

At the same time, several of Perez's entourage finally snatched Castillo by the shirt and dragged him away from the fracas.

Adolph recalled, "Somebody grabbed his ass and drug him out of there. I remember it was a Hispanic guy, because he knew exactly what he said to me." He added, "The only reason he said it in Spanish is because about eighty-five percent of the people there were white and they wouldn't have known what he was saying."

When asked if Castillo's reaction was unintentional, Adolph knew better. "He knew exactly who I was and he said it just loud enough so that I could hear it. And it was his stepdad, of all people."

Once the feuding families were separated, the police attempted to restore order in the courthouse. "Court is still going on here," a young police officer pleaded. "So lower your voices, please."

Andy Kahan surmised that Castillo's actions were revealing. "Efrain Perez is where he is today because of parents who don't hold him accountable for his actions. And that was certainly proved here today."

Sandra Ertman later commented on the fury that she witnessed in her husband at Castillo's insensitivity. "I saw the rage come out in him," she stated.

"In life and in death, he will protect Jen."

Unfortunately, the outrage would not end anytime soon. Immediately after Perez's stepfather was escorted out of the building, Perez's defense attorney, Ricardo Rodriguez, stepped into the hallway. The attorney, with his overgrown Snidely Whiplash handlebar mustache, enjoyed being in front of the cameras. Beside him stood Andy Kahan.

When asked what he thought about his client's stepfather's statement, Rodriguez opined, "I know that they're upset and they have every right to be upset, but I'll say this—and you may not like it—but the parents bear some responsibility, too." The lawyer started to walk away.

Kahan and the reporters standing around Rodriguez were stunned.

A reporter shouted out, "Whose parents?"

Rodriguez returned to the cameras and microphones to clarify: "The parents of the victims." Then he darted off.

Andy Kahan was stunned by Rodriguez's comment. "I'll never forget because I was standing right there by him. I said, 'What?'

"The reporter went, 'Did you just hear what he just said?'"

Rodriguez immediately turned tail, but he would not be alone for long. Kahan took off after the defense attorney. "I ended up chasing him. We ended up in a foot chase into another courtroom. I think he realized that *Oops! I said something I shouldn't have said,* and I started running after him down the hallway, and he ran into a courtroom and ran all the way into the back room. That's the first time I've ever run after anybody in the courthouse."

Kahan continued on, "Of course, the media reported it, and the next day, we all had a protest at Rodriguez's office. Pam Lychner and I were out there demanding an apology. He finally ended up saying that he'd only meet with the families."

There were at least fifty protestors outside Rodriguez's office expressing their displeasure with the mustachioed one.

"That son of a bitch, what did my wife call him? One day, she went up to the courthouse and she got into the elevator with that son of a bitch, and he knew exactly who she was and just liked freaked out when he saw her. Melissa doesn't say much or yell too much at anybody, but it just so happened that this guy pushed the right button and she got off all over his ass for saying what he said about us and our daughter," Adolph Pena remarked.

"Years later, we get in that same damn elevator in that courthouse and he sees Melissa again. You know what he did? He starts pushing buttons so he can get the hell out of there on the next floor, once he saw Melissa get on there.

"She said, 'You chickenshit son of a bitch!' to him.

"My wife won't get pissed too much, but he said just the right thing to set her off and she got pissed that day. That's for sure."

Adolph added, "I still see that little son of a bitch downtown. He's got that long handlebar mustache. Probably four or five or six years ago, I seen him down there. He's got his little briefcase.

"I was driving my car and I saw him. I rolled down my window, honked my horn at him. He looks over at me and I go"—Adolph slowly lifted his middle finger—"I said, 'Fuck you!' He takes off and runs inside. I know he knew who I was." Adolph laughed.

Adolph Pena recalled the day after the death penalty sentences came down. "I opened up the *Houston Chronicle* and it said something like FIVE DEATH SENTENCES, in big bold letters on the front page." Adolph marveled at the headline; however, he had a bad feeling. "I said, 'You know what? This is too good to be true. I won't believe it until I see it.'"

Adolph spoke to the media about his doubts as to whether or not all five death sentences would be upheld. "It's all fine and dandy that you've got these five death sentences and all, but until I see it, I won't believe it."

Adolph added, "I wanted to accept it that every one of them was going to die someday, and then everybody would be just fine, but I just knew that it was too good to be true. Every day, the judicial system can change from one minute to the next. From one judge to the next. It'd be nice, but I don't think it's going to happen."

Adolph's prophetic abilities would be seriously tested.

Chapter 42

Later that evening, Randy Ertman and Andy Kahan appeared before the monthly meeting of the Houston chapter for the Parents of Murdered Children. Kahan spoke to the group and informed them of his next fight—to make sure family members of victims have the option of witnessing their loved ones' killer's execution.

According to Kahan, at that time, only the state of Louisiana allowed the families of victims the opportunity to view an execution.

"I plan on Texas being the second state to allow this," he informed the crowd.

After the meeting, Randy spoke of his desire to see all five killers' executions. "It will please me," he stated very clearly. "I'm not a morbid person. I know it won't bring my daughter back, but I think it's just plain justice."

Randy added, "We have the right, as victims, to watch that . . . ," he paused, rolling his eyes, and continued, "individual who murdered our children, we have the right to watch him die."

"When Randy asked me that question in the hallway after the Cantu trial," Kahan recalled, "he said, 'I'd really like to be there when they execute these guys. Can I do that?' Now, trust me, if you know Randy, you know he didn't say it so politely.

"I said, 'That's a good question. I don't know.' I found out that victims' families were specifically prohibited as a part of policy." On the other hand, defendants were allowed to have up to five family members present in the death chamber with them.

"So that's when we got the bill sponsored. Did some research on who had been witnessing executions. Did all that background research. That's how we got the bill sponsored just from that one question. One question in the hallway."

Getting the bill passed, however, was not so easy.

The following year, Kahan, the Ertmans, and Melissa Pena all traveled to Austin to appear in front of the Criminal Justice Committee. Randy Ertman informed the committee he wanted to view the executions of the young men who killed his daughter. In no time, the committee agreed and said no problem, consider it done.

Everything was smooth sailing. But, eventually, another obstacle reared its ugly head. Texas politics at the most ridiculous level entered the fray. According to Kahan, "All of a sudden, you've got personalities to play into it, and next thing I know, they're shitcanning it and buried it so we didn't even get a full vote. All because Mark Stiles, the chairman of the Calendar's Committee, was feuding with John Culberson, who was the cosponsor of the bill."

Kahan was flabbergasted at the behind-the-scenes

machinations that led to the premature burial of the bill. "No one testified against it, it was smooth. It was the smoothest thing I ever did, until I got that phone call from (House sponsor) Kevin Bailey's office. He said, 'We've got a problem.'

"I said, 'What problem?'"

"Mark Stiles," Bailey informed Kahan, "is in a feud with a cosponsor of the bill, and unless he removes his name from that bill, he's going to bury it."

"You've got to be kidding me," Kahan replied exasperatedly.

Sure enough, according to Kahan, "the issue never came up for a vote, and it died. Time ran out. Stiles stuck it on the bottom of the calendar and it disappeared.

"So I called the chairman of the Board of Criminal Justice, Alan Polunsky, and asked him what we could do. I reminded him that no one was against it, the Texas Department of Corrections said we could do it.

"If we can't get the law changed, how about if we change the policy?" Kahan asked.

In September 1995, the Penas, the Ertmans, and Kahan all traveled together to the coastal town of Corpus Christi, Texas. Polunsky told Kahan there was a board meeting coming up and he would call him back. "He called me back," Kahan remembered, "and said we are going to put you guys on the agenda. And he did."

Kahan added, "He put us on the agenda to testify in front of the Board of Criminal Justice. We all drove down there. Testified as to why we thought it was important. They all listened to us. There were some other families that came down, too. And next thing you know, they voted unanimously to change the dang policy."

There has never been a problem with the policy

since. "Seventy-five percent of families have witnessed the executions. And all we wanted to do was to give them the option as to whether they wanted to be there or not. I was shocked how many people would watch. Which tells me we did a good thing."

Chapter 43

Three years after the murders, the first of several appeals came across the transom. Efrain Perez's appeal was denied.

Yuni Medellin was eventually transferred from a youth facility to an adult prison. The judge cited the heinous nature of the murders and opted to make Yuni serve out his entire forty-year sentence. The hearing went by very quickly. The judge read the sentence, informed Yuni that he would be transferred to an adult prison, and banged his gavel. It was over almost as soon as it had begun.

According to Adolph Pena, the judge said, "'Put the cuffs back on and send him back to the big house. You got sentenced to forty years—you're going to serve forty years.'"

Adolph simply said, "Hallelujah! See ya later. Now you got to go up there with the big boys. You ain't gonna go to no little penitentiary."

According to Andy Kahan, Yuni Medellin has been up

for parole twice since he was sent to an adult prison; he has been denied both times.

The second appeal was heard—this time for Raul Villarreal. The end result was the same: verdict upheld.

The third appeal was heard—this time for Sean O'Brien. The end result was the same: verdict upheld.

The fourth appeal was heard—this time for Peter Cantu. The end result was the same: verdict upheld.

The fifth appeal was heard—this time for Joe Medellin. The end result was the same: verdict upheld.

Chapter 44

Five years after the murder of their only child, Randy and Sandy Ertman decided they had had enough of Houston. Everywhere they looked, they faced painful reminders of their lovely daughter, Jennifer. Whether it was the stuffed animals hanging in a hammock in her untouched bedroom, or if they saw a blond teenager wearing jewelry and shopping at the nearby mall, they could not escape the pain.

Randy had given up on his days as a crime victims' advocate. The pain that others experienced cut quickly and deeply every time he experienced it with them. It became too much to bear. He admitted he turned to alcohol to ease his pain. His consumption level increased each year he was removed from the loss of his daughter. He admitted to drinking nearly twenty-four beers a day.

The Ertmans had to do something about it.

They packed their bags, including all of Jennifer's belongings, and moved to a tiny little town near Lake Somerville, called Lyons, Texas. They bought a quaint cabin near the lake and kept to themselves.

It was the start of a positive recovery for the couple.

* * *

Wednesday, June 24, 1998
T. C. Jester Park
T. C. Jester Boulevard and West Thirty-fourth Street
Houston, Texas

Adolph and Melissa Pena gathered some of their clos-est friends and family members together at the memo-rial benches for the girls. Several of the girls' friends from high school, most of them now in college or off in the working world, made sure to stop by to support the Penas.

It was a joyous and solemn ceremony. People tried to focus on the positive aspects of the girls' short lives. It was not easy knowing their final resting place was a mere two hundred feet away on the other side of White Oak Bayou.

To honor the girls' memories, Melissa and Adolph re-leased a large batch of pink and white balloons to sym-bolize innocence and purity, and to acknowledge that we cannot always hold on to those qualities for our dearest loved ones, no matter how hard we try.

Chapter 45

As the years passed, and the families waited for execution dates to be set for the convicted killers, strange little tremors erupted here and there to remind everyone about the case.

Six years after the murders, Efrain Perez stabbed a guard while inside his prison cell. Luckily, the guard survived.

One year later, Don Davis, defense attorney for Peter Cantu, committed suicide. Some of his associates believed it was because his first batch of death row clients had recently been executed and it hit him hard. In addition, he recently had two legal complaints filed against him with the Texas Bar, and he was potentially on the verge of facing disciplinary action.

Davis was discovered dead in his bathroom from a single gunshot to the abdomen.

More tragedy occurred that same year. One of Jennifer Ertman's best friends, Annie Caballero, and her three-year-old daughter were killed in a fire in their Heights-area home, not far from where Jennifer lived.

Annie's daughter was named Jennifer, after her mother's slain friend.

Chapter 46

In the summer of 2003, more than ten years after Elizabeth Pena and Jennifer Ertman were murdered, a judge finally set an execution date for one of the five killers on death row. Judge Mike Anderson scheduled Raul Villarreal's execution for June 24, 2004, the eleventh anniversary of the girls' murders.

Judge Anderson informed Villarreal that he wanted him to dread that day as much as the Penas and the Ertmans had to for the past ten years.

The following day, Judge Jim Wallace set an execution date for Efrain Perez for June 23, 2004, the day before the anniversary. Judge Wallace wanted to make it more convenient for the Penas and Ertmans so they could witness both executions without having to deal with all the attendant hassles.

Chapter 47

During January 2004, the United States Supreme Court agreed to review the case of *Roper* v. *Simmons,* in which Christopher Simmons, who planned and executed a murder when he was seventeen, was given a death sentence when he turned eighteen. The case would be argued before the Supreme Court in October 2004. If the Supreme Court decided that executing a minor would violate that defendant's constitutional rights, several cases, including Raul Villarreal's and Efrain Perez's, could be adversely affected.

The Pena and Ertman families were devastated when they heard the news. They had waited so long for the executions to come, and the first two convicts up to bat—Villarreal and Perez—were both seventeen at the time of the murders.

When October finally arrived, the Penas traveled to Washington, D.C., to attend the Supreme Court hearings for Perez and Villarreal. Texas attorney general Greg Abbott made sure the Penas received passes so they could attend the hearings. They were accompanied by their youngest daughter, Rachael, and also Dianne

Clements, from the crime victims' advocacy group Justice for All.

The Ertmans were unable to make the trip.

"I was scared to death of going inside the Supreme Court," Pena recalled. "I was scared to death, but mostly I was scared that they were going to be against me. That was my fear."

Adolph's fears were not without merit.

Several months later, in March 2005, the Supreme Court ruled against them, by the slimmest of margins, 5–4, and in favor of murderers who were aged seventeen at the time they committed their murders.

Adolph stated he was sick and tired of hearing the arguments as to why minors should not be executed. "It's that part of the brain that's not developed. They didn't really know what they were doing because they were too young. How many times did we go through that shit? Yeah, a seventeen-year-old's mind is not completely developed, so there is no way he knew what he was doing when he was murdering these girls. A six-year-old knows not to kill somebody! C'mon, give me a break."

In addition to taking two of the murderers of Elizabeth Pena and Jennifer Ertman off death row, the Supreme Court also allowed another famous Texas death row inmate to escape the needle. Robert Burns Springsteen IV, one of two teenagers convicted in the 1991 Austin, Texas, yogurt shop murders, was only seventeen at the time of the massacre. He, too, was released from death row. (See Corey Mitchell's *Murdered Innocents*, Kensington/Pinnacle 2005, for more history.)

Adolph spoke about the decision made by the Supreme Court. "You talk about being pissed," the angry father spat out. "I said, 'Here we go again.' Would have been nice to take them back the day after they got their sentences and executed all five of them right there. Back in the day, they used to hang them from the oak tree in front of the courthouse.

"I was just outraged," Adolph recalled. "I had my three-hundred-dollar suit on. I need some freakin' cameras. I'm ready to say something." Adolph, who had been the less vocal of the two fathers during the trials back in 1994, was finally coming out of his shell. He was furious at the Supreme Court's decision and wanted everyone in the country to know how he felt.

Apparently, the media were interviewing a few people before him, and one television crew member told Adolph in a snotty tone, "You're just going to have to wait, Mr. Pena."

"I was about to bust a vein. I was gonna be last and I was gonna let them have it."

He did.

Adolph ripped into the United States Supreme Court for siding with the killers, not only of his and Randy's daughters, but also of the sons and daughters of hundreds more affected by the ruling.

"It must have made an impact"—Adolph shrugged—"because I received more phone calls about the case after that interview than anything I had ever done before. People were calling me up and complimenting me for going after the Supreme Court. They said, 'You kicked some ass!'"

In the end, it did not matter. "Them sons of bitches," Adolph said, referring to the members of the Supreme Court, "they just pissed me off.

"I'm just this little bitty guy who grew up in San Antonio and I'm up against the Supreme Court of the United States. Going up there to raise some damn hell. Somebody's going to hear what I've got to say."

* * *

After the letdown from America's highest court, the Penas did not see how things could get any worse.

They did. Quickly.

That same month, Joe Medellin, now using his given name of "Jose," claimed that since he was born in Mexico, he should have been considered a Mexican national at the time of his arrest. Because of this, he should have been afforded the opportunity to contact the Mexican consulate, which could have been by his side and prevented him from confessing to the police.

Miraculously, the United States Supreme Court agreed to hear his case as well, along with fifty other Mexican nationals on death row.

That November, the Penas dutifully traveled back to Washington, D.C., to sit in on the Supreme Court. Powerful, broad-ranging arguments about international intercession, American rights in foreign countries, and more were raised.

Afterward, Adolph was determined to have his voice heard on behalf of his murdered daughter, Elizabeth. There was a large Mexican news contingent present for the Medellin hearings.

"I had to bone up on my Spanish that day." Adolph laughed. "Those [guys] were from Mexico, and the Mexican people wanted to hear what I had to say about the Supreme Court's decision to hear these cases. They speak the good Spanish. I polished up my teeth and spoke in Spanish."

Afterward, the reporters told him that he did a good job and they wished him luck and hoped things would work out for him.

Two months later, the Supreme Court dismissed the case and said they never should have taken it in the first place. In addition, the Fifth Circuit Court of Appeals decision that Medellin did not assert his treaty-based claim on time was upheld.

Joe Medellin would get his execution date after all.

Any chance for celebration for the families of the victims was short-lived, however—thanks to President George W. Bush. The former governor of Texas intervened in the Joe Medellin case and ordered the state of Texas (and several additional states) to hold hearings for the fifty-one Mexican nationals imprisoned for the death penalty, which included Jose Medellin.

One week later, Condoleezza Rice informed the international community that the United States would be withdrawing from the section of the Vienna Convention on Consular Relations that allows consular access to occur. The international community was up in arms at the latest nose-thumbing by the president.

Echoing Natalie Maines, of the Dixie Chicks, Adolph Pena said of Bush, "I'm just ashamed that son of a bitch is from Texas. I am really ashamed that that boy is from Texas." Adolph added, "My wife said that if something happened to one of his kids, he wouldn't go through this shit. If somebody was to murder one of his daughters, I bet you he wouldn't think the same way. Until it hits you right there. Until you actually are the one who got damaged from the killings, you have no earthly idea what it does to not only an individual, but to a whole family and a whole lifestyle. You don't have any idea."

Adolph was incensed by the angle Medellin was using, claiming he was a Mexican national, even though he spent as much time in the United States as he had in Mexico. "If that son of a bitch doesn't like our laws over here, he shouldn't have crossed the border. They want to kill people and get away with it and send them back over there because they don't have a death penalty. If you don't like our laws, don't come to our country. That's the bottom line."

Andy Kahan added, "What's so oxymoronic to me is that Bush, who presided over the state with the largest amount of executions—they were always calling Bush 'the Executioner,' flip-flops all of a sudden and then does a one-eighty. That really floored me."

"It just pisses me off when I see that son of a bitch," Adolph continued on about Bush. "I voted for him the first time." He shook his head at the memory. "I didn't vote for him the second time. That son of a bitch, I can't stand to look at him because of what he is doing."

Kahan also marveled: "I don't think there has ever been a standing president that ever intervened in a death penalty case, with the exception of this." Kahan again could not believe that another ridiculous obstacle had been thrown up in this case. "It's just one thing on top of another."

Chapter 48

December 29, 2005

The families of the girls finally had something to be thankful for after so many obstacles. Sean O'Brien lost his death penalty appeal. A judge set his execution date for May 16, 2006. The first execution of one of the girls' killers would finally take place, almost thirteen years later.

Adolph and Melissa Pena, along with Randy Ertman, were already making plans to attend.

Despite being scheduled to die, O'Brien was still afforded the occasional perk. The biggest one was that he was allowed to marry a female pen pal from Finland.

Chapter 49

Sunday, May 14, 2006
Pena residence
Hockley, Texas

Two days before Sean O'Brien's scheduled execution, he received a miracle from the Texas Court of Criminal Appeals. His attorney filed a motion that claimed death by lethal injection should be considered cruel and unusual punishment. The basis for the argument was a recent scientific article that stated the painkilling drug in the lethal cocktail used to execute a prisoner wore off too quickly; as a result, the killer would feel too much pain.

The Penas and the Ertmans were flabbergasted. The roller coaster they had been on for almost thirteen years continued to give them whiplash at every turn.

Adolph Pena talked about gearing up to witness O'Brien's execution. "We were ready. We thought it was a done deal."

Originally, ABC affiliate channel 13 planned on following the Pena family around as they prepared to drive to Huntsville and view the execution of one of their daughter's killers. A sort of "Day in the Life in the Viewing of an Execution." It was sweeps month after all.

"They were going to do a feature," Adolph recalled, "that would follow us throughout the day as we prepared to go to Huntsville to view O'Brien's execution. They were going to come over here in the morning when we woke up and drank coffee.

"My wife was dreading that from day one. My brother and my sister-in-law were here. They didn't want to have nothing to do with the media. I just told them to go upstairs and watch TV while we're doing the interviews. Then we'll get ready to go and they'll get in the truck with us and head on over to Huntsville."

Adolph's sister-in-law begged off. "She started freaking out. She didn't want to have anything to do with them."

Andy Kahan was planning on heading over to the Penas for dinner. At approximately 3:00 P.M., he received another dreaded phone call. This from the county general's office telling him that the Texas Court of Criminal Appeals, by a vote of 5–4, decided they were going to take up the issue of lethal injection!

"You've got to be shitting me!" Kahan screamed into the phone. "They just made this decision two days ago on another case that a guy was just executed for, and now they want to take the issue up on *this case*!"

Once Kahan realized the decision was not a joke, he contacted Randy Ertman and Adolph Pena to break the bad news.

Adolph also received a call from Mark Garay, a reporter with channel 13 news division, who informed him he would not be coming over to shoot the piece.

Adolph was, however, interviewed by several local media outlets and he went off on the higher courts of Texas. "It wasn't the first time," he stated, unleashing on the Texas judicial system, "and it probably won't be the last time."

Soon thereafter, longtime Houston television newscaster Deborah Duncan called Adolph on the telephone.

"I'm glad you called me because I've got plenty of shit to say," Adolph informed her in a very frustrated and angry tone. She asked him to come down to her studio, which he did, along with Kahan.

Once on the air, it was the same old saw repeated over and over again. "It was just mind-boggling to me that the court would make this type of decision."

Kahan added, "We understand that the United States Supreme Court is going to take a look at this issue down the road, but why is a higher court in Texas, who already made a decision two days earlier on another case that wasn't an issue, decide that this is the case that we're going to make it an issue out of?"

Kahan later added, "This is the first time I have ever done this. I picked up the phone and I called two judges (involved in the decision). I was so livid." Kahan contacted Judge Sharon Keller, who asked Kahan if he "would please tell everybody that [she] voted against this. Will [he] make sure everybody knows that?"

When Adolph heard Judge Keller's comment, he offered, "Bless her soul."

"Not even forty-eight hours later, not even two full days, they go back and reverse their decision," Andy Kahan recalled of the court. "Again, I've never seen anything like that. And then they had to reset the date."

The new date was July 11, 2006.

Chapter 50

Tuesday, July 11, 2006—6:00 P.M.
Walls Unit
Huntsville State Prison
Huntsville, Texas

"I knew it was going to happen this time," Pena predicted. "I knew there was nobody gonna stop this thing now."

The Penas made a day trip of it. When they arrived at Huntsville, the family was immediately escorted to a private holding room. Once inside, they were asked to remain quiet.

After several minutes of waiting, they were taken, this time, to the death house, also known as the Walls Unit. The family was taken to another big, large room near the warden's office.

Adolph Pena had a quick laugh. "While we were waiting, they brought in these homemade cookies. They were made by the prisoners. They looked like something made in a gourmet shop. They call them 'Condolence Cookies.'

Something about the other prisoners are sharing their condolences to us for the loss of our loved ones. The prisoners took the time out of their day to make cookies to give to us."

Adolph was a bit hesitant to take a bite. "The prisoners made this?" he asked one of the guards. "You don't think they put something in here, did they?"

The guard smiled and replied, "No, sir. I can guarantee you that there is nothing in there but cookie ingredients."

Adolph smiled back and took a big bite of his Condolence Cookie. "Those were some damn good cookies."

The staff also provided the family members with drinks, ranging from tea to soda to water. "They just really took care of us. They treated us like royalty. I had no idea they were going to treat us like that. They weren't exceptionally nice, but they were real professional. Very, very professional."

Sandra Ertman never had a desire to witness O'Brien's execution. By the time it was finally set, and actually going to happen, even Randy Ertman started to balk at the idea.

Adolph, frankly, was surprised that Randy went. "He told me, 'Oh, I might be fishing that day.' I told him, 'I'm figuring you're gonna go to the execution, brother. Fishing's going to be there every day. The execution, you ain't gonna see one every day.' Sure enough, he went."

The victims' family representatives who made it to the viewing were Adolph and Melissa Pena, Randy Ertman, and also Sergeant Ray Zaragoza, who worked on the case.

Despite all of his work and efforts to get the policy changed, and despite all of the support he lent the Pena and Ertmans families, Andy Kahan was not allowed to view the execution since he was not a member of the families.

* * *

The process for a victim's family to be able to witness the execution of their loved one's killer is fairly simple in Texas. The Texas Department of Corrections (TDC) sends the surviving family members documentation, which requests the name of three family members who want to view the execution. They fill out the documents and mail them back to TDC and wait until execution day.

Once the surviving family members arrive at the Walls Unit in Huntsville, they are treated with dignity and the utmost respect.

At about 4:30 or 5:00 P.M., the Pena and Ertman families were released from the large building for their "debriefing." They were placed into a vehicle that shuttled them over to the Walls Unit, where the execution would actually take place. When the families of Elizabeth and Jennifer drove up to the Walls Unit, the streets were lined with other family members and friends of the girls. Several people were adorned in white T-shirts with a beautiful picture of Elizabeth that said JUSTICE FOR ELIZABETH. The crowd waved and smiled at the occupants of the transport vehicle.

The caravan pulled up right to the front of the Walls Unit, parked, and everyone stepped out of the vehicle. They had direct access to the entrance.

Everyone got out of the car and were greeted by their family and friends. They spent a few moments together just chitchatting, then the families were led inside the unit. At this point, Kahan was asked to remain back with the crowd. He complied and wished the Penas and Randy well.

Off they went inside. The members of the media were practically foaming at the mouth to get to the families. One reporter asked Adolph the typical lazy-reporter question, "How do you feel?"

"You don't know how bad I've been wanting to do this number," Adolph whispered to Randy as they walked in, ignoring the reporter. He decided to keep his real opinion close to the vest, as far as the media were concerned. He did not comment at all on the walk in, but he did look over at Houston news reporter Mark Garay and gave him the thumbs-up sign.

By the time they got inside the Walls Unit, it was approximately 5:00 P.M. All that was left to do was sit and wait for a last-minute phone call from Texas governor Rick Perry. As Adolph put it, "If you didn't hear that red phone ring, buddy, your time's up."

The families were made to wait in a hallway located next to the execution chamber's viewing room.

"That's when I kind of started getting nervous," recalled Adolph. "They were telling us to do this and don't do that." The process started to fade in and out of his consciousness. He was concerned O'Brien would get a last-second phone call. He hoped to God there was no final stay of execution. "I wanted to get the shit over with and make sure that damn phone didn't ring." Adolph shook his head. "I just knew that at any minute they were gonna do it again."

Adolph, an avid fisherman, described his anxiety in angler terms. "It's like waiting for that bobber to go up and down in the water. The anticipation of waiting for the fish to take the bait. You're just sitting there waiting and watching it and watching it. I'm just sitting there literally watching that phone and waiting for it to ring."

After a tension-filled hour, one of the guards came in and informed the families that the governor did not call. "Y'all can go in now." The guard nodded toward the door to the viewing section of the execution chamber.

"It's over now." Adolph sighed. "I knew that there was no more stopping because there's been so much bullshit that we've been through. It'll make you old. Quick. This shit took its toll on us. It does. It does."

The families made their way into the viewing room. The room was much larger than what Adolph had expected. "I thought we were going to be packed in there like sardines," based on what the guards had told him. Instead, the room measured approximately twenty feet by six feet, and all of the witnesses on the girls' side had plenty of room. There were no seats in the viewing room.

Located next to the victims' families' viewing room, but separated by a wall, is the killer's family's viewing room. Adolph was not sure, but he thought he spied O'Brien's wife and his mother, Ella Jones.

As Adolph familiarized himself with the surroundings, he noticed a large glass window at the front and center of the room. Behind the window, he could see the reason why they were all brought together on this day: Sean O'Brien lay on his back on an elevated gurney. His arms and legs were all strapped in. He wore his thick studious-looking glasses. His feet were closest to the window, while his head was positioned farther away. O'Brien looked up toward the ceiling, ignoring the people being ushered in.

Adolph and Randy took their positions at the front of the glass window. Both men wanted to make sure that the last faces O'Brien saw were those of the fathers who had lost their little girls by his hands. They were joined up front by Officer Zaragoza. Melissa stood slightly behind, and to the side of her husband.

Warden Charles O'Reilly, who rarely comes into the chamber before an execution, made it a point to walk into the room and inspect O'Brien. O'Reilly moved toward the edge of the gurney, near O'Brien's head.

Adolph was surprised by O'Reilly's appearance in the chamber. "I surely didn't expect to see him in there. I don't know if it was because of the case, if it got to him, or what. But I was surprised. It must have affected him somehow."

Adolph did, however, have another bout of anxiety. Unsure if the warden came in to pull the plug, Adolph recalled, "I kind of freaked out. I just thought there was going to be the preacher man and O'Brien. The preacher man was already in there. He was standing close to him with his Bible. But when the warden walked in, I thought, 'Uh-oh, he's putting a stop to this.'"

After nearly a minute with Warden O'Reilly standing next to O'Brien, Adolph felt a sense of relief. O'Reilly did not make any motions to indicate he was going to halt the execution. Instead, he looked at O'Brien and asked, "Do you have any last words?"

"I do," O'Brien assured the warden. He craned his head up to make eye contact with the families of the girls. He quietly began to speak to the Penas and Randy Ertman. "I am sorry. I have always been sorry. It is the worst mistake that I ever made in my whole life. Not because I am here, but because of what I did and I hurt a lot of people—you, and my family. I am sorry. I have always been sorry. I am sorry."

O'Brien turned away from the victims' families and attempted to look in the general direction of his own family. "You look after each other. I love you all. Be there for one another. All right. But I am sorry, very sorry."

O'Brien's new wife mouthed, "I love you" to him through a stream of tears.

"I love you, too," he said back to her in hushed tones.

"All right," he declared, followed by a large sigh. He was ready.

Adolph believed Sean O'Brien's sentiments were genuine. "I believe he really did mean that. You could see it in his eyes. He had hurt in his eyes. I don't know if it was because he was going to die, or did he really mean it? But I believe he really did mean it.

"Just shortly after that, it had started." Adolph watched the execution. "To actually see him sigh real big and then die . . . there is nothing inhumane about it."

Conventional wisdom is that a death caused by lethal injection takes six to eight minutes for the prisoner to die. Adolph disagreed. "It just takes literally seconds for him to stop breathing. You know when it's going in, because his body kind of freaks out. You see him gasping for air. He then said, 'Wow,' or something like that. He felt something when it went in. Then, right then, he just closed his eyes and he stopped moving. You couldn't even see his stomach moving.

"I knew he was dead. He's not breathing. That quick. I mean seconds. He was dead in twenty seconds. I guaran-damn-tee you, he was dead in twenty seconds. Because if you're not breathing, I don't know how you could be alive."

After suffering through the stay of execution in May, due to a legal discussion as to whether or not death by lethal injection is considered to be inhumane, Adolph laughed. "The guy just closed his eyes and went to sleep. It's pretty painless. For me and him." He added, "Everything was by the book. It kind of freaked me out how smoothly it all went. It was a cakewalk."

Adolph believed the punishment was too mild. "I wished to God that my daughter could have died that easy. Put a needle in her arm and just go to sleep. I wish to hell he could have died the way she died. That's justice. You want to talk about justice? That would be justice."

Adolph recalled that they did not stay in the viewing room very long. "I don't think we were in there even five minutes. Then the warden walked out of the chamber. A guy came into the room where we were and told us to step out of the room."

The families of the victims were the first to be released. O'Brien's family was allowed to spend more time in their room.

After the families left the viewing area, they were whisked away across the street to the administrative building and an organized press conference set up inside a large room in the prison. Randy opted out, while Adolph agreed to attend. Melissa also opted out; however, she walked over with Adolph and stood next to him as he spoke. According to Adolph, "She ended up talking as well. I don't remember what I said. I'm sure it was good." Most of the local Houston television news stations were present, along with several cable news channels, including CNN.

Adolph could see his group of supporters standing outside dressed in their Elizabeth T-shirts. "There was someone there representing Patricia Lopez," Adolph recalled, mentioning the young lady who was allegedly murdered by O'Brien.

"There was somebody outside over there with my group, Justice for Elizabeth, that was either her sister or her mother, I can't remember. She came up to me and told me, 'My last name is Lopez.' I said, 'He killed your daughter, too?' She said, 'Yep. But I just want to be here for you.' I said, 'No, vice versa. I want to be here for you. Me getting him executed was justice for you. You didn't even get a real trial for your daughter. We didn't even know about your daughter until we started going through the punishment stages. And that's probably not the only person. That's just the only one we know about.'"

Adolph also spotted a smattering of anti–death penalty supporters. One was a professor from a Texas college where Rachael Pena attended. Later, Adolph told his youngest daughter that when she went back to school that if she saw the professor to "kick that son of a bitch."

Adolph reflected on the execution of O'Brien. "How long did that guy get to stay in prison and live? Fourteen, fifteen years. I wished to God my daughter could have had another fifteen years. I'd have seen her kids, my grandkids, get to see her graduate, go to college, her wedding. But at sixteen, hell, you haven't even lived none of your life. You're just a child at sixteen. She never had a chance to live. Hell, I would have been pleased if she could have lived thirty years. I would have been pleased with that."

"I don't wish this on anybody," Adolph added. "But, hopefully, you make a little good from the bad. Hopefully, I can help somebody down the road."

When asked how long it took to come to the realization that he did not want to bottle up his emotions and keep everything inside, Adolph stated, "A long time. It took me a long time not wanting to get over not wanting to kill somebody.

One of the claims that death penalty opponents make in regard to an execution of a killer is that it does not bring closure to the families of the victims. That clearly was not the case for Adolph and Melissa Pena.

"He's dead and gone. He paid for what he did to my daughter. If there was any kind of closure, it did mean something to me when he told me that he was sorry," Adolph admitted.

"It looked to me like he meant it. It just looked like he was hurting," when he apologized, "and that he meant what he said and it did help me a little bit.

"After he was dead, I said, 'You know what? That did mean something to me. It kind of helped me when he did that.'"

Pena looked at this book's author and added, "That's the first time I ever told that to anybody." He grinned and added, "And that will probably be the last time I ever tell that to anybody again.

"I could tell [O'Brien] really, really, really meant it when he said it."

Adolph also looked forward to the time when he will get to witness Peter Cantu's execution. "Oh, that son of a bitch. It's going to be real hard for me not to say something to that bastard when he's sitting there getting executed.

"They always tell you, 'Don't say nothing, don't say nothing because you're not supposed to say anything to them.' I'm thinking I might need to put something over my mouth like duct tape, because it's going to be hard for me not to say something to that son of a bitch."

Adolph was furious Peter Cantu had never bothered to show remorse for killing his daughter, Elizabeth, and Jennifer Ertman after all these years. He was also appalled Cantu has had so many luxuries and freedoms—despite being behind bars for more than fourteen years.

"He's supposedly got him a bunch of followers in prison and some groupies and Web sites. It's disgusting."

Chapter 51

The United States Supreme Court, led by George W. Bush–appointee Chief Justice John Roberts, delivered yet another nearly lethal blow to the Pena and Ertman families, when it agreed to accept the case of Joe Medellin during the 2007 fall session.

The justices had previously agreed to hear Medellin's case back in 2005, until President George W. Bush stepped in and declared that the case should receive a state court review. According to the Associated Press, "the justices reserved the right to hear the appeal again once the case had run its full course, as it now has, in state court."

Several dyed-in-red-wool Conservatives were furious at the decision made by the Supreme Court and the man they voted to be president twice. The ultra-conservative *Lone Star Times* message board was fired up the following day. One of the calmer commentators, stwilhelm, wrote in to voice what many people around the country felt to be true, denouncing the president's decision, and calling for others to make their voices heard.

The United States Supreme Court is expected to reveal its decision in Joe Medellin's case in March 2008.

According to Randy Ertman he has been clean and sober for more than five years.

At the time of publication, Adolph's own son, Michael, is in prison for drugs. He has been in and out of jails and prisons more than a dozen times since the murder of his sister. Adolph believes the majority of his problems stem from his failure to deal with Elizabeth's death.

Adolph and Melissa Pena will continue to fight to have their voices heard regarding their daughter Elizabeth. "We're all she has. We are her lone voice. We don't want her life to be for nothing. Hopefully, something good can come from her death and somebody out there can learn from this. Maybe someone's life can be saved." Adolph paused momentarily in his heartfelt remarks.

Suddenly his solemn visage turned animated.

"In the meantime, I'm gonna make goddamn sure those other sons of bitches get executed."

JA! DAS ISS GOOT.

In Memoriam

Elizabeth Pena

Jennifer Ertman

Patricia Lopez

Jose Ariel Acosta

Corey Mitchell will donate a portion
of his royalties for *Pure Murder*
to the Heidi Search Center (San Antonio, Texas).

Feel free to visit their site and consider donating:
http://www.heidisearchcenter.com/
For *Pure Murder* updates and extras, please visit:
www.coreymitchell.com
www.myspace.com/coreymitchell
Corey Mitchell is the founder of and
contributor to In Cold Blog
http://incoldblogger.blogspot.com/
Corey Mitchell is also a contributing blogger for
Investigation Discovery, part of the Discovery Channel
http://blogs.discovery.com/hollywood/

Acknowledgments

This book would not have been written were it not for Andy Kahan. Andy and I spoke at a luncheon together one day before Sean O'Brien's first scheduled execution. Andy found out about O'Brien's stay the day before and was livid. I only briefly knew about Elizabeth Pena and Jennifer Ertman's story because I mentioned them in my previous book, *Strangler,* when I wrote about Diana Rebollar's murder by Anthony Allen Shore in the same neighborhood where Jennifer lived.

I was living in San Antonio and had just finished my first year of law school when the girls were murdered. As a result of my One L immersion, I was unaware of the case at that time.

Andy filled me in on the details and I quickly became intrigued by all the twists and turns of the story *after* the murders. I could not believe the incredible journey the Penas and Ertmans had to take to finally see justice for their daughters. Of course, that fight still continues, not only for their families but for thousands more out there who have lost someone to violent crime.

So, here's to Andy Kahan for fighting the good fight and clueing me in to one of the most fascinating cases I could have ever been a part of.

* * *

Much gratitude goes out to Adolph and Melissa Pena. They welcomed me into their warm home and shared their pain and suffering, as well as their love and caring for their daughter Elizabeth. I admire the sense of humor y'all display and wish you the best on your never-ending journey to seek justice for Elizabeth.

Thank you to Randy and Sandra Ertman, who reluctantly agreed to speak with me about their lovely daughter, Jennifer. I hope both continue to find peace and hope.

A big thank-you to my MySpace friends. I gave you guys five stories to pick from for my next book and this is the one you chose. Great job! I hope you enjoyed it.

Barbara Anderson, from the Harris County District Clerk's Office, was an invaluable help as usual. The ladies in the office including, but not limited to, Diane and Colleen, always welcome me with open arms and make my research feel like a vacation.

Attorney K. S. "Gator" Dunn provided several laughs and was kind enough to open his office doors to me. P.S., I know it's not about your briefcase.

Assistant District Attorney Kelly Siegler, again, thanks for your legal insight and sense of humor.

Thanks to Nora Fontenot and Fabiola Medina for helping me out in Brownsville.

As always, thank you to Michaela Hamilton. Your patience is incredible. Also, thanks to everyone at Kensington for their hard work and dedication to quality writing. Also, to Adam Korn. Sorry to see you go. Special thanks to Mike Shohl and Stephanie Finnegan for their editorial expertise.

Eardrum mayhem provided by Divine Pustulence, Ian Brady Bunch, Project E.L.F. (Thanks, Roach), P.J. Harvey, Lustmord (I can't believe I just now discovered this), Nachtmystium, Bergraven, Swallow the Sun, Watain, Funeral Pyre, Horna, Behemoth, the Field, Cliff Martinez, Jesu, Urgehal, Autechre, Red Sparowes, Caribou, Explosions in the Sky, seefeel, Global Communication, the Black Dog, Plaid, Plaid and Bob Jaroc, Boards of Canada, Arovane, Amber Asylum, Murcof, Plastikman, Trentemoller, Ulrich Schnauss, the Album Leaf, Knife, Moonsorrow, Novembers Doom, Mors Principium Est, Omnium Gatherum, Dodheimsgard (DHG), Dark Tranquillity, Hacride, Grails, Beyond the Massacre, Despised Icon, Burzum, Dimmu Borgir, Amon Amarth, Pelican, Destroy the Runner, Mekong Delta, Richie Hawtin, Vapourspace, Funeral Mist, Possessed, Xasthur, Hatebreed, NIN, Daath, Brian Eno, Neurosis, ISIS, Throne of Molok, Devildriver, Scarve, 16 Volt, Angkor Wat, Skrew, Bathory, Darkthrone, Agalloch, Rosetta, Gregor Samsa, Pantera, Dimebag (RIP), Watchtower, Dread, Zero Tolerance, Russian Circles, *The Fountain* s/t, *Solaris* s/t, Cattle Decapitation, Dawn of Azazel, Macabre, Arvo Part, Cephalic Carnage, Marduk, Queens of the Stone Age, Carcass, Celtic Frost, Iron Maiden, Gojira, *Decibel* magazine, Botch, Giant Squid, the Human Abstract, Tim Heckler, Phutureprimitive, Sounds from the Ground, The End, Machine Head, Poison the Well, Cult of Luna, Unearthly Trance, Akercocke, *Perfume* s/t, Pete Namlook, Auricular, Ministry, Goatwhore, Genghis Tron, Made out of Babies, Aphex Twin, AFX, SOD, Viking Crown, Naglfar, Belphegor, Stars of the Lid, the Dead Texan, Cro-Mags, Crumbsuckers, Slayer, Gescom, Leng Tch'e, Zombi, Loscil, Mimi + Boyd, Mouse on

Mars, Carpet Musics, here, Aix Em Klemm, Hate Eternal, D.R.I., Napalm Death, Deicide, Mortiis, Evile, Between the Buried and Me, Glass Casket, dead horse, and Bush Laden.

To my fellow In Cold Bloggers: Carol Anne Davis, John Ditmars, Joseph Foy, Ron Franscell, Michelle Gray, Dale Hudson, Steve Huff, Laura James, Andy Kahan, Brian Karem, Paul LaRosa, Gary Lavergne, David Lohr, Steven Long, Dennis McDougal, Gregg Olsen, Donna Pendergast, M. William Phelps, Katherine Ramsland, Simon Read, Fred Rosen, Harriett Semander, John Semander, Mike Stinski, and Carlton Stowers. Extra thanks to Sam, John, Michelle, Steven Long, and Gregg for moral support.

Thanks to Gregg Olsen, Roy Hazelwood, Dennis McDougal, Joyce King, Steven Long, Dale Hudson, and Del Howison for the wonderful blurbs for *Strangler*.

For my friends Ray Seggern and Kelly Nugent, Peter Soria, Lupe Garcia, Mike and Lynette Sheppard, Knox and Heather Williams, Ricky and Shirin Butler, Trey and Missy Chase, Clint and Cathy Stephen, Phil and Karen Savoie, Kevin and Shana Fowler (Go Dazed and Confused!), Chris and Beverly Goldrup, Dennis and Sharon McDougal, Aphrodite Jones, Poppy Z. Brite, Kirk and Teresa Morris, Drew and Sarah Stride, Mike and Sarah Stinski.

To my incredible in-laws, the Burkes. Thank you for all the help, love, and support you offer us. We would not be able to cope without you. Dennis, Margaret, Denise, and Leah—I love you all.

For my wonderful parents, who always manage to keep their sense of humor through life's travails, I love you both so very much. To the dedicatees of this book, my brothers, Kyle and Darrin Mitchell, thanks for not kicking my ass too much when I was young. To my sister-in-law, Ramona, and all of my Mitchell nieces and nephew, Julie, Kaylee, Madison, and Ronnie. Also Bill and Renee Runyan, Todd Solomon, and Jeremy Frey. RIP Max and Lucas. Hello, Dallas and the newest Mitchell family member, Tamale.

For Lisa, my late wife, it's hard to believe that you will have been gone for six years by the time this book comes out. I could not have done any of this without your support and belief. I will always love you.

For my darling daughter, Emma. Having you one year older actually made this my hardest book to write. I cannot imagine my life without you being the biggest part of it. I look forward to the day when you can read my books and go out into the world and make a difference. In the meantime, have fun, be safe, and stop throwing your food. I love you forever.

For my incredible wife, Audra. I don't know how you do it. Supermom, breadwinner, funny lady. I have truly been blessed to be able to remarry and find another wonderful woman like you. I admire you for so many things, but the greatest is how you manage to do it all and still smile. Thank you for all of your love, support, and laughter. I truly would not be able to do any of this without you. You have my heart forever.